Absolutism in Central Europe

Historical Connections

Series editors
Tom Scott, *University of Liverpool*
Geoffrey Crossick, *University of Essex*
John Davis, *University of Connecticut*
Joanna Innes, *Somerville College, University of Oxford*

Titles in the series

Absolutism in Central Europe

Peter H. Wilson

London and New York

First published 2000
by Routledge
11 New Fetter Lane, London EC4P 4EE

Simultaneously published in the USA and Canada
by Routledge
29 West 35th Street, New York, NY 10001

Routledge is an imprint of the Taylor & Francis Group

Typeset in Times by BC Typesetting, Bristol
Printed and bound in Great Britain by MPG Books Ltd, Bodmin

British Library Cataloguing in Publication Data
A catalogue record for this book is available from the British Library

Library of Congress Cataloging in Publication Data
Wilson, Peter H. (Peter Hamish)
    Absolutism in central Europe/Peter Wilson.
        p.   cm. – (Historical connections)
    ISBN 0–415–23351-8 (hb) – ISBN 0–415–15043–4 (pbk)
        1. Europe, central–Politics and government.   2. Despotism–Europe,
    central.   I. Title.   II. Series.
    DAW1047.W55 2000
    320.943–dc21   99-085981

ISBN 0–415–23351–8 (hbk)
ISBN 0–415–15043–4 (pbk)

For Tom

Contents

Series editors' preface

Historical Connections is a series of short books on important historical topics and debates, written primarily for those studying and teaching history. The books offer original and challenging works of synthesis that will make new themes accessible, or old themes accessible in new ways, build bridges between different chronological periods and different historical debates, and encourage comparative discussion in history.

If the study of history is to remain exciting and creative, then the tendency to fragmentation must be resisted. The inflexibility of older assumptions about the relationship between economic, social, cultural and political history has been exposed by recent historical writing, but the impression has sometimes been left that history is little more than a chapter of accidents. This series will insist on the importance of processes of historical change, and it will explore the connections within history: connections between different layers and forms of historical experience, as well as connections that resist the fragmentary consequences of new forms of specialism in historical research.

Historical Connections will put the search for these connections back at the top of the agenda by exploring new ways of uniting the different strands of historical experience, and by affirming the importance of studying change and movement in history.

Geoffrey Crossick
John Davis
Joanna Innes
Tom Scott

Acknowledgements

This is a book about the form of European monarchy known as absolutism, how it was defined by contemporaries, how it emerged and developed, and how it has been interpreted by historians and political and social scientists. No historical work stands in isolation, and while my conclusions derive partly from my own research into politics and war in early modern Europe, they have also benefited from an engagement with many other scholars to whose views I have tried to do justice in my discussion. This has been a long process stretching back to well before this book was conceived, and I would like to take this opportunity to thank in particular Jeremy Black, Tim Blanning, Michael Hochedlinger, Derek McKay and Hamish Scott for many fruitful debates. Tom Scott and Joanna Innes read an initial draft and provided numerous helpful comments, while Heather McCallum, Gillian Oliver and the staff at Routledge have been supportive throughout. Eliane, Alec, Tom and now Nina have endured my often prolonged absence with good humour, and have, as usual, rendered the greatest assistance and inspiration.

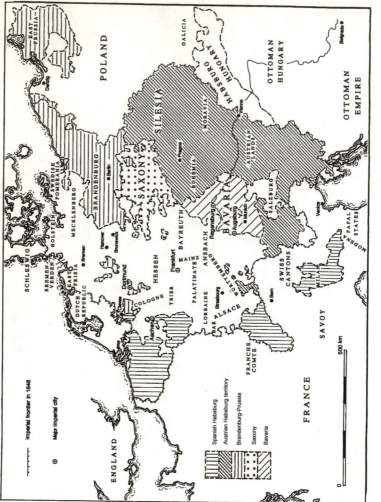

Map 1 The Reich in 1648

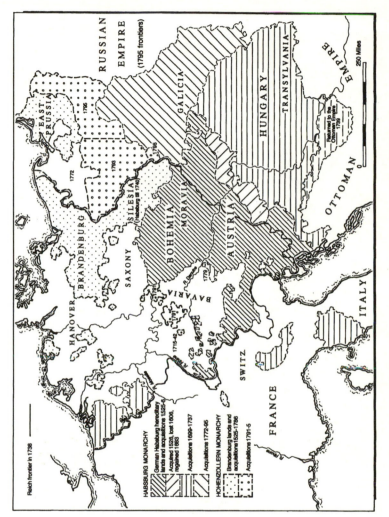

Map 2 The Habsburg and Hohenzollern monarchies

Introduction

Absolutism was once a certainty. It was seen as a distinct form of monarchy that dominated the European continent and defined an entire age. It coordinated and centralised power, pushing political development towards the modern state. While broadly associated with the defence of aristocratic privilege, it nonetheless fostered the conditions for social and economic change, assisting in the monumental transition from feudalism to capitalism. It was personified by self-confident monarchs, stamping their mark on their nations' histories. High in the firmament was Louis XIV, the dazzling 'Sun King', builder of Versailles and archetype of all absolute monarchs, but competing for the attention of posterity with the representatives of the later 'enlightened' rule, like Frederick the Great or Joseph II. If such figures lent colour and grandeur to their countries' pasts, they also served as symbols of despotism and authoritarian rule; the sort of power that right-thinking Britons had so gloriously overthrown in the seventeenth century and which the French were to do in 1789, ending the age of absolutism and starting modern history.

Where are these certainties now? Generations of historians have been chipping away at an edifice which, even if its precise shape was in dispute, at least had seemed solid enough and its basic dimensions agreed by all. The hammers and chisels have been replaced by power tools, and what seemed so imposing has been revealed as nothing more than a stucco façade. As the plaster falls away, the once omnipotent inhabitants of the palace are exposed as frauds who disguised their lack of real power with a lot of showy display. Robbed of their grand coverings, they appear little different from rulers elsewhere in Europe's history, bound by customary and practical constraints to consult traditional institutions and important social groups. Far from pushing history forward, or indeed holding it back, they meander instead, buffeted this way and that by the harsh winds of change out of their control. Finally, the last of the demolition team swings the wrecking ball and the whole construct disappears in a puff of smoke, leaving behind only a myth.[1]

What are we to make of this? At the very time when historians are queuing up to wave 'goodbye to absolutism',[2] social and political scientists still use the term with confidence, raising the question that either they are lagging behind or that the recent historical discussion is simply a case of revisionism pushed too far. This book addresses these issues directly. It investigates how scholars from a variety of disciplines have defined and explained political development across what was formerly known as the 'age of absolutism'. It assesses whether the term still has utility as a tool of analysis and it explores the wider ramifications of the process of state formation from the experience of central Europe from the early seventeenth century to the start of the nineteenth. Chapter 1 unravels the controversy over when absolutism may have begun and what caused it to emerge. Chapter 2 looks at how contemporaries defined monarchical and political power and how these definitions changed over the centuries under review. The practice of government and its relationship to society form the focus of Chapter 3, while Chapter 4 investigates the longstanding belief that absolutism was transformed in the later eighteenth century through its relationship with enlightened thought, and considers how this may have affected its ability to confront the forces unleashed by the French Revolution.

Before we can proceed, however, we need to examine the full implications of the assertion that what we are dealing with here is a myth – a fabrication of political and historical debate – rather than a reflection of verifiable historical processes. The notion that the past is constructed and deconstructed by the process of writing and discussing it is highly fashionable and applies not only to the study of absolutism, but to the rest of human history. This broader challenge cannot be ignored here, even if its wider implications lie beyond the scope of this book. In particular, it suggests that there is more to the 'myth of absolutism' than has hitherto been believed.

Three dimensions can be identified within this wider conception of the myth. The first is familiar and has long provided the staple for historical debate as well as the fuel for the recent controversy. This is the 'myth of absolute royal power'. Historians had always known that the achievements of such monarchs as Louis XIV fell far short of their pretensions. The extent of these failings became ever more apparent as the scope of historical analysis broadened out from its initial preoccupation with diplomatic and political affairs. Further studies of royal taxation, as well as the composition of the French court and its ties with the localities, demonstrated the limited nature of Louis XIV's power. Far from commanding absolute obedience and exercising close supervision through a network of loyal officials, royal authority had been patchy, dependent on a small, corrupt and inefficient administration riddled with faction and completely lacking any progressive, modernising drive. Rather than absolutism, historians began to talk simply of a 'shift to the centre' as executive authority gravitated towards groups and institutions based in and around Paris, rather than those out in the provinces. Exercise of this authority nonetheless still depended on the cooperation of other 'power holders' in the localities, while significant aspects of daily life remained scarcely touched by high political decisions.[3]

By the early 1990s such revisionism had gone well beyond modifying details to undermine the whole basis of absolutism as a historical concept. The conclusion that it was all a myth was drawn first by Nicholas Henshall in 1992, who argued forcefully that not only did Louis and his fellow monarchs fail to deliver an absolutist agenda, but that they had never had such pretensions.[4] All European monarchies were simply variations on a universal theme of 'consultative monarchy', whereby royal power was always limited by practical and theoretical constraints. Henshall starts with the origins of the term 'absolutism' in the political debates of the early nineteenth century, rather than those of the seventeenth or eighteenth, and traces how it became interwoven with notions of 'English exceptionalism' to become the antithesis of British liberal parliamentary development. Absolutism acquired the definition of being intrinsically despotic, autocratic, bureaucratic and definitely not English. This clearer appreciation of the term's etymology permits Henshall to go beyond the now familiar relativising of absolutism as 'always in the making but never made', to question whether it ever existed even in theory. A comparison between Britain and France reveals that Louis XIV and his successors were not despotic since they continued to respect the corporate rights of privileged social groups and even, on occasion, extended them. Nor were they autocratic, since despite their centralisation of executive authority they still relied on consultation and consent in the practical exercise of power. Finally, the French state was far from bureaucratic as its administrative infrastructure remained rooted in local, regional and national networks of patronage and clientelism. If any European monarchy deserves the label 'absolute', it has to be the British, not the French, since the powers of the English kings and their ability to put decisions into practice far exceeded those of their continental contemporaries.

The belief that absolutism constituted a progressive, modernising force constitutes the second element of its myth. A number of impulses have contributed to this view. The German historical school of the nineteenth century regarded the creation of homogeneous nation states as the aim of the historical process. Many scholars were attracted by what they saw as dramatic, dynamic historical personalities, and these scholars' reliance on dynastic and administrative archives for sources, as well as political sensibilities, contributed to the magnification of the roles played by individual monarchs. Such rulers and their regimes appeared to embody the uncompromising and determined principles of efficiency, rationality and power thought necessary to drive political development forward. It is important to remember that not all these historians were outright apologists for a conservative, authoritarian, militarised 'power state' (*Machtstaat*). Johann Gustav Droysen, for instance, was critical of what he perceived as the 'selfish dynastic interests' of many absolute monarchs, and instead favoured a constitutional monarchy as the best means of realising a true nation state.[5] French historians generally went further in their condemnation of the excesses of royal rule and understandably stressed the significance of the revolutions of 1789, 1830 and 1848 in the creation of modern France. However, despite political disagreements, few dissented from the belief that absolutist centralisation had been a modernising force and that absolute monarchy should be interpreted as the creator of the 'modern state'.[6] Other perspectives reinforced this view. The sociological school that grew out of the work of Max Weber emphasised the 'rationalisation' inherent in absolutism's transformation of medieval 'office holding' into modern bureaucracy, while Marx and Engels both attributed a key role to its promotion, albeit largely unwittingly, of 'progressive' social forces behind the fundamental shift to capitalism and modernity.

A reaction set in during the twentieth century, particularly after the experience of fascism and Soviet communism discredited the glorification of strong states and national traditions. Moreover, the disorders and destruction of the first half of the century heightened awareness that political centralisation did not necessarily mean rationalisation and modernisation. The persistence of earlier liberal historical traditions combined with the practical need to legitimise new states, such as the two German republics established in 1949, to encourage fresh research into the non-absolutist elements of the allegedly absolute monarchies. Such work not only served to undermine the myth of absolute royal power, but to suggest that early modern representative institutions and popular resistance had also contributed positively to political development. Meanwhile, Marxist scholarship in both the West and the Soviet bloc moved away from Marx's original emphasis on absolutism's association with progressive bourgeois forces, to stress instead its role as 'feudal reaction' in delaying modernisation. Some non-Marxists also argued that absolutism retarded political development by contributing to the persistence of aristocratic power into the nineteenth century. Far from propelling German history forward, it may have pushed it down a deviant, 'special path' (*Sonderweg*) of historical development, culminating in the disasters of the Nazi era. Faced with such conclusions, the idea of absolutism as a progressive historical force appears to be a myth.[7]

The third dimension to the myth was the idea that absolutism formed a distinct and important part of Western historical development. The argument that it constituted a progressive force in political development implied that it formed a necessary stage on the road to modernity. Earlier interpretations of 'English exceptionalism' only reinforced the belief that absolutism was the normal route to modern statehood within the European historical experience. At the very least, absolute monarchy appeared to be the predominant form among a very narrow range of possible paths to the same destination. While political and social scientists still wrestle with defining these variations,[8] postmodernists have become increasingly critical of the basic underlying premise that history has a singular ending. Such grand explanations have been rejected as 'master narratives' which impose order on an essentially formless and unknowable past. Absolutism has to be rejected as part of these grand schemes, regardless of whether they have portrayed it as the political superstructure of the transition from feudalism to capitalism, as in the Marxist 'narrative', or as the progressive, rationalising force of more conservative interpretations.[9]

The history of central Europe from the seventeenth to the nineteenth century offers a particularly fruitful area to explore these three dimensions. First, discussion of the myth of absolute royal power has been largely confined till now to the study of France and its comparison with early modern Britain. Most historians have accepted Henshall's assertion that if the notion can be disproved for France, history's pre-eminent absolute monarchy, then the same must be true for the rest of Europe. Unfortunately, this inadvertently perpetuates the entrenched Franco-centric bias in the study of absolutism which measures everything against standards set by Louis XIV and the Bourbon dynasty in general. It is time that this imbalance was redressed, and the central European monarchies considered on their own terms and not as pale imitations of the court of Versailles.

The case for investigating central Europe grows stronger still when we shift our focus from historical writing and towards the work of political and social scientists for whom Brandenburg-Prussia often assumes greater importance than France in models of absolutism, bureaucracy and feudal reaction. Even those historians who are prepared to accept that French royal power may have been limited often regard that of German monarchs as corresponding more closely to the traditional conception of absolutism. The preoccupation of German scholars with the state has also left an important legacy that requires consideration in this context, particularly given the issue of absolutism as a distinct phase in European development. Finally, within the framework of the old Reich, or Holy Roman Empire, central Europe contained the bulk of the continent's smaller states which have rarely featured in theoretical discussions of absolutism, but which some historians believe were more absolute than the great monarchies.

The Reich deserves particular attention because it does not fit the conventional trajectory of European state development. The fact that it was neither an absolute monarchy nor a nation state led to its history either being grossly distorted or written out almost entirely from discussions of central European politics. This has changed substantially since the 1960s as a growing body of scholarship points to a new interpretation of the old Reich as not only historically significant, but a vibrant political entity even in the late eighteenth century. Since this picture has not yet fully penetrated the Anglophone world some further clarification is required here. The Reich encompassed most of central and much of western Europe, even in the seventeenth century when it stretched from the Low Countries in the west to the Hungarian frontier in the east, and from Holstein in the north to Tuscany in the south (see Map 1). Little of this huge area was under the emperor's direct control since he was only the immediate ruler of his own hereditary lands, while the remainder was governed by a variety of territorial lords, generally known collectively as the princes, even though many did not in fact enjoy this title. Apparent continuity of rule was provided by the fact that the Austrian Habsburg dynasty monopolised the imperial title between 1440 and 1806 with the sole exception of 1742–5. This title was not hereditary, however, and each succession had to be negotiated with the eight or so electoral princes (*Kurfürsten*) who enjoyed the unique privilege of choosing the next emperor.

Traditionally, imperial politics has been interpreted as a dualism between the emperor, who became progressively weaker as he lost powers to the electors, and other important princes whose strength increased correspondingly. The most powerful of these, notably

Prussia, but also the Habsburgs in their capacity as territorial rulers of Austria and its associated lands, gradually evolved as distinct, increasingly absolutist monarchies, allegedly leaving the Reich an empty shell after 1648. This is now refuted by a growing weight of evidence that reveals not just the continued significance of myriad lesser rulers, but the presence and vitality of imperial institutions that provided a forum for common action and could develop a momentum of their own. The most important of these institutions was the imperial diet, or Reichstag, which served as an assembly for the territorial rulers to debate policy with the emperor and which met in permanent session after 1663. Other assemblies existed at an intermediary level of the imperial circles, or *Kreise*, which were regional groupings of the territories for defence coordination and other collective action. The two imperial supreme courts also functioned to preserve the Reich's structure as a hierarchy subject to the emperor's overall authority but not under his direct control. Despite internal and external pressures, the Reich continued to survive and develop after the Thirty Years War (1618–48), with the emperor and imperial institutions experiencing periodic revivals in their influence, particularly in the later seventeenth century. Austro-Prussian rivalry combined with the French Revolutionary Wars (1792–1801) to precipitate the collapse of the Reich after 1802 and pave the way for the Napoleonic reorganisation of Germany between 1803 and 1813.

The elective principle inherent in the imperial title was also present in the ecclesiastical territories where the cathedral or abbey chapter chose each new ruler from a list of candidate churchmen. These constituted a significant proportion of the territories despite annexations and secularisations during the sixteenth century, and as late as 1792 still comprised 3 electorates, 31 prince bishoprics and archbishoprics, and 40 abbeys. Hereditary rule held sway in the other 5 electorates, 61 principalities and 99 counties, though, as with the ecclesiastical territories, there were huge discrepancies in size, ranging from the electorate of Bavaria with 41,580 square kilometres and 1.2 million inhabitants to the count of Isenburg-Meerholz, who ruled a mere 82 square kilometres and 1,500 people in the late eighteenth century. In addition to these miniature monarchies, the Reich encompassed the fifty-one urban republics, or imperial cities, which, while under the emperor's over-lordship, also had their own small dependent territories. Some of these could be larger than many principalities, such as Hamburg which contained over 100,000 people in 1792.

Only about 25 of these 290 electorates, principalities, counties, abbeys and cities were ever of more than local political and military importance, though by acting collectively through imperial institutions they could still make their presence felt, even internationally. Those capable of some independent action included the three ecclesiastical electorates of Mainz, Cologne and Trier, and their five secular counterparts: Bohemia, Brandenburg, Saxony, Bavaria and the Palatinate. Of these, Bohemia was ruled by the Habsburgs and Brandenburg by the Prussian Hohenzollerns. Saxony was held by the Wettin dynasty while two branches of the Wittelsbach house governed Bavaria and the Palatinate. All these families had junior branches holding other lesser territories and often, thanks to election, important ecclesiastical principalities. The most important of these included Münster, Würzburg, Bamberg and Salzburg, while the leading secular principalities comprised Württemberg, Hessen-Kassel, Hessen-Darmstadt, Mecklenburg, Ansbach, Bayreuth, and East Frisia. Other, much smaller territories, such as Weimar, Dessau, Bückeburg and Lippe, might assume only temporary political significance but could nonetheless become significant cultural centres. We will meet these territories periodically throughout this study.[10]

Like absolutism, 'central Europe' is a contested term that requires definition. It will be used here simply as a convenient label for that part of Europe encompassed politically by the Reich and the monarchies based within it. This includes all the German principalities discussed above, as well as the dynastic monarchies of the Austrian Habsburgs and Prussian Hohenzollerns which stretched beyond the Reich to the south and east (see Map 2). The word 'German' is also used loosely to describe those ruling houses based within the Reich, though the actual background of their members was frequently cosmopolitan, while their subjects could include many who spoke another language. The north Italian territories that were still within the formal orbit of the Reich as 'Imperial Italy' until 1802 will be excluded, as will those areas ruled by lesser German dynasties at times during the period under review. The most significant of these is Poland, which was ruled by the Saxon Wettin dynasty between 1697–1763, and which is variously interpreted as an aristocratic commonwealth, or a form of constitutional monarchy.[11]

The historiography of this region has contributed one further dimension to the absolutism myth that this book will address. The myriad lesser principalities that made up the German political patchwork have provided a fertile source of examples for the 'myth of petty despotism' (*Kleinstaaterei*). This concept also has its origins in nineteenth-century political and historical debates, but has received scant treatment in studies of absolutism, to which it is clearly related.

Just as France has so often served as a stereotype for all absolute monarchies, Brandenburg-Prussia has fulfilled the same function with regard to the German states which are assumed to have followed its general pattern of development while failing to achieve its degree of modernity before the nineteenth century.[12]

Frequently, the degree of divergence is exaggerated to the point that the lesser territories are portrayed as deviating from Prussia's path of rationalisation and centralisation, in order to pursue an alternative modelled on France. Evidence for this is provided by none other than Frederick II of Prussia, who criticised the lesser German princes for slavishly copying Louis XIV.[13] Other late eighteenth-century thinkers extended the range of pejorative terms when they argued that the smaller territories were more prone to 'despotism', 'tyranny' and 'sultanism' than their larger, more enlightened neighbours. The fact that many of these princes hired their soldiers as mercenaries to foreign powers only served to corroborate this criticism. The image of backward, petty tyrannies served both liberal and nationalist agendas in early nineteenth-century Germany and was propagated by those seeking constitutional checks on princely power, as well as those demanding an end to political fragmentation and its replacement by unification under Prussian leadership.[14] Even historians with no particular political purpose have continued this interpretation. A few examples will suffice to illustrate the tone of such work. The German princes were 'a host of little tyrants' who only 'had two main preoccupations in life; to satisfy their vanity and to affirm their absolute power'. Despite ruling realms of microscopic proportions, 'their vanity knew no bounds' and 'there was no limit to their power' over their unfortunate subjects.[15] Frequently this descends into caricature and can just as easily produce rosy pictures of benevolent, comic-opera princedoms as deliver the stock images of evil tyrants.

Whatever the precise configuration of this myth of petty despotism, the underlying premise is always the same. The lesser territories are always more extreme versions of the larger, absolute monarchies: either they are more backward, 'feudal' or 'reactionary', their rulers more tyrannical, extravagant and vain, or they are models of enlightened government, free of the great power pretensions that wasted the resources of their larger neighbours. It remains to be seen whether there is anything in this particular element of the 'myth', or whether the difference between the larger and smaller German principalities was fundamentally simply one of scale.

1 Emergence

Simply a matter of centralisation of the time period or was it an Eldest? example of Modern Government of a Ordered hierarchy throughout the federal Local Principality

DATES AND PHASES

The various dimensions of the myth of absolutism contribute to the present uncertainty surrounding its origins and development. There seems little agreement as to when it emerged, what drove it forward, whether it progressed through distinct phases and when it came to an end. These issues are often clouded further by a failure to distinguish clearly between the impulses behind the political transformations variously identified as absolutism, and the justifications and means employed by contemporaries to advance political centralisation. Finally, there has been a tendency to generalise from specific examples, and to impose rigid theoretical models on disparate historical experiences. This chapter intends to remove these difficulties by unravelling the controversies and identifying what may be specific for central European state formation, and what is of more general application for the continent.

Discussions of absolutism's emergence have a long history, but one which starts after the period it seeks to explain. Most German theorists of the seventeenth and eighteenth centuries discussed politics as variations on a single theme of monarchy limited by the presence and participation of territorial estates (*Landstände*) who acted as the representatives of the inhabitants in dealings with the ruler. Disputes centred on the relative positions of the monarch, or prince, and the estates, and raised specific questions such as which social groups should be represented in the estates, whether they should have the right of self-assembly, and how far the ruler should be bound by their advice. This balance between princely power and estates' restraint was regarded as something common throughout Europe and not peculiar to the Reich or its constituent territories. France was the only exception, as its monarchy was widely thought to be truly despotic, or free from restraint. Far from being applauded, this was taken as a sign of weakness and not something that German princes should adopt. These convictions were reinforced when the neo-medieval French monarchy collapsed in 1789 while the 'modern' German principalities remained largely untroubled by serious internal unrest.

However, a number of commentators had grown dissatisfied with the accepted terms by the 1790s and in place of variations on a common theme were now discussing politics as a set of stark alternatives: tyranny or freedom, despotism or the rule of law. Though it took time for these ideas to gain ground, they set the framework for the early nineteenth-century debate on the liberal constitutional state. Like those elsewhere on the continent, German liberals regarded their ideal state as 'modern', but one which combined elements from the past in its balance between a hereditary monarch and a truly representative assembly replacing the old territorial estates which were now condemned as bastions of oligarchy and aristocratic privilege. The term 'absolutism' only entered the political lexicography in the 1820s to define the sort of narrow, unrepresentative monarchy the liberals were seeking to abolish. It was not until the next decade that any-one applied it to the period before 1789, let alone used it as a term synonymous with the entire pre-revolutionary 'old regime'.[1] However, this does not mean that absolutism itself was only invented in the early nineteenth century. The idea and even the words 'absolute monarchy' were familiar to writers such as John Locke long before and, as this book will argue, absolutism existed as a real form of monarchy. What was new was its use as an abstraction to systematise an entire period in European history and to provide a rhetorical counterpoint to liberal models of constitutional government.

If liberal constitutionalism both introduced the term and announced its demise as a form of government, it still left the date of its emergence unidentified. German academic interest in the origins of what was rapidly being termed the 'modern state' encouraged the search for absolutism's emergence. The traumatic experience of the Thirty Years War (1618–48) appeared a plausible starting point as it had clearly encouraged the process of centralisation in many important German principalities. By happy coincidence, the war also saw the reign of Frederick William, the 'Great Elector' of Brandenburg-Prussia (1640–88), whom nineteenth-century historians had identified as the founder of the modern Hohenzollern state. The Treaty of Westphalia in 1648 provided a convenient general turning-point from which to date the beginnings of what had become the 'age of absolutism', as it not only concluded the Thirty Years War in a major European peace settlement confirming France as a major power, but strengthened the German princes by weakening the authority of the Holy Roman Emperor. Many historians continue to accept the period 1648–1789 as a distinct phase in European history and one which can be defined by absolutism.[2]

Others, however, were not to be confined to a mere 150 years. The process of political centralisation had clearly begun much earlier than the mid-seventeenth century and historians were aware that earlier monarchs had often set precedents or laid foundations upon which later successors had built. Scholars of central Europe noted that the upheavals of the Reformation had strengthened the power of the territorial princes in the early sixteenth century and so possibly set in motion the trends which others had detected during the Thirty Years War. Comparison with the rest of Europe revealed that rulers elsewhere were engaged in similar processes of internal political consolidation at the expense of previously autonomous regions and privileged social groups, while simultaneously delineating and expanding their external frontiers in wars with neighbouring kingdoms. The French Valois dynasty expelled the English and brought Brittany and Burgundy under their control, while Ferdinand of Aragon and Isabella of Castille united the Spanish kingdoms and drove the Moors from Iberia. Even England appeared to participate in the general European trend as the Tudor dynasty ended civil war and consolidated the power of the crown. The novelty of these late fifteenth-century political transformations was magnified by their coincidence with the new intellectual climate associated with the Renaissance. Altogether, there seemed to be sufficient evidence to justify calling these rulers 'new monarchs' and the direct precursors of the absolute kings.[3]

Like the proverbial dog chasing its tail, the search for absolutism's origins seemed to have no end. Other historians pointed out that medieval monarchs, such as the Staufer dynast Emperor Frederick II (1212–50), had also accumulated and centralised power. Classicists argued that absolutism rested on foundations laid by imperial Rome and the Greek city states, while others began questioning whether it had really been swept away by the French Revolution. A recent biography of the Austrian emperor Franz Joseph (1848–1916) terms Habsburg rule absolutism until the 1848 revolution, followed by 'neo-absolutism' 1851–9, 'quasi-absolutism' 1860–97 and finally 'bureaucratic' or 'parliamentary' absolutism until 1918.[4] Such claims do have a historical basis, as do those that see Napoleon as the last of the absolute monarchs, but other interpretations that apply the term to the regimes of twentieth-century inter-war Europe, or range outside the continent to embrace Chinese or Indian history, are clearly stretching it beyond breaking point.[5] Those who claim absolutism is merely a myth are right that it has been misused simply as a byword for political centralisation.

The dating of absolutism is closely related to questions about its own evolution and whether it constituted a unique stage in wider historical development. The latter have already been highlighted in the Introduction as the second and third dimensions to the absolutism myth. The view that held absolutism to be a progressive, modernising historical force regarded it as a *necessary* stage in historical development. While shying away from the moral judgements implicit in such interpretations, others have nonetheless argued that it still constituted a *transitional* stage through which many European societies have passed. There are two main variants to this view. One regards absolutism in political terms as the intermediary stage between the medieval and modern state. In this interpretation, absolutism is frequently depicted as 'modernising' the medieval 'feudal state' and so paving the way for the fully modern constitutional state.[6] The other perspective sees the transition in socio-economic terms with absolutism as the intermediary between feudal and capitalist society. This has featured prominently in Marxist interpretations of absolutism, as we shall see shortly, and gave rise to the designation 'late feudal epoch' applied by historians in the former German Democratic Republic to what their Western colleagues generally termed the early modern period (*Die Frühe Neuzeit*).

Within this broader periodisation, absolutism is often seen as itself progressing through several stages. The current scheme used to explain state formation in the German-speaking parts of central Europe places absolutism as the final stage of 'early modern' political development and encompasses much of what other scholars have discussed as the early phases of absolutism itself. German political development is described as a process of 'territorialisation' (*Territorialisierung*), whereby authority became concentrated in the hands of the princes and lesser lords ruling increasingly distinct parts of the Reich. This had its origins in the twelfth to fourteenth century as it became clear that the elective German imperial monarchy was unable to assert effective control across the wide expanse of the Reich. The public order problems of the fifteenth and sixteenth centuries gave a considerable boost to these developments which then entered a second stage characterised by the consolidation of the so-called *Ständestaat*. This is described as a dualistic balance between a hereditary prince wielding executive authority but dependent on the advice and cooperation of the territorial estates, who entrenched their position by bargaining rights and privileges in return for assisting in the development of a fiscal infrastructure. Many princes gradually displaced their estates, especially during the turmoil of the Thirty Years War, throwing them on to the defensive and ushering in the third, absolutist stage. This in turn gave way to the modern constitutional state in the wake of the Napoleonic reorganisation of Germany and the process of unification in the nineteenth century.[7]

Many historians divide the last of these three stages into two subperiods based on the now classic scheme elaborated for European absolutism in general by Wilhelm Roscher in 1847. Roscher also used a tripartite model starting with the phase of 'confessional absolutism' between 1517 and 1648, characterised by the phrase taken from the Religious Peace of Augsburg in 1555 which permitted the German princes to determine the faiths of their territories (*cuius regio, eius religio*). Roscher saw rulers such as the Emperor Ferdinand II (1618–37) and the Spanish Habsburg King Philip II (1556–98) as consolidating their political power in alliance with militant churchmen who sought their help in the great struggles of the Reformation and Counter Reformation era. A new stage of 'courtly' or 'classical absolutism' began as religious passions subsided after the Thirty Years War and so also corresponded with the start of absolutism according to the territorialisation model of German political development. This age was distinguished by the personification of political power by the monarch, as expressed in the famous phrase (falsely) attributed to Louis XIV: 'I am the state' (*L'état c'est moi*). 'Enlightened absolutism' formed the last stage, according to Roscher's model, and was characterised by the subordination of the monarch to the wider good, exemplified by Frederick II and Joseph II and their claims to be 'the first servant of the state' (*Le premier serviteur de l'état*).[8]

Roscher's periodisation has been extremely influential but was never watertight. It has been pointed out that not all countries progressed through the three stages at the same time, if they did so at all. This has encouraged a search for typologies rather than chronological phases. Reinhold Koser suggested distinguishing between 'practical absolutism' involving the concentration of power in royal hands, 'fundamental absolutism' as it removed all barriers to rule, and 'enlightened absolutism' as it became tempered with the new intellectual currents of the later eighteenth century.[9] These efforts continued into the 1950s, but met increasing resistance from those who felt it impossible to define meaningful categories, though, as we shall see in

Chapter 4, many still clung to the idea of a distinct type or phase of enlightened absolutism.

A possible way forward has been suggested recently by Wayne te Brake, who has criticised the term 'old regime' used to describe the period before the French Revolution. Like absolutism, the notion of an old regime post-dates the events it describes and is a product of the political controversies following the collapse of the French monarchy. Absolutism has long been regarded as the defining characteristic of the old regime, and despite the progressive tendencies ascribed to it, shares the assumption that both are essentially reactionary phenomena, deeply rooted in a pre-modern past. Without losing sight of important continuities, te Brake argues that so much changed during the great religious and political struggles of the sixteenth and early seventeenth centuries to merit the term 'new regime' for the period after about 1660.[10]

There is much to recommend this idea. As will be demonstrated throughout this work, political developments in central Europe did enter a distinct phase roughly during the first half of the seventeenth century. The exercise of political power changed considerably within one to two generations, establishing a general direction that was followed with varying degrees of consistency across the German territories and, indeed, elsewhere throughout the eighteenth century and, in some respects, well into the nineteenth. It is the contention of this book that it is appropriate to label these developments 'absolutism'. The purpose of using this term is not to resurrect the generalised, abstract models that have dominated past discussion, but to develop a new one from contemporary definitions of absolute monarchy. These rested on a specific set of justifications and theories, to be explored in Chapter 2, as well as a variety of ways to project an aura of omnipotence and seek the subordination and cooperation of the rest of society that forms the focus of Chapter 3. Before we can explore what constituted these further, we have to explain why political development took this new course in the seventeenth century.

ABSOLUTISM AS THE PRODUCT OF CRISIS

Many general explanations for the emergence of absolutism take what might be described as the eclectic long view, stressing a variety of factors behind the gradual centralisation of power in royal hands since the Reformation. This can be summed up as follows for central European absolutism, though most of the factors feature prominently in explanations for its emergence elsewhere. The impact of the religious conflicts of the sixteenth and early seventeenth centuries are said to have secured the extension of secular authority over ecclesiastical institutions and fostered an ideology of obedience. The development of permanent standing armies during the Thirty Years War 'provided princes with a reliable instrument of coercion against refractory bodies' like the territorial estates. The implementation of mercantilist protectionist economic policies helped transcend parochialism and provided additional revenue for the princely treasury. This was now administered more efficiently than before thanks to the creation of a new, more professional bureaucracy which expanded, acquired new functions and extended state authority into previously private spheres of life. Finally, old corporate social relations were eroded through the introduction of new, codified law codes emphasising common subordination to a singular, increasingly depersonalised state authority.[11]

The main problem with this view is that it highlights the means of centralisation, not the motivation behind it. Those who do go beyond description to explain causes generally see absolutism as a response to some sort of 'crisis'. This too is a retrospective concept that originates in the upheavals following the French Revolution. The depiction of Napoleon as the saviour of France from the chaos of revolution was a powerful image that gained ground in the mid-nineteenth century through the writings of historians like Ranke. There seemed to be a plausible parallel between Napoleon's return to stability in alliance with the Catholic Church and other representatives of conservative order and the actions of earlier rulers like Louis XIII and Louis XIV, who restored relative domestic tranquillity after decades of civil war and religious strife. Further evidence was provided by many contemporary political theorists who argued that the crown had reserve absolute powers that could be employed in such emergencies as civil unrest or foreign invasion. The idea of absolutism as 'emergency dictatorship' proved attractive to conservative historians during the Weimar era (1919–33) when Germany struggled, ultimately unsuccessfully, to form a stable, democratically elected government.[12]

More recently, the concept of absolutism as a product of crisis has broadened to encompass three distinct elements: a moral and intellectual crisis, an international and military crisis, and a socio-economic crisis. Varying degrees of emphasis have been placed on each, and they are often combined in different proportions as a 'general crisis of the seventeenth century' credited with fundamentally transforming European society.[13]

The concept of a moral and intellectual crisis interprets absolutism as a response to the eschatological uncertainties of the late fifteenth and early sixteenth centuries. The new intellectual currents known as the Renaissance, Reformation and Scientific Revolution combined to shatter medieval orthodoxy and reopen the debate on the ultimate fate of mankind and the universe. The previous basis for political authority collapsed as its ideological underpinnings were called into question. The debate over the best form of government was immediately complicated by the wider disputes over the 'true religion' and meaning of the world, contributing to the violence and ferocity with which these questions were settled.

However, the intellectual turmoil also threw up potential solutions. One was the alliance between throne and altar that is generally regarded as an essential prop for absolutism. The religious conflict forced all Churches regardless of confession into alliance with the crown in order to defeat their rivals and enforce their version of Christianity. This process is termed 'confessionalisation' (*Konfessionalisierung*) for central Europe and is regarded as an important factor in the wider process whereby political power became territorialised within the Reich.[14] The relationship between ruler and ruled was redefined to emphasise the sanctity, not of the person of the monarch, but of his political power and the virtues of subordination and the maintenance of order. Other solutions derived directly from the new scientific and intellectual currents. The Renaissance promoted the rediscovery and elaboration of ancient classical learning and its application to the problems of the present. One example was the revival of Roman law, under way since the twelfth century, but which only achieved a significant reception in the Reich with its dissemination by humanist scholars from the 1480s. Roman law promoted political centralisation partly because it contained numerous authoritarian principles, but mainly through its preference for rationalised, schematic structures as opposed to individual special pleading. The basis for privileges and preferential treatment was weakened, particularly where these could be portrayed as disruptive and harmful to the general good. Science provided a further boost to this by defining the natural world as a harmonious and rational order, guided by clear underlying principles.[15]

Thus, although many of the challenges to authority lay in the practical worlds of political, social, economic, military and religious affairs, the crisis and its solution were essentially cognitive. The rapid changes affecting late fifteenth- and early sixteenth-century Europe disrupted existing explanations of the world and engendered a new quest to render it comprehensible again by defining, labelling, categorising and regulating life. Only those who could solve these problems would emerge strengthened from the crisis. All the authorities charged in the late medieval world with this function failed the test; for central Europe this included imperial institutions like the Reichstag (imperial diet) and imperial courts, as well as the Church, guilds, urban governments and territorial estates. This left the territorial princes within the Reich and the monarchy in major states like France as the sole powers capable of providing the sense of order that was so desperately sought.[16]

By contrast, the second variant on the crisis theory stresses the world of practical politics and military conflict. Absolutism is explained as the product of wider shifts in the European balance of power and means of international competition. Two distinct elements can be detected that receive varying degrees of emphasis in these explanations. One is the fragmentation of the medieval states system and the rise of a new European order based increasingly on sovereign states with clearly delineated frontiers.[17] Absolutism emerged as the form of government best suited to the task of internal consolidation necessary to facilitate survival and growth in this hostile international environment. This argument has a long heritage, particularly in German-language scholarship where it is known as the 'primacy of foreign policy' theory (*Primät der Aussenpolitik*). External pressures and the geopolitical position of a given country are regarded as fundamentally more important factors in its development than domestic concerns or its social and economic structure. In a classic and sophisticated formulation by the late nineteenth-century German historian and political sociologist Otto Hintze, the 'pushing and pulling' of continental European states encouraged the emergence of absolutism, whereas countries on the periphery of great power struggles, or those like Britain which were protected by geography, were able to develop differently.[18] After falling out of fashion with the rise of social history after 1945, this interpretation has been revived recently and reaffirmed with a new cultural dimension. Most princes and European monarchs were not concerned with the minutiae of domestic reforms but with securing and retaining universal recognition of their personal grandeur and that of their dynasty and court. This required constant intervention in wider affairs to impress fellow rulers, in turn necessitating a high level of military and court spending. Political centralisation and intervention in social and economic relations were simply means to this end.[19]

The changes in warfare known as the 'military revolution' constitute the second element of the international and military crisis. The spread of gunpowder technology during the later fifteenth century, combined with the introduction of other improved infantry weapons, changed the way wars were fought. In place of the aristocratic armoured knight, the battlefield was now dominated by large masses of common footsoldiers employing the new pikes and firearms in disciplined formations. These tactical and technological changes increased the scale and cost of warfare as skilled expertise and scarce resources were required, particularly with respec to the heavy cannon needed to counter improvements in fortification techniques. Those princes who managed to master and monopolise the new means of waging war secured a decisive advantage over their internal and external rivals. The retinues of the powerful magnates proved no match for the new royal and princely forces which were not only larger, but better disciplined and equipped, and frequently recruited from areas outside the territory, such as Switzerland or the Low Countries.

Like all such grand concepts, the idea of a military revolution in early modern Europe sparked considerable controversy when it was first advanced in 1956. While some historians now dispute the idea altogether, most still see the changes of the century after 1450 as significant, and certainly more important than those between 1560 and 1660, which were identified initially as the timespan of the 'revolution'.[20] Some social theorists arrived at these conclusions independently. The social psychologist Norbert Elias, writing in the 1930s, already identified the rise of gunpowder technology and new infantry tactics as factors behind the decline of the aristocracy and the emergence of absolutism.[21] Other theorists have borrowed more directly from the historical model, notably Brian Downing, Anthony Giddens and the political scientist Bruce Porter, while Michael Mann, Charles Tilly and Thomas Ertman have also emphasised military developments in their explanations of absolutism.[22] Underlying all these interpretations is a reliance on Max Weber's definition of the state as the monopoly of legitimate violence within a given territory. Political centralisation and the accumulation of military power are thus two aspects of the same process of absolutist state formation.

The third form of crisis interprets absolutism as the political product of social and economic pressures. Some explanations take the long view, arguing that the growth of royal power was a response to a series of crises in the fourteenth and fifteenth centuries, including the demographic impact of the Black Death, the gradual shift to a money economy and the rise of capitalism following the expansion and integration of European markets, and the advent of global commerce with the discovery of the New World.[23] Others highlight the more specific economic problems of the early seventeenth century which are associated with the broader concept of a 'General Crisis'. These include the shifts in production at the end of the sixteenth century that are believed to be behind the intensification of feudal agriculture in central and eastern Europe known as 'second serfdom', as well as the dislocation in the continental pattern of trade following the growth of the 'Atlantic economy' focused on western European countries with better access to the markets of the New World and colonies.[24] The attempts of various pre-modern elites to cope with these changes provide the social dimension. In this interpretation, absolutism becomes the political framework through which groups such as the feudal aristocracy hold on to their domestic economic and social pre-eminence during this period of fundamental change.

The variety in state structures throughout Europe is explained by the different outcomes of these crises, usually exemplified by a comparison between England and France. Both were rocked by turmoil in the first half of the seventeenth century but the outcome was clearly different. One influential viewpoint interprets England's constitutional monarchy and powerful Parliament as the product of a successful 'political revolution' during the English Civil War. At the same time attempts to broaden the base of political participation were frustrated in the failed 'social revolution' of the Levellers and other radical groups of the 1640s. By contrast, absolutism resolved the crisis in France left by the failure to develop late medieval constitutionalism in the unsuccessful political revolution of the Fronde between 1648 and 1653.[25] The impact of international pressures and military change is often emphasised as decisive in explaining these different outcomes. Brian Downing develops Hintze's arguments that those states that escaped conflict at the time of the military revolution were better able to preserve and develop their late medieval constitutions and so avoid absolutism. Thomas Ertman has considerably extended such arguments by recognising that the onset of prolonged international conflict could act as an important variable since the methods for waging war were in a constant state of evolution. Depending on the timing of such conflict and how it interacted with the nature of existing local government and representative assemblies like the estates, he detects four possible outcomes: patrimonial constitutionalism (Poland, Hungary), bureaucratic constitutionalism (Britain, Sweden), patrimonial absolutism (France and the rest of Latin Europe) and bureaucratic absolutism (Denmark and the German states).[26]

Cutting across such interpretations based on the tripartite notion of crisis are two further perspectives reflecting the twin poles of Western social philosophy variously expressed as the dichotomy between structure and action, macro and micro, or society and the individual. Neither perspective is exclusively associated with any one of the three crises, but instead tend to be combined in varying proportions with each to produce a broad spectrum of interpretations.

Micro perspectives emphasise human agency and see absolutism resulting from individual action. Wider pressures do not disappear from the equation, but are seen as subordinate to the activities of a few key figures who are credited with influencing events, if not actually shaping them. This accounts for the preference for the term 'state-building' rather than formation, to emphasise the conscious and deliberate actions behind political change. Even where wider circumstance is given greater prominence, human error and miscalculation are perceived as significant factors.

Micro perspectives are frequently found in combination with the concept of an intellectual and moral crisis. Whether responding to external pressures, or acting on their own initiative, key figures such as individual rulers, bureaucrats or political theorists all sought new methods of government and, in so doing, became themselves forces for change. The most extreme version of this approach interprets absolutism 'by blueprint' as the implementation of a plan derived from the new intellectual currents and emulation of systems in place elsewhere. There is some evidence for this view, notably in Russia where Peter the Great obtained copies of Swedish government ordinances and imposed them on his own administration and subjects. This interpretation features prominently in the work of those historians who have drawn extensively on central government records and the private papers of individual monarchs and their officials whose actions often seem more rational and planned to posterity than to their contemporaries.[27]

The other main variant is the 'Great Men' school of history in which dynamic figures stamp their mark on their age by military victories, architectural and artistic achievements, domestic reforms and sheer force of personality. Despite its popular label, the interpretation is not exclusively male dominated, as indicated by the significance ascribed to Catherine II, Maria Theresa and a string of French royal mistresses. Understandably, historical biography is the most common form expressing this view of absolutism, but the role of dynamic individuals surfaces in a surprisingly wide range of interpretations. The most important example is the Great Elector, Frederick William of Brandenburg-Prussia, who is repeatedly credited with founding the modern state by scholars who otherwise give prominence to broader, impersonal forces.[28]

These forces are at the heart of the macro perspective which emphasises the underlying structural features largely beyond individual human control. When combined with the concept of an intellectual and moral crisis, the macro perspective interprets absolutism as the response to wider pressures with the new intellectual currents merely providing the means to make sense of this process. Instead of shaping change, political theorists simply responded to it by using the language of science and philosophy to explain the new forms of state. Similarly, rulers and their apologists borrowed absolutist rhetoric and theory to justify what they were already doing as they centralised power. Whereas the micro perspective on international pressures emphasises the relative ability of such rulers as the Great Elector to defeat their enemies, the macro variant robs them of most of their influence and instead stresses the underlying trend towards powerful sovereign states to which each country had to respond or go under. The history of Poland appears to provide an example. Though not short on able individuals, the elective Polish monarchy was unable to overcome the structural constraints imposed by the entrenched power of a strong aristocracy and the interference of foreign powers, and was ultimately incapable of resisting extinction by partition between 1772 and 1795. Such explanations also point to the third type of macro perspective, which is combined with the notion of a socio-economic crisis. This has spawned a detailed and complex literature that merits more extensive treatment in the next section.

ABSOLUTISM IN MARXIST INTERPRETATIONS

Socio-economic factors feature most prominently in those explanations equating absolutism with the transition from feudalism to capitalism. These include both Marxist historiography and the approach associated with the French Annales school. Of the two, the Marxist perspective is by far the more important, not least because Annales historians have tended to downplay high political developments to the extent that they virtually disappear altogether from some of their studies. Furthermore, the Annales approach has generally been applied to France and the Mediterranean region, whereas Marxist historiography addresses central European history directly.[29]

However, there is no such thing as *the* Marxist explanation of absolutism. Whereas Marx referred to absolutism as the 'direct agent of capitalism', Engels developed a more sophisticated model of the crown as mediator between a declining feudal aristocracy and a rising capitalist bourgeoisie. He believed that the position of the two classes had reached a rough equilibrium by the seventeenth century, creating an opportunity for the crown to free itself from the constraints of late medieval constitutionalism by siding with the bourgeoisie and bringing them into its expanding administration. However, when these upstarts began making political demands for their class, the monarch fell back on the nobility as his 'natural' allies in the 'feudal reaction' of the eighteenth century. This attempt to hold up the historical process was doomed to failure because changes in the mode of production were shifting real power away from the feudal landowners and placing it in the hands of merchants, manufacturers and professionals. The political superstructure of the absolutist state gave way in the fundamental social realignment of the French Revolution which ushered in new forms more attuned to the interests of bourgeois capitalism.

Though this scheme loosely fits the course of French history, it suffers from fundamental problems, not least the absence of concrete evidence that social and economic structures were developing as Engels believed, and it seems even less applicable to the situation in central Europe.[30] Neither Marx nor Engels was primarily interested in history, and their references to absolutism remain fragments scattered throughout works on entirely different topics and are often contradictory. This is a perennial source of frustration to some Marxist scholars who have expended much energy disputing what the Great Men might have meant. Fortunately, most have had the good sense to use these ideas as starting points for their own explanations which, since 1945, have tended to revolve around variations of 'Western' and 'Eastern' models of European absolutism.

Discussions of the Western model generally follow Engels's concept of the crown as arbiter of social disputes, siding initially with the bourgeoisie before closing ranks with the aristocracy in the feudal reaction some time in the eighteenth century. Britain and the Dutch Republic are interpreted as having escaped this process by undergoing 'early bourgeois revolutions', enabling a more advanced and commercially active bourgeoisie to modernise the state more directly. This occurred during the Eighty Years War (1568–1648) when the Dutch overthrew Spanish rule and established an independent republic, while the Civil War and 1688's Glorious Revolution secured a similar advance for Britain within the framework of a constitutional monarchy.

The Eastern model encompasses not only Russia, but Prussia, Austria and the German states and draws on Marx's belief that these countries experienced a 'stunted' (*verkrüppelter*) version of Western progressive development. The growth of capitalist forms of production in Britain, the Dutch Republic and absolutist France compelled the less well-developed states of central and eastern Europe to adapt or suffer in international political and economic competition. Their monarchies responded by introducing reforms intended to enforce tighter regulation of agriculture and commerce. Since these measures left little room for the development of a large and vibrant bourgeoisie, the crown was compelled to accommodate itself with the still powerful feudal aristocracy. This compromise was at the expense of the peasants who were obliged to work harder for the nobles and pay war taxes to the crown. Soviet historians such as Boris Porshnev added a second subsidiary strand to this model by arguing that the gradual transition to capitalism heightened class conflict and caused the crown and aristocracy to draw together and defend themselves. They established powerful standing armies, officered by reliable nobles and recruited, allegedly, from foreign mercenaries who could be trusted to crush peasant opposition and serve in external wars of conquest and plunder.[31]

East German Marxist scholars responded to Western critics who pointed to the relative absence of large-scale risings while absolutism was being established. They argued that this was due to the deterrent effect of the new mercenary armies, which had already proved their utility in defeating popular protest during the Peasants' War of 1524–6, and to the fact that the opposition to absolutism had passed to bourgeois intellectual circles. The peasants were reduced to 'lower forms of class struggle' such as sabotage, arson, malingering and emigration.[32]

However, the fiercest disputes raged within Marxist circles and centred on disagreements on the role attributed to economic factors. Orthodox Marxist theory places absolutist theory and institutions in the 'superstructure' that is determined by the economic 'base'. Changes occur within the base, especially in the mode of production, as people develop new ways of making, distributing and consuming goods and services. These changes trigger tensions in the 'relations of production', or the social distribution of economic power. Specifically, the growth of capitalist forms of production disturb society as previously privileged and wealthy groups are displaced by those profiting from the new economic practices. These tensions mount until they can only be resolved by transforming the political, cultural and ideological superstructure to bring it in line with the new mode of production. The perennial problem with this theoretical insight lies in relating it to the available evidence. It is far from clear that direct or even indirect links can be drawn from changes in the western and central European economy and the apparently differing political outcomes. This has alienated not only non-Marxists, but those wishing to remain within the tradition of Historical Materialism. The work of Perry Anderson and Robert Brenner represents the most important response to this problem. Anderson's ideas are older and better known, but Brenner's have sparked the fiercest controversy and are the source of the most recent Marxist contribution to the debate on central European absolutism.[33]

Anderson criticised older Marxist studies for their generic use of the term 'economic' to refer to the material base of the mode of production and argued that this only makes sense for capitalism where 'surplus extraction' is truly economic in the form of profit taking. The rest of social life has to be considered for feudalism since the extraction by those in power extended beyond the purely economic to include military and labour services as well as political loyalty. Through this 'extra-economic coercion', things normally attributed to the super-structure now define the base; in short, a key tenet of orthodox Marxist theory is turned on its head. 'The "superstructures" of kinship, religion, law or the state necessarily enter into the constitutive structure of the mode of production in pre-capitalist society' and it is not until the advent of capitalism that they are fully bounced upwards from the base to the superstructure. 'In consequence, pre-capitalist modes of production cannot be defined *except* via their political, legal and ideological superstructures, since they are what determines the type of extra-economic coercion that specifies them'.[34]

In addition to this fundamentally different conception of feudalism, Anderson rejects the orthodox Marxist linear stage theory whereby the inherent contradictions of one mode of production force a transformation into the next. Instead of seeing capitalism as emerging from the contradictions within feudalism, he argues that it stemmed from the complex interrelationship of at least two previous modes of production, adding 'antiquity' to feudalism. The former had disappeared by the Middle Ages but the period from the fourteenth to the nineteenth century saw the coexistence of both feudalism and capitalism.[35]

These theoretical foundations underpin Anderson's version of the Marxist Eastern and Western models of absolutism. His Western model remains fairly true to the 'economistic' interpretations described above in that it interprets the demise of serfdom and the growth of an

urban bourgeoisie as reducing aristocratic control over wealth pro-
ducers. 'The result was a *displacement* of politico-legal coercion
upwards towards a centralised, militarised summit – The Absolutist
State' which compensated the nobles for their loss of economic
power by defending their class status.[36] Anderson's model has been
subjected to severe criticism, including from fellow Marxists who
claim that it merely describes absolutism's functions rather than
explains its origins.[37]

His Eastern model has, however, received a more favourable reception. International competition receives a greater than usual emphasis,
with the impact of Swedish expansionism in the mid-seventeenth
century highlighted as a factor behind Russian and Prussian absolutism, alongside the more customary references to the threat posed by
the expanding capitalist economies of Britain, France and the Dutch
Republic. The eastern European monarchies responded to these
pressures through a direct compact between crown and aristocracy,
whereby the latter surrendered political power in return for the imposition of serfdom, often in areas where it had not previously existed.
Anderson's Eastern model is thus the exact opposite of that for the
West; in the former absolutism is 'a device for the consolidation of
serfdom', whereas in the latter it served as 'compensation for the dis-
appearance of serfdom'.[38]

As will be apparent from this discussion, despite its different theoretical premise and important points of detail, Anderson's East/West
model shares much in common with the other Marxist viewpoints.
All have a root in Historical Materialism, including its sense of the
motive force and direction of history and the belief that human
development passes through successive stages. Absolutism is always
identified as a key transitional phase between two of the most important of these stages: feudalism and capitalism. The concept of tensions
between base and superstructure is present in the view that absolutism
was riddled with contradictions, fostering the very developments that
would bring about its demise: 'Absolutist states helped perpetuate
feudalism, but they also facilitated the growth of capitalism within
it'.[39] The disagreements are on how this came about. Finally, absolutism is interpreted as essentially 'reactionary'. Though it fostered
the progressive forces of capitalism, it was ultimately identified with
the feudal social elite and served their interests.

This is apparent in Anderson's distinction between the social and
economic characteristics of absolutism. While arguing for the coexistence of both feudal and capitalist forms of production during
the period, Anderson nonetheless firmly associates the former with

aristocratic agrarian domination and the absolutist state, while identifying the latter with the urban bourgeoisie and international capital
accumulation. Absolutism thus fostered capitalism only indirectly by
stabilising feudal agrarian domination and so preventing the landed
aristocracy from becoming entrepreneurial farmers. This permitted
the growth of a separate urban bourgeoisie within the relative security
provided by the militarised absolutist state, though the nature of the
crown–aristocratic alliance mitigated against this in the East. Others
share this broad interpretation, and for this reason associate absolutism with political reaction and economic backwardness, even in
western Europe where monarchies like France are viewed as being
increasingly outpaced by the 'bourgeois regimes' in Britain and the
Dutch Republic.[40]

This position predetermines Anderson's discussion of social relations
in Prussia – the area of central Europe to which he devotes the most
coverage. The presence of capitalist elements in 'feudal' Prussia is
denied, though it should be mentioned that most of the research that
demonstrates their growth in the eighteenth century was published
after Anderson completed his work.[41] According to Anderson, the
Prussian Junkers were not 'agrarian capitalists' as some theorists
have claimed, but still essentially feudal landlords, only switching to
more market-orientated production in the Reform Era (1806–13), as
the Hohenzollern monarchy supposedly reorientated itself from East
to West in the wake of defeat by Napoleonic France and the subsequent
acquisition of the industrialising Rhineland in 1814/15.[42]

An attempt has been made recently to address some of these
problems while preserving a Marxist interpretation of absolutism.
Building on the work of Robert Brenner, Colin Mooers has tried to
integrate the different patterns of German, French and British state
formation within a broader account of the emergence of capitalism.
In a series of highly controversial articles, Brenner tried to link the different routes to capitalism with divergencies in feudal class relationships which he believed already divided east and west Europe in the
Middle Ages. The late fourteenth-century feudal crisis benefited
many Western peasants who gained rights over land. Where prices
were high and peasants had access to markets, small-scale commercial
farming could develop. Brenner regarded this 'petty commodity production' as crucial to capitalism's development, because the emergence
of a 'middling sort' of yeoman farmers caused tensions within peasant
communities. As village solidarity broke down, enterprising lords were
able to consolidate their estates at the expense of the marginalised,
weaker peasants and engage in large-scale commercial farming. This

took off in Britain, but remained stalled in France and elsewhere due to the nature of political developments, including absolutism.

Mooers extends Brenner's analysis by giving greater coverage to central Europe and expanding his account of state formation. In a direct challenge to Anderson's theory, Mooers seeks to relocate absolutism's origins in the economic base rather than the politico-cultural superstructure. He draws on Brenner's concept of 'political accumulation' which roughly corresponds to what social theorists label 'monopoly formation'. Since feudal production was relatively inflexible, Brenner argues, the only way to increase yields significantly was to expand the control of people and land by accumulating coercive means such as legal rights and military power. Political accumulation made the state a 'class-like phenomenon' since it became 'an independent surplus-extractor' using its coercive powers to take a significant slice of peasant production through taxation.[43]

This model is then related to Brenner's discussion of petty commodity production to account for the different paths to capitalism and the modern state in Britain, France and Germany. Britain supposedly avoided absolutism and took a shortcut to capitalism because the landed gentry had 'unchallenged control of the state' after the 'English Revolution' of 1640, reducing Parliament to a 'committee of landlords' governing in the interests of capitalism. It was a 'bourgeois revolution', even though it was not made by the bourgeoisie. The presence of a strong yeoman class further served to promote capitalism and acted as a buffer between the gentry and the mass of landless peasants. The spread of share cropping prevented the growth of a comparable class in France, exposing the aristocracy to the threat of popular unrest and so forcing them to seek protection from an absolute monarchy. German, or rather Prussian, absolutism is explained is largely similar terms. The absence of a strong yeoman class heightened class tension and forced the nobles to seek the crown's protection against peasant revolts, while the monarchy also defended them against rival lords in other countries. In contrast to the supposed fusion of the state and gentry in Britain, the Prussian monarchy acted in Brenner's manner as a class, competing for a share of the relatively inflexible peasant production with the nobility. As the Junkers were able to prevent the crown from significantly diminishing their share of this surplus extraction, the Hohenzollerns were allegedly driven to conquer new lands from their neighbours.

There are a number of serious flaws in this scheme. While it differs from Anderson's model, it still rests on an exaggerated East–West divide in European economic and political history and neither Brenner nor Mooers took sufficient account of the recent research on East Elbian social and agrarian relations.[44] In some places the facts appear to be made to fit the theory: for instance, there is little evidence that Hohenzollern expansionism was propelled by the crown's inability to reduce the Junkers' share of peasant production. On the contrary, it was the involvement in international competition that demanded ever more resources and caused them to intervene in social relations. More usually, however, it seems as if theory is stretched to accommodate awkward facts to the point that it is doubtful if such a varied and diverse experience can be encompassed within the original concepts. This was already apparent in the debate surrounding Brenner's original thesis which became increasingly abstract and detached from what it was supposed to be explaining.[45]

These arguments have been explored in detail because they reveal the assumption underlying all Marxist theories of the state: that it always represents the interests of the dominant class. The absolutist state is thus a 'captured state', created and controlled by the feudal aristocracy, despite whatever fragmentary autonomy individual monarchs may have exercised. This permits Anderson and Mooers to reconcile their interpretations with the essentially traditional historiography from which they draw their material for central Europe. Prussian domination of Germany is as inevitable for Anderson as it was for many conservative and nationalist historians, though the basis for this assertion is radically different. In place of micro perspectives, such as the glorification of the Hohenzollern dynasty, or more traditional macro viewpoints emphasising geopolitics, Anderson argues that only Prussia could emerge as a strong absolutist state, because only it had the necessary precondition of 'an economically strong and stable landowning class'.[46]

THE HISTORIC COMPROMISE

The importance of the Prussian example to Marxist and other explanations of central European absolutism necessitates its further investigation. All versions of the Eastern model of absolutism stress a compromise between crown and aristocracy as fundamental to the consolidation and extension of royal power. Many nineteenth-century historians had already detected this and identified its key element as the Recess, or concluding agreement, between the Great Elector and the Brandenburg estates, dated 5 August 1653.[47] This document confirmed various old rights previously granted by past electors to the

Brandenburg estates, including the right to advise on external relations. Other provisions legalised the condition of hereditary subordination (*Erbuntertänigheit*) that had been developing since the early sixteenth century and which permitted the extension of formal serfdom over all those who could not prove they were legally freemen. Since most peasants lacked such documentation, or had lost it during the confusion of the Thirty Years War, this measure appeared to strengthen the nobles' position considerably. In addition, earlier privileges exempting the nobility from taxation and extending their jurisdiction over the peasants were confirmed, while further clauses consolidated aristocratic access to landownership by making it harder for foreigners or commoners to acquire noble estates. In return for these concessions the Brandenburg nobility dominating the estates voted war taxes totalling 530,000 taler over six years, or sufficient for Frederick William to maintain a modest standing army of 5,000 men.

The money is widely regarded as crucial as it gave the elector a measure of practical power which he quickly consolidated and extended as his lands became embroiled in the Northern War between Sweden and Poland (1655–60). Troops funded by one Hohenzollern province were deployed to intimidate the estates of another, notably those in the western enclaves of Cleve and Mark, and later those of the duchy of East Prussia. Meanwhile, the general emergency permitted Frederick William to levy more soldiers and taxes, reinforcing his diplomatic position and allowing him to extract important concessions from both the warring parties. He continued to strengthen his domestic position after 1660 by introducing two distinct forms of taxation designed to split the estates. An indirect excise (*Akzise*) was imposed on the towns, while a direct war tax (*Kontribution*) was levied in the countryside. The former retarded the growth of a commercial bourgeoisie, but the latter preserved the compromise since the nobles could offload payment on to the peasants. The subsequent expansion of the Hohenzollern army and administration further reconciled the nobles to absolutism by providing careers and other rewards.[48]

Similar examples can be detected in other important German territories. Elector Johann Georg III secured the agreement of the Saxon estates to fund his army in 1682 by granting concessions reinforcing aristocratic privilege and exclusivity, including preferential treatment in appointments as army officers.[49] However, it is the Brandenburg Recess of 1653 that has attracted by far the most attention. Perry Anderson describes it as 'the beginnings of the social pact between the Elector and the aristocracy which was to provide the foundation of Prussian Absolutism', while others call it the 'foundation-stone of the Brandenburg-Prussian military state' and the origin of later Prusso-German militarism.[50] Disagreement centres on the precise consequences of this 'Historic Compromise'. One school of thought believes there was a shift of power between the parties in favour of the crown, reducing the aristocracy to a 'service nobility', reconciled to their loss of political influence by the preservation of their socio-economic privileges and the extension of alternative career opportunities within the army and bureaucracy.[51] By contrast, most Marxists regard this shift as of little importance since it took place within the same 'ruling elite'. The compromise was an intra-class agreement and the state remained essentially feudal.

The existence of such an explicit compromise is now being called into question by recent historical research. The critique concentrates on the two fundamental elements of supposed class solidarity and the consolidation of noble power. Though they did grant their ruler new taxes in 1653, the Brandenburg nobility remained opposed to the idea of a standing army and state service. Long after the permanence of both the army and its funding arrangements had become established, many Brandenburg nobles refused to serve in it or assist in its recruitment. Frederick William and his three immediate successors relied heavily on nobles born outside their domains to provide essential expertise, particularly while absolutism was being established during the later seventeenth century: French Huguenot refugees accounted for fully one-third of all army officers in 1689. Native nobles remained, by and large, opponents of absolutism rather than its collaborators and several historians now suspect that the extent of their discontent has been masked by the way in which nineteenth-century editors compiled important published collections of such Prussian documents as the *Acta Borussica*. Aristocratic criticism persisted well into the eighteenth century and its targets included measures like the canton system of military recruitment, which was also widely identified as an element of the compromise.[52]

Comparison with other German territories has relativised the claims made for the power of the Brandenburg-Prussian Junkers. The nobles in Mecklenburg and Swedish Pomerania were able to introduce comparable large-scale estate farming with dependent serf labour without needing the help of an absolute monarch. Indeed, one empirically based Marxist study has concluded that the Mecklenburg nobles opposed their duke in order to defend their socio-economic pre-eminence.[53] Perhaps more fundamentally, the concept of a powerful

Junker class dealing with the elector as equal partners has been called into question by the work of William Hagen and other scholars reappraising agrarian relations east of the River Elbe.[54]

The economic position of the Junkers had certainly been strong during the sixteenth and early seventeenth centuries prior to the customary start date for Prussian absolutism. However, their situation was not as prosperous as previously thought, for though they commanded a substantial workforce, there were still many independent peasant farms protected by crown legislation. Brandenburg's involvement in the Thirty Years War after 1626 precipitated a crisis that proved disastrous for many nobles who, far from being able to make gains at the expanse of the peasants, suffered severe losses. The decline in population reduced the workforce while increasing the bargaining power of the survivors. Peasants refused to accept the customary subordination, especially (and understandably) because the elector and Junkers had failed in their duty to protect them from foreign invasion. Where they had previously been compelled to work they now demanded wages, while those who had been paid insisted on a raise. Official wage rates were nearly double those of 1551 by 1635 and many Junkers paid well above this to secure scarce labour. The return of relative calm in the 1640s brought no respite and the Junkers were compelled to offer further concessions to retain workers and attract new ones. Some Brandenburg peasants were sufficiently emboldened by 1646 to arm themselves against regular troops and by 1651 the nobles were clamouring for crown intervention to restore the subordination and respect they considered appropriate.

Thus, the Brandenburg nobles negotiated the 1653 Recess from a position of weakness rather than strength and this is reflected in the true nature of the agreement. Far from consolidating and extending aristocratic power and privilege, the terms largely restored a position that had been recently eroded. More importantly, the crown inserted itself as mediator between nobles and peasants by granting the latter the right to appeal beyond the Junkers' local jurisdiction to the state courts. The balance had shifted against the nobles and it is clear that they derived no substantial benefits from the Recess. Though the elector issued further decrees in 1670 and 1683 stiffening their formal powers to force their tenants to work, in practice the Junkers were unable to return to the old system of unpaid labour. It was openly admitted that the rules were being ignored and attempts to reduce or limit wage levels also failed, and it was not until the 1720s that the nobles recovered their former position. The chief factor behind this was not the support of the crown but the general demographic recovery following the Thirty Years War. By 1713 population levels had returned to those of 1614. Peasant bargaining power was reduced as pressure on land increased, forcing a rise in the minimum marriage age to reach twenty-five by 1735, and creating a pool of unmarried younger men who could be exploited as unpaid labour on the Junkers' estates.

However, the crown had gained significantly in the meantime, indicating that it, not the nobility, was the chief beneficiary of the alleged compromise. It entrenched its position as mediator between nobles, peasants and other social groups, and extended its power over the population by breaking the landlords' monopoly of peasant labour with the introduction of limited conscription through the canton system by 1733. Noble opposition persisted but was worn down through the employment of foreign aristocrats and non-noble specialists. No less than 259 Brandenburg aristocratic families died out from natural causes between 1540 and the early eighteenth century, creating opportunities for the elector to choose newcomers as servants. Many of these came from other German territories, or from France, but the sheer size of the indigenous nobility ensured that the elector did not have to rely on recalcitrant families for crucial roles. Indeed, the concept of a service nobility must be questioned given that there were no more than 500 higher civil posts in the entire monarchy as late as 1720, while even at the end of the century two-thirds of all nobles had no prospect of a government or military appointment. The incorporation of numerous lesser nobles through the acquisition of parts of Poland after 1772 meant that although the officer corps increased from 3,100 in 1740 to 5,500 forty years later, the proportion of the total nobility this represented declined from one-seventh to one-tenth.[55]

The evidence for Brandenburg-Prussia can be supported by broadly similar findings from the Habsburg monarchy, which is often in danger of being unduly neglected in this context. Crown–noble relations within the Habsburg territories also underwent a significant reordering in the early seventeenth century, though the precise pattern was different due to the ethnic and religious diversity of the various aristocracies. Family feuds had weakened the Habsburg dynasty by the 1590s and left it ill-equipped to tackle the serious international and domestic pressures it faced. Fragile alliances between sections of the Hungarian, Austrian and Bohemian nobilities and disaffected members of the dynasty allowed the different territorial estates to underpin their political autonomy with guarantees for religious freedom. The crisis peaked in the Bohemian revolt of 1618 which is generally taken as the start of the Thirty Years War. However, the Habsburg victory at the Battle of White Mountain in 1620 created the first of several opportunities to recover lost authority. Significantly, this was done in conjunction with other sections of the nobility who, because of kinship, religious sympathies or ethnic origin, were considered more reliable. Habsburg opponents were dispossessed and their estates redistributed to loyal supporters, often based originally in another part of the monarchy and almost invariably adherents of Catholicism. The consensus under-pinning and legitimising the regime was refounded on this more partisan confessional basis, strengthening the monarchy and raising its profile internationally.

However, there were clear limits to how far this could be pushed. Attempts to extend it into the Reich to revive imperial authority encountered stiff opposition. Habsburg victories encouraged Emperor Ferdinand II to pass the Edict of Restitution in 1629, legitimising a redistribution of confiscated Protestant land to his supporters within the German territories. A further effort was made at the Peace of Prague in 1635 which tried to integrate most of the territorial armies into a single force controlled by the emperor and his chief supporters. Swedish and then French intervention in the Reich frustrated these measures and eventually forced Ferdinand's successor to conclude peace at Westphalia in 1648. Nonetheless, the final treaty confirmed the relative autonomy of the Habsburg lands within the Reich and left the emperor free to continue to reward loyal clients at the expense of recalcitrant or refractory opponents. Throughout, the crown sought, as in Brandenburg-Prussia, to widen its freedom of action and extend the basis of its legitimacy by acting as mediator between significant social groups.[56]

The process of compromise thus looks far less straightforward than some explanations would suggest. Crucially, there is little evidence that the nobility collectively sought a stronger monarchy, though sections certainly demanded assistance in mastering the peasants. Closer examination reveals the fallacy of regarding the nobility, or indeed the peasants and any other section of society, as a homogeneous, undif-ferentiated group with uniform aims and interests. Absolute monarchy certainly served aristocratic interests, but not those of a single *aristocracy*. Neither was it controlled by a group defined by their rela-tionship to a particular form of production. These conclusions suggest that we need to reconsider the questions posed at the start of this chapter as to what prompted absolutism's emergence and when this occurred.

PRELIMINARY CONCLUSIONS

The question of dates is important since, if we are to believe that absolutism was the product of crisis, it is essential to know which crisis. As the opening discussion of absolutism's origins and periodisation has shown, there is no agreement on this issue. Part of the problem is the imprecision in the definition of absolutism itself, a question to which we will return in the following two chapters. These will indicate that it is not simply a label for political centralisation, but a *distinct form* of monarchical rule which emerged in the early to mid-seventeenth century. We can thus dispense with the almost impossible task of explaining all political centralisation and address the more specific question of why central European rulers changed the way they conducted and justified their actions during the seventeenth century.

The tripartite concept of crisis suggests that we need to look at the military and international shifts associated with the Thirty Years War, along with the concomitant intellectual turmoil, sense of uncertainty and economic dislocation and change. The macro and micro perspectives indicate the relative importance of wider, structural factors, as well as the role of individual personality, human error and chance. At this point we should also remember an important warning posed by those who claim absolutism is a myth. The assumption that absolutism is the product of crisis clearly belongs to one of the 'master narratives' of European history, depicting the state as the resolver of strife, guarantor of order and engine of progress. The state also *caused* disorder, principally by waging destructive wars and disrupting established customs and behaviour in its effort to fund these.

Such considerations suggest a way out of what might otherwise become a rather sterile debate and help avoid a futile pursuit of the holy grail of historical theory: the search for the 'ultimate primacy' or fundamental driving force of human history. Like all political forms, absolutism emerged through human interaction, especially within the overlapping matrices of collaboration and competition to exploit and enjoy scarce resources. Such activity takes place at all levels of human society and a full discussion would break the bounds of this brief study. For present purposes, the varied nature of absolutism, and its degree of completeness or absence, can be explained by the specific nature of a matrix of three broad arenas of human interaction with the three key elements of political power.

The international arena provided the level of interaction between territories and states. For central Europe this included the overarching framework of the Reich, as well as the wider European states system.

The Reich remained an important factor throughout the period under review, leading some German historians to argue that the smaller territories were never absolutist because princely authority remained circumscribed by imperial law and institutions.[57] The state served as a second arena, to be defined not only by its formal institutions, but by the people who composed and controlled them. Like the international arena, the state is not itself a single actor, but simultaneously a forum and a force for action. The third arena of interaction was the society, or inhabitants of a given territory or state. This can be usefully broken down into local and regional levels, defined by the particular social and spatial distribution of power in each territory. An important part of the development of absolute rule, as with the general process of political centralisation in early modern Europe, was the state's containment of autonomous action within this arena through the practical and ideological articulation of sovereignty to sever formal connections between local and regional power-holders in one territory with those in another.

The first element of political power consists of the power to command, or executive authority. The process of state formation is also the process of monopoly formation as executive authority in the key areas of judicial, fiscal and military power (or organised coercion, or violence) becomes concentrated in a clearly defined political centre. This is related to the definition of state sovereignty and is a process which looks simultaneously outwards and inwards as the authority of external powers is excluded, while those within the territory are brought under unitary control. The formation of state sovereignty is a gradual process, even in crucial areas like the control of extra-territorial violence, and is arguably never completed.[58] It is also dependent on the second element of political power, which concerns the infrastructure necessary to put executive authority into practice. Infrastructural power includes not only the formal institutions of the state administration, but the social composition of its staff and the technologies they employ, such as a written culture and methods of record keeping. Both executive authority and the effectiveness of its infrastructure are further dependent on the degree to which they are deemed legitimate. Legitimacy thus constitutes the third element of political power and embraces the values used to justify the social distribution of power and the extent to which these are accepted or contested within society.

The next chapter explores how this third element of political power was defined under absolutism, while Chapter 3 examines the practical extent of executive authority and the state infrastructure. This chapter has indicated that we need to move beyond the association of the formation of absolutism with a particular social group or class. Importantly, we must not lose sight of the fact that the so-called 'ordinary people' played a part in political change before the advent of participatory democracy. This has been partially obscured by micro perspectives of the top-down, Great Men approach to the past, as well as by macro interpretations stressing underlying, impersonal forces. The absolutist state was not captured by a single class, nor was it detached from society, standing benevolently above it as some nineteenth-century conservative models would have us believe. Instead it faced pressures both from the external international arena and the internal society. The constant interaction of these pressures is best understood as a bargaining process, as different forces, states, groups and individuals collaborated and competed with one another. Bargaining too needs to be considered in its widest sense, involving not only formal channels like the territorial estates or courts of law, but active and passive informal pressure, such as popular protest, revolts and religious nonconformity. The language of the bargaining process could also be cryptic and opaque, as both the next chapter and the later section on the absolutist court will illustrate.

2 Theory

POLITICAL THEORY IN EARLY MODERN CENTRAL EUROPE

Discussions of absolutism as a theory are beset by the general problems affecting analysis of it as a historical concept. This is particularly true for central Europe where the example of Prussia distorts the wider picture and obscures the continued role of the Reich. Coverage of the German conception of absolutism frequently concentrates on the means to impose it, rather than the ideas themselves, and often goes no further than general references to rule by the grace of God (*Gottesgnadentum*).

These deficiencies may be explained by a misunderstanding of the role of political theory in early modern Europe. Theorists sought definitions and worked largely within the accepted categories borrowed from classical philosophy and Christian theology. Some were apologists for monarchs, while others opposed stronger royal rule. However, all wrote with at least one eye on their contemporary world and were conscious of the potential consequences of their writings. Some were deliberately vague, particularly those who favoured absolutism and found it impossible to place limits on omnipotence. More importantly, we should abandon the idea that the theorists posterity has thought worthy of study were necessarily representative of their age. Ideas were in a constant state of flux and varied over time and space. Even writers who were genuinely influential at the time changed their minds, contradicted themselves and were open to different interpretations. There is thus a danger of constructing a retrospective, generic and singular 'theory' of absolutism from a set of very disparate and changing components. We need instead to broaden our definition of theory to embrace other currents that shaped the minds of those who exercised power. Such ideas were often not to be found within the

pages of learned treatises, but in state papers, private corre
and the 'political testaments' drawn up to instruct future rul

Finally, the categories that structure our thought tod
frequently understood differently in the past. Modern political
makes extensive use of binary opposites to define the range of po
systems and ideas, including monarchy versus republic and despo..ism
versus freedom. The theorists and political actors of the late sixteenth
and early seventeenth centuries constructed their discussions differently. They worked within the legacy of Aristotle and the ancient
world as mediated by medieval scholasticism and the humanist
'rediscovery' of classical thought. The debate on government was not
presented as a stark choice between competing systems, but as an argument over the relative merits of different levels of monarchical rule.

The two predominant schools of thought were both essentially
monarchist, but differed on how far royal power should be restricted.
They recognised two categories of monarchy. Despotism (*monarchia
herilis*) was characterised by rule primarily in the self-interest of the
monarch and only secondarily in that of the people. Limited monarchy
(*monarchia limitata*) restricted the total and absolute political power
of the ruler by permitting other formally constituted bodies, such as
the estates, to exercise certain rights and share in the administration.
Absolutism was conspicuous by its absence. It emerged not from
despotism, which was rejected as a desirable form, but from the debate
over the ideal sort of limited monarchy.

One side of this debate was represented by those who became known
as the monarchomachs. The leading central European proponents of
this view, Johannes Althusius (1557–1638) and Hermann Conring
(1606–81), quickly distanced themselves from this term, which was
associated with radicalism and subversion. They were not advocating
democratic or republican government but a distinctly early modern
form of representation that remained within the framework of limited
monarchy. Their ideal was a mixed monarchy (*monarchia mixta*) where
the estates would share the exercise of power on a more equal basis with
the monarch. They stressed the limits to royal rule and argued that
formal agreements between the monarch and estates should be binding
on both parties and could not be renounced unilaterally by either side.

Absolutism emerged as the alternative view and its exponents tended
to be labelled Machiavellians or Hobbesians by their opponents. At
first, discussions made little distinction between hereditary or elective
monarchy, mainly because Aristotle had not done so. However, in
the course of the seventeenth century the former became increasingly
identified with the absolutist position, while the latter was associated

with the monarchomachs. These remained cautious in their theoretical elaborations of elective monarchy, hanging back from developing it as a sort of life presidency and remaining vague as to what powers the estates should have in choosing each king.

Matters were complicated in central Europe by the overarching presence of the Reich, which engendered a second area of debate over the respective powers of the emperor and German princes. Two broad positions emerged, mirroring those on the question of monarchical, or princely, power. The monarchomach view was represented in imperial politics by those who argued the princes, acting collectively in the Reichstag, could participate in the governance of the Reich. This princely (*Fürstenerianer*) position was countered by the imperial, caeserist (*Caeserianer*) argument emphasising the supreme power and authority of the emperor and the princes' subordinate status as his vassals. Neither position was monolithic. The princes in particular were divided as to whether to limit imperial power through a narrow electoral oligarchy of the seven or so rulers with the exclusive right to choose the emperor's successor, or to act in concert through the wider institution of the Reichstag. Further difficulties were posed by the presence of lesser rulers, like the imperial counts and prelates who were denied full votes at the Reichstag, and the autonomous imperial cities which only secured participation as a separate college in 1648.[1]

The existence of this second level of debate contributed to the generally authoritarian tendency within most German political thought. The multilayered structure of the Reich placed princes as representatives of authority in their own territory, but also as symbols of its autonomy within imperial politics. This produced a paradoxical concept of liberty (*Libertät*) which associated freedom and autonomy with state authority, since the princes were the guardians of their subjects' laws and protected them from the spectre of 'imperial absolutism'. The authoritarian trend was reinforced by the close relationship between political theorists and state patronage and employment, and by the long legacy of Aristotelian relativism which saw legitimacy in terms of efficient discharge of essential functions rather than dependent on a particular form of government.[2]

INDIVISIBLE SOVEREIGNTY AND TERRITORIAL SOVEREIGNTY

Many discussions of the theory of absolutism rightly start with the concept of indivisible sovereignty, which is regarded as a key attribute of the modern state and the 'lynchpin' of absolute monarchy.[3] The French theorist Jean Bodin (1530–96) was the first to articulate this view of sovereignty as resting with a single monarch and incapable of division or dispersal among other authorities. The royal monopoly of power was to be exclusive and free from internal or external interference.[4] Bodin's ideas are regarded as fundamental to French absolutist thought, but were difficult for contemporaries to reconcile with the fragmented character of imperial politics.

There was a long tradition of absolute imperial authority which derived from ancient Rome, but reached the seventeenth century through the experience of the Merovingian (511–752) and Carolingian (687–911) kingdoms and the medieval past of the Reich. Charlemagne had retained some Roman features of Merovingian kingship when he founded the Reich in 800, including the ruler's strong prerogatives in defence, justice and legislation. These were reinforced by the Christian emphasis on the preservation of peace and order and the promotion of the public good as duties of a good king. Prolonged conflicts with the papacy encouraged the view that the emperor should be free from all restraints so that he could fulfil his proper role, while the rediscovery and articulation of the body of Roman law provided additional arguments for unrestrained central authority. None of this, however, was absolutism in the seventeenth-century sense. Moreover, it was never implemented in practice. Various emperors attempted to convert indirect lordship into more direct forms of rule from the twelfth century, but all failed to displace the families that controlled the component fiefdoms constituting the Reich. Unlike the French and English kings, the emperor never established an exclusive monopoly of power, but instead continued to share it, or, more properly, construct it jointly with the territorial rulers.[5]

Contemporaries had difficulty making sense of these developments. Prior to the seventeenth century, all German theorists believed the Reich was a monarchy with the emperor as its sole head wielding supreme jurisdiction over the entire area. However, they also acknowledged that these powers could only be exercised in conjunction with the territorial rulers as constituent imperial estates (*Reichsstände*). For this reason they rejected both Bodin's concept of indivisible sovereignty and his claim that the Reich was an aristocracy, not a monarchy, and the emperor was like the doge of Venice, merely the first among equals.

The confessional and political strife of the Thirty Years War intensified the debate and polarised German viewpoints. The revival of Habsburg power after 1620 and the more aggressive policies of

Ascending view

Emperor Ferdinand II encouraged a growth in the princely interpretation of imperial politics. Under the influence of Swedish and
pro-Swedish propaganda, many Protestant theorists abandoned the
idea of the Reich as a monarchy and argued instead that supreme
power lay with the imperial estates, not the emperor. They created an
image of 'Spanish (i.e. Habsburg) tyranny' that was roughly comparable to later English charges of 'French absolutism' and was equally
used to condemn political opponents.[6]

Greater emphasis was placed on the elective character of the
imperial title and on what had become known as territorial sovereignty
(*Landeshoheit*) by the mid-seventeenth century. The latter was a product of the territorialisation process that politicised the geographical
concept of territory (*Land*). It was first mentioned in 1231 as *domini
terrae* and was subsequently expressed in a growing range of derivative
terms: territorial law (*Landrecht*), territorial prince (*Landesfürst*), territorial rule (*Landesherrschaft*), territorial estates (*Landstände, Land-
schaft*) and the less translatable *Landesvater* (literally, father of the
territory) and *Landeskinder* (children of the territory, i.e. subjects).

The presence of the estates among these concepts serves as a warning
not to see the emergence of territorial sovereignty as the inevitable process of the accumulation of power in princely hands. Nor was it simply
a question of the gradual erosion of imperial power and sovereignty
and their usurpation by territorial rulers. The latter did take place as
the charters of 1220, 1230–1 and 1356 all transferred to the princes
prerogatives once reserved exclusively for the emperor. These included
the right to build castles, receive certain forms of tribute and taxes, and
to exercise various judicial powers.[7] However, this was only one aspect
of the development of territorial sovereignty as other powers evolved
from below or were developed in response to new situations. Examples
of the latter included the police and military functions assumed during
the later fifteenth and early sixteenth centuries in response to public
disorders and inter-territorial feuds.

The emergence of territorial sovereignty thus mirrored the general
political developments within the Reich. As the territories became
more distinct, their rulers eliminated external interference from rivals
and other agencies, acquiring the status of *Reichsunmittelbarkeit*, sig-
nifying that a territorial ruler had no overlord other than the emperor.
In practice other imperial institutions, notably the two supreme courts
established at the end of the fifteenth century, continued to exercise
varying degrees of jurisdiction, while the papacy and Catholic
Church also played an important role, particularly in the ecclesiastical
principalities known collectively as the Imperial Church (*Reichskirche*).

Nonetheless, this status of 'immediacy' was an important mark of political autonomy, especially when it was combined with that of imperial estate (*Reichsstandschaft*), which brought with it voting rights at the Reichstag and other imperial institutions like the *Kreise*, or 'circles' which coordinated inter-territorial activity on a regional basis. The imperial knights (*Reichssritter*) ruling minor fiefdoms enjoyed the status of immediacy, but failed to acquire that of imperial estate, and they remained overshadowed by the other territorial rulers.

The other dimension of territorial sovereignty looked inwards and reflected the ruler's gradual accumulation of prerogatives and the exclusion of other bodies within the territory from the exercise of executive authority. This dimension underwent an important transformation that only became fully apparent from the mid-seventeenth century. Originally, the exercise of such rights had made an individual a territorial ruler (*Landesherr*) and distinguished him or her from the lesser vassals and corporate bodies within the territory that lacked immediacy. The ruler remained a subordinate, though distinguished, member of the Reich's complex political hierarchy. However, the idea evolved beyond a collection of exclusive rights to signify a semi-sovereign position. The original relationship was reversed, with the rights no longer identifying who was ruler, but now flowing automatically from that position. The Treaty of Westphalia gave this process a considerable boost by specifying a uniform set of prerogatives enjoyed by all rulers with the status of imperial estate, irrespective of whatever local customs or arrangements existed in their territories. Most of these rights had long been exercised, at least in practice, by the majority of princes, but now the territorial estates were specifically excluded from such powers. Though full sovereignty was still reserved for the emperor, the text explicitly used the terms territorial rights (*ius territoriale*) and territorial sovereignty (*superioritas territorialis*) to define this position.[8] It was not until the eighteenth century that the implications of this transformation were fully appreciated and articulated, but the growth of territorial sovereignty nonetheless lent a new and distinctive quality to later seventeenth-century princely rule.

HEREDITARY RIGHT

The elective character of the imperial title was far from unusual in medieval and early modern European monarchy, but it did set it apart from absolutism, where hereditary right determined who was to be sovereign. The right of primogeniture developed in France in the tenth century for both kings and nobles and was taken to England by the Normans in 1066. French monarchs retained it even after they began endowing their numerous offspring with appanages from the thirteenth century, since these remained subordinate to the overall royal patrimony. It was endorsed in the seminal text on French absolutism by Bishop Jacques Bénique Bossuet (1627–1704), tutor to the princes at Louis XIV's court: 'Of all monarchies the best is the successive or hereditary, above all when it passes from male to male and from eldest to eldest.' Bossuet's reasons were threefold: it was 'the most natural' form of monarchy since it was self-perpetuating, it gave the king a personal interest in working for the state, and it encouraged popular loyalty.[9]

Despite the elective imperial title, primogeniture was not incompatible with imperial politics, where it was encouraged by the feudal system and concept of imperial estates as it was advantageous to the German nobility that the fiefs and associated political rights pass from father to son. This had been sanctioned by Emperor Frederick Barbarossa in 1158, when he agreed that existing vassals could apportion their fiefs among their children. The Golden Bull of 1356 extended these rights for the seven electorates which were now deemed indivisible, while the four secular ones were henceforth always to pass to the eldest male heir. However, other imperial laws contradicted these provisions, notably the *Statutum in favourem principem* of 1232 which confirmed considerable freedom for the princes in the internal management of their territories. The ambiguities of Roman law reinforced this and many dynasties continued to favour partiable inheritance and split their holdings among their offspring.

Though this had a number of advantages, it furthered political fragmentation within the Reich and was increasingly being abandoned prior to the Reformation. However, the process of conversion halted this after 1517 and now, with rare exceptions, Protestant princes retained, or returned to, partiable inheritance with the result that divisions were more pronounced among Lutheran and Calvinist dynasties between 1525 and 1650 than they were among those who had remained Catholic. Religious and personal sensibilities account for this discrepancy. Catholic families still had access to the lands of the Imperial Church which provided suitable opportunities for junior princes as high clerics. The secularisation of church land by Protestant rulers and their natural exclusion from the remaining ecclesiastical principalities denied these options to their children. Many Protestant princes took their Church's teachings on fatherly responsibility seriously and so continued to partition their lands among their children. This proved a political liability during the Thirty Years War, particularly where rivalry between Lutheran and Calvinist branches of the same family caused additional strife, as in Hessen. Continued warfare against France and the Ottoman Turks in the later seventeenth century reinforced the necessity of preserving a large resource base, while changes enacted at the Reichstag in 1654 meant that the status of imperial estate was firmly associated with distinct territories and could not be acquired through subdivision of existing ones. Protestant rulers and theorists abandoned their religious arguments and now endorsed primogeniture on utilitarian grounds.[10]

German thought had thus moved close to a key tenet of French absolutism and now considered hereditary right the most 'natural' method of selecting rulers.[11] Frederick the Great echoed Bossuet by claiming that 'hereditary kingdoms are the easiest to govern' because 'the right of inheritance is joined to the power of time'.[12] Both the Habsburgs and the Bavarian Wittelsbachs commissioned historical and genealogical research to legitimise their political pretensions. Duke (later Elector) Maximilian I of Bavaria (1597–1651) revived the legend that Charlemagne was the direct ancestor of the Wittelsbachs and glorified the memory of Ludwig IV (1314–47), the one emperor who had been chosen from his house.[13] Nonetheless, primogeniture remained far from unproblematic, even for Catholics. The lack of a male heir posed fundamental problems for the Austrian Habsburgs by the early eighteenth century and necessitated the rewriting of their inheritance law in the Pragmatic Sanction of 1713 to permit Charles VI's daughter, Maria Theresa, to succeed. The uncertainty surrounding this change is indicated by the great lengths to which Charles VI was driven to secure German and international recognition, most of which proved worthless as many guarantors contested the arrangements during the War of the Austrian Succession (1740–48).[14]

The Habsburgs faced additional difficulties in their two kingdoms of Bohemia and Hungary that had been acquired in 1526. Both had powerful territorial estates with long traditions of resistance to overmighty monarchs. The conversion of many Bohemian and Hungarian nobles to Protestantism reinforced these traditions in the sixteenth century and contributed to the outbreak of the Thirty Years War. However, the elective character of both monarchies was ambiguous and disputed by the Habsburgs who imposed hereditary right by military force in Bohemia in 1627 and in Hungary sixty years later.[15] Thus, despite certain difficulties, hereditary right became a fundamental prop for central European absolutism. However, its absence did not preclude absolutism. The German ecclesiastical principalities lacked hereditary rule, but nonetheless embraced the other elements of absolutist thought and practice. A factor in their ability to do this was the strong relationship between religion and political power in central Europe.

DIVINE RIGHT

The divine right of kings is commonly regarded as a key element of absolutism but in fact stems from the more general principle that all political power derived ultimately from God. The most famous articulation of this belief in an absolutist sense is that by Bishop Bossuet, who buttressed historical and rational claims for the rule by one person with biblical arguments and examples: 'All power comes from God [and] thus princes act as ministers of God, and his lieutenants on earth.' These claims reaffirmed the sacral element inherent in early modern monarchy. As 'the Lord's anointed', monarchs were the representatives on earth of the supreme, heavenly king of kings.[16]

Like Bodin's indivisible sovereignty, this tenet of French absolutism was not well received in central Europe, except in the duchy of Lorraine, which was under French occupation for much of the seventeenth century and fully lost to the Reich in 1738. There was no German equivalent of the French 'royal touch' and only the emperor was considered a sacral monarch who was crowned in a religious ceremony involving a high cleric.[17] The influence of the Jesuits also retarded reception of French divine right theory since they controlled much of Catholic education and were inherently hostile to anything that reduced the pope's role as sole intermediary between humanity and God. The furthest that Catholic German writers would go was to stress the general links between monarchy and the divinely sanctioned political hierarchy, and they usually restricted themselves to discussions of practical rather than spiritual power.

The rejection of French-style divine right gave greater scope for other, arguably more effective, religious impulses to shape the style and content of German absolutism. The belief in France and England of the sacral royal body that lay behind divine right was always problematic and became more so during the sixteenth century. Unavoidable royal mortality had long conflicted with divine right's claims of eternal royal power and dignity, while the impact of reformed Christianity in both its Protestant and Catholic forms heightened the association of the human body with sin and corruption. Largely unencumbered with ideas of a sacral royal person, German monarchical thought was able to absorb the impact of these shifts and harness their potential to underpin a new belief in princes as God's agents on earth to defend the true faith and combat the wickedness of the world.[18]

The impulses behind this were diverse and included ideas borrowed from pagan antiquity as well as Christianity. There were also different confessional styles among Catholics, Lutherans and Calvinists, while even the authorship of some of the key documents is in dispute.[19] Nonetheless, it is possible to detect the emergence by the 1620s of what can be labelled a distinctly baroque absolutist interpretation of kingship. This advocated that politics had a moral and spiritual purpose with the aim of the state being to assist humanity's search for virtue, happiness and eternal salvation by providing the material basis for this quest. The best way to achieve this was to rule as a Christian prince (*princeps Christianus*) as defined by the great Christian humanist scholar Erasmus in the late fifteenth century.

Erasmus identified three guiding principles for an ideal Christian prince. His first purpose was to uphold the true religion; something which took on different connotations following the schisms of the Reformation and Counter Reformation. Second, he was to live by the five classic virtues of *pietas, justitia, prudentia, constantia* and *fortitudo* which derived from ideas put forward by Plato and adopted by the early church fathers. Third, he was to use Christianity as a guide in all his dealings with his subjects and other Christian rulers. These ideas continued to be elaborated into the eighteenth century through the *Fürstenspiegel* literature which provided compendia of advice on how best to rule to generations of German princes.

Much of this will resurface later in this chapter as we encounter other elements of German absolutist theory. However, the influence of religion is seen most directly in the role of piety in political ideas. This was expressed most clearly in the baroque Catholic articulation of the ideal of *pietas* which was pronounced in both Bavaria and the Habsburg monarchy after the early seventeenth century. Piety began at the top with the ruler's personal behaviour. It had to be genuine and Catholic writers like Adam Contzen attacked the Machiavellian notion that a prince could fool his subjects with a semblance of virtue. True piety was essential for the subjects' well-being, vital to retaining their loyalty and possibly crucial to defeating external foes. Both the Habsburgs and the Wittelsbachs took the Madonna as their patron saint. Their daily lives were punctuated by religious observance and many, like Emperor Ferdinand II, went on personal pilgrimages to holy shrines. The great conflicts against the Ottomans, which resumed with the Habsburg reconquest of Turkish Hungary after 1683, retained an air of a crusade and Austrian ministers seriously entertained dreams of liberating Jerusalem and the Holy Land.[20]

The baroque stress on external appearances meant that piety also had to be demonstrated through endowments for the Church, veneration of appropriate symbols and the construction of suitable monuments. Leopold I built the famous Plague Column (*Pestsäule*) as thanksgiving for the deliverance of Vienna, while the consecration of the St Charles Church on 22 October 1713 commemorated the end of a further epidemic. The Habsburgs paid particular attention to veneration of the Holy Cross and Eucharist, and fostered the cult of selected saints like St Leopold, St Charles Borromaeus and John Nepomak.[21] The demonstrative dimension of piety had been heightened by the Catholic renewal associated with the Counter Reformation, but this did not extend to an advocacy of external aggression or the extermination of heretics. Rather, it advocated prayer and good works as the secrets of successful politics and the advance of the true faith. Both rulers and their advisers stressed the need to retain God's support. God raised and promoted a dynasty because it honoured the true faith, not because of the personal attributes or actions of its individual members. Piety was simply a recognition that God had chosen a dynasty for His holy purpose, and not something that could secure secular reward.

The baroque concept of *pietas* thus implied distinct limits to secular power. Political power indeed derived from God, but was not given freely and had to be earned by adhering to the true Christian principles of rule. Princes were still mortal and would not only be held accountable to God on Judgement Day, but throughout their lives remained dependent on divine grace and favour. As this could be denied them, the possibility of failure remained ever present and the profundity with which these beliefs were held by the Habsburgs, at least until 1711, helps account for their often excessive caution in international affairs.[22]

Protestants broadly shared these beliefs, indicating that the concerns and pressures of seventeenth-century kingship ignored confessional boundaries. Some important differences remained. Protestant theorists added *heros* to the five Erasmian princely virtues, implying that the ruler should take the initiative in furthering the common good. Rulers' political testaments also placed a heavy emphasis on religious duties, replacing the often perfunctory biblical references that appeared before the Reformation with lengthy extracts from the key articles of faith, like the Confession of Augsburg from 1530. Detailed arrangements continued to be made as late as the eighteenth century to ensure that a prince's children were brought up as true believers.

The secular element was perhaps also more pronounced in Protestant thought, though it shared Catholicism's heavy emphasis on the need to adhere to Christian principles and the uncertainty of divine grace. The Reformation strengthened belief in the division of powers where the state oversaw the secular, material external world (*Externa*), leaving the Church free for internal, spiritual matters (*Interna*). This legitimised an expansion of princely power as Protestant rulers established new administrative bodies, known as consistories, to manage the personnel and economic affairs of their new territorial Churches. Whereas Protestant English monarchs had to adapt coronation rites that stemmed from the medieval Catholic Church, German princes were spared this dilemma as they already took office without clerical involvement. The problem of a coronation first appeared in Protestant Germany when Elector Frederick III/I of Brandenburg acquired a royal title for his sovereign duchy of East Prussia in 1701. He asserted royal authority by distancing himself from Catholic ritual and placing the crown on his own head, symbolising that there was no intermediary between himself and God.[23]

The nature of German Calvinism provided a further distinction between central Europe and many Western countries. German Calvinism was a phenomenon of the social elite and developed a different organisation than in Scotland, England and the Dutch Republic where the congregation, not the prince, held power. Initially, some German Calvinists had been outspoken advocates of the power of territorial estates, but this had exposed them to charges of being monarchomachs during the Thirty Years War. That conflict also emphasised that the survival of their faith depended on the patronage of key princes like the Brandenburg Hohenzollerns and encouraged Calvinist theologians to emphasise the supremacy of secular over clerical authority. The Pietist fundamentalist movement, which sprang from orthodox Lutheranism in the later seventeenth century, also contained elements inimical to absolutism and contributed to the opposition to princely power in some territories like the duchy of Württemberg. However, its emphasis on obedience allowed it to be reconciled with absolutism where it received princely favour, as we shall see later in this chapter.[24]

MAJESTY

The quality of majesty (*majestas*) had long been present in monarchy, but as late as Bodin and his followers was regarded as simply an element of state power. Bossuet and other French writers elevated it as an element of the semi-divine nature of kingship. Pomp and circumstance were but mere reflections of true majesty, which was 'the image of the greatness of God in a prince'. Majesty did not 'reside in the prince' but was 'borrowed from God, who entrusts it to the prince for the good of his people'. The prince thus remained merely the earthly reflection of the commanding position of God in heaven and Bossuet reminded rulers that though majesty elevated them above their subjects, it nonetheless still 'leaves you mortal, it leaves you still sinners, and it lays upon you a heavier charge to render to God' in the responsibility to promote the common good.[25]

Bossuet's arguments had less direct influence in central Europe than those of the late humanist scholar Justus Lipsius (1547–1606), who related majesty to the superhuman charisma of the prince that underpinned the growth of baroque court culture that will be explored in the next chapter. However, most princes echoed Bossuet in stressing their mortality and their duty to the common good. The true prince was to be a role model to his subjects and was to prove his worth by displaying proper Christain virtues and leading a moral life. Whereas the initial emphasis had been placed on finding the appropriate balance between hard work and necessary relaxation, writers in the later seventeenth century placed increasing emphasis on the need to acquire knowledge and expertise, rather than the alleged possession of innate qualities to rule.[26]

THE MYSTERIES OF STATE

The idea that knowledge is power and should therefore be restricted to those in authority was a key tenet of central European absolutism and underpinned its ideology of the aura of government. Only the monarch, elevated above the mass of the population thanks to his office, was capable of understanding the mysteries of state (*arcana imperii*). In contrast, his subjects were unable to see beyond their narrow class or local interests and so should be denied access to executive authority which they would only misuse for their selfish ends.

This concept was peculiar to the early modern age and was associated with a shift in the understanding of 'secrecy' due to changes in theology and the debate surrounding the role of deceit in politics. Theologians rejected the medieval notion of a 'transparent' world where divine intentions were revealed and visible to all since this implicitly made God the servant of His own creation. By portraying God as mysterious they made Him seem more powerful, but in doing so they helped change political thought. Previously, royal actions were perceived as direct demonstrations of divine will, while the 'open' concept of government regarded the king as still linked to his vassals and obliged to consult them before reaching a decision. The image of a mysterious God undermined these beliefs and fostered the idea that power was beyond ordinary comprehension and should be restricted to those who could properly understand it.[27]

Such ideas were controversial, even in the seventeenth century, and were attacked as Machiavellian, contrary to Christianity and amounting to deceit. However, a growing number of writers endorsed the idea by the 1640s that the business of government should remain secret. Their arguments rested on the baroque notion of prudence (*prudentia*) that became the absolutist equivalent of the modern term 'state security'. By treading an often tortuous line between necessary caution and outright deceit, both Catholic and Protestant theorists such as Contzen and Lipsius believed they could reconcile secrecy with Christian virtue. They distinguished three graduations of deception starting with slight deceit (*fraus levis*), which involved a cautious mistrust of others' intentions and a degree of dissimulation to hide one's own through silence, but not ambiguous words or lies. Moderate deceit (*fraus media*) included persuasion (*conciliatio*), bribery (*corruptio*) and deception (*deceptio*), which could be condoned provided they served a good cause. Grave deceit (*fraus gravis*) posed difficulties for both Contzen and Lipsius since it involved violation of treaties (*perfidia*) and the disregard of laws and rights (*injustitia*). However, both accepted that even these actions might be necessary in extreme emergencies. Under absolutism, the concept of secrecy had become morally neutral, far removed from its earlier association with deceit and dependent now on the use to which it was put. The influence of the baroque concept of prudence extended well beyond the exclusive world of absolute princes in the contemporary concept of politeness; the façade of good manners that concealed thoughts and true intentions.[28]

FUNCTIONS

The moral ambivalence inherent in baroque prudence was also present in the discussion of absolutism's functions. Influenced by Aristotle, many medieval and early modern thinkers had related good government to the performance of essential functions. Advocates of absolutism not only claimed that rule by one man did this best, but that it could also do more. Absolutism was characterised by a considerable expansion of state functions and the elaboration of new justifications for the ever-increasing intrusion into previously private or autonomous spheres of life.

The list of functions was at first sight comparatively traditional and differed most prominently in the degree of activity now expected from the ruler. Defence was most prominent and, unlike Bossuet's stress on the biblical origins of the state, such leading German philosophers as Samuel Pufendorf (1632–94) or Gottfried Wilhelm Leibniz (1646–1716) regarded the desire for mutual security as the basis for all political organisation.[29] Imperial law reinforced this by identifying territorial rulers as responsible for the provision of military contingents to the collective defence of the Reich. It also required them to assist in the maintenance of the public peace, while the Christian virtues of justice and piety underpinned their roles as judges and defenders of the faith. The widest function was the promotion of the common good (*bonum commune* or *Gemeinwohl*) which had traditionally been present, but was revitalised under absolutism. Finally, the new emphasis on majesty and the ruler's charisma added the obligation for the prince to defend and enhance his own status and that of his dynasty and subjects (*la gloire*).

A number of new intellectual currents added to the practical pressures behind the move to this more active form of kingship in the mid-seventeenth century. The debate on imperial politics had produced the paradoxical notion of German liberty where the prince protected the freedoms of all while the estates and other corporate groups merely defended their own privileges. The scientific and philosophical search for an underlying order to the universe encouraged a similar quest in the political world. Louis XIV distinguished between 'nature as it ought to be', as ordained by God, and 'nature as it is', disrupted by human activity. As the new, distant and mysterious God no longer intervened directly in the natural order, it fell to the monarch to uphold 'nature as it ought to be' and prevent it disintegrating into disorder.[30] Such views gained ground in central Europe during the destruction wrought by the Thirty Years War. As fields were abandoned and farms fell into disrepair it was easy to believe in a natural force of entropy that could only be held at bay by determined and coordinated action.

German Natural Law theory developed these ideas in the later seventeenth century through the writings of Pufendorf, Christian Thomasius (1655–1728) and Christian Wolff (1679–1754). Natural Law had a long heritage in central Europe, dating back to the influence of Luther and Melanchthon in the Reformation. At its heart was a particular notion of a social contract between ruler and ruled. People banded together for mutual protection and voluntarily accepted a degree of subordination to a properly constituted authority in return for its protection and promotion of the common good. In its seventeenth-century articulation, this contract was monarchical and not a basis for popular sovereignty. It was considered mutually binding and could not be cancelled except by common consent. It encouraged absolutism because it implied that no king could be expected to perform the difficult task of ruling unless given absolute authority. The people were no more competent to supervise the ruler than to govern by themselves.

The functions assigned by Natural Law were still fairly traditional, limited, according to Pufendorf, to external defence, internal order and maintenance of public morality.[31] However, by grounding political legitimacy in rationality, not theology, Natural Law implicitly encouraged an expansion of monarchical functions to embrace all aspects of human happiness and so provided a foundation on which later, so-called enlightened, absolutism was to build. It is also important to note that those contemporaries who were critical of Natural Law also placed an emphasis on the ruler assuming a more active role. For example, Leibniz stressed that it was not sufficient for a prince merely to prevent misery; he had to strive actively to promote improvement.[32]

The more active role led to growing efforts to regulate social and economic life that lent further distinctive characteristics to central European political thought. Such efforts can be detected from the fifteenth century, well before absolutism had emerged, and became known as policing (*Polizei*), a term first used in 1464. There was a practical need to confront new problems, such as those posed to public health by the expansion of urban centres, or the civil and religious disturbances associated with the Reformation. The reception of Roman law and its dissemination through imperial institutions encouraged this, especially by providing model legislation that could be adapted at territorial level to suit local circumstances. Good examples are the three imperial police ordinances (*Reichspolizeiordnungen*) issued by the Reichstag in 1530, 1548 and 1577 that continued to influence territorial legislation well into the eighteenth century. Protestant theology provided a further basis for regulatory action by reviving and developing Aristotle's concept of happiness. Luther and Melanchthon elaborated a doctrine of eudemonism, that the basis of moral and rational action should be its capacity to bring about personal well-being and happiness. This called for more active political intervention since the ruler now had a duty to promote happiness and not merely uphold order. State action was given moral and ethical force, raising the dignity and profile of the ruler and encouraging the growth of paternalism since the subjects were now considered incapable of achieving happiness without the assistance of their benevolent prince.[33]

Taken together, these ideas indicate that absolutism represented, in theory at least, the concentration not only of authority, but of responsibility. This had important implications for the wider conception of the state. The idea of a territory as the personal and private patrimony of its ruler was gradually displaced by the concept of the timeless, impersonal state that transcended the lives of mere mortals. This process was far from complete by the end of the eighteenth century, but it was nonetheless a feature of both French and especially central European absolutism.

In the classic formulation of French absolutism, the king is the personification of the state. This is an oversimplified cliché: Louis XIV never said 'I am the state' and throughout his reign French laws and royal decrees carefully distinguished between the monarch and the kingdom. Bossuet came closer to personifying the state through the monarch when he claimed that 'the whole state is to be found in the person of the prince'. Nonetheless, he stressed the patriarchal duties of the king who 'is not born for himself, but for the public' and argued that only a tyrant thought for himself. On his deathbed, Louis XIV remarked that 'I am leaving you, but the state will remain for ever' ('*Je m'en vais, mais l'Etat demeurera toujours*').[34]

German princes expressed similar views. Margrave Christian Ernst of Bayreuth told Strasbourg University in 1659 that 'a good prince must always remember that the supreme law is the good of the state. The state is not to serve the ruler, but instead the prince must disappear within it [*ganz im Staate aufgehen*].'[35] The adoption of primogeniture encouraged the belief that the territory was a public trust which a ruler must pass safely on to his successor, while theology added further moral responsibility. The obligations of Natural Law's social contract also required that a prince 'forgo pursuits that have no bearing on his office' and 'must believe that nothing is good for them privately that is not good for the state'.[36] While individual rulers continued to behave irresponsibly, in theory absolutism already required them to subordinate their personal desires to the greater good well before enlightened philosophers asked them to do so in the eighteenth century.

OBEDIENCE

Absolutism implied not only the monarch's power to command but the subject's duty to obey. This was expressed most forcefully by Wilhelm von Schröder (1640–88), a converted Lutheran who entered Austrian Habsburg service in 1673 and published an influential guide on fiscal and administrative policy entitled *Fürstliche Schatz- und Rentkammer* in 1686. Schröder's harsh, authoritarian views were grounded on a desire for order and efficiency that was widespread in the seventeenth century and has been taken as evidence for the general yearning for stability after decades of civil and religious strife. Bossuet was equally forthright: 'subjects owe their prince complete obedience' because 'if the prince is not scrupulously obeyed, public order is overthrown. And there is no further unity, and in consequence no further cooperation or peace in the state.' While Bossuet limited justified disobedience solely on religious grounds if the prince broke the commandments, some German thinkers like Leibniz were prepared to condone it on utilitarian grounds if the ruler's actions endangered the state. Nonetheless, Leibniz still believed 'that as a rule one must obey, the evil of revolt ordinarily being incomparably greater than that which causes it'.[37]

There was also a strong religious foundation for obedience to secular authority, though there was far from complete agreement among the theologians or between confessions. Discussions of central Europe have often made much of Lutheran authoritarianism as a factor behind Prussian absolutism. Lutheran attitudes to obedience were contradictory and rooted not only in Luther's reading of the Bible, but Melanchthon's interpretation of Aristotle, Greek Stoicism and Roman jurisprudence. The practical experience of the sixteenth century made a profound impact and contributed to the anti-authoritarian character of much of Luther's early writings. Given the opposition of the papacy and Catholic princes to his ideas, Luther developed a theory of justified resistance to tyranny but retracted much of it when he perceived its misuse by the peasants in opposing their landlords in 1525. Nonetheless, the tradition of justifiable resistance was retained by the princes who had converted to the new faith and felt threatened by the still Catholic emperor and his allies. This element fused with the princely version of monarchomach thought and was used to legitimise the formation of the Schmalkaldic League of Protestant princes in 1531. The combination of justified defence of religious freedom and political privilege resurfaced during the Thirty Years War as a counter to what were interpreted as Habsburg attmepts to impose absolute imperial rule. Echoes of it could still be found in the eighteenth century and were at times manipulated by Prussia to legitimise its policies of blocking Habsburg initiatives in the imperial institutions.[38]

A separate tradition of Lutheran authoritarianism had developed meanwhile which emphasised absolute obedience to secular authority. Following the experience of 1525, Luther drew on New Testament images to depict the emperor as an absolute monarch. This could scarcely be reconciled with the contemporary opposition to Charles V through the Schmalkaldic League and was dropped in favour of ideas advanced by Melanchthon. Whilst stressing the advantages of limited monarchy where the prince was bound by fundamental laws, Melanchthon nonetheless argued that, as sovereign, a ruler must be obeyed. Subjects must have faith in God and were to suffer princely transgressions in silence as further tests of their piety and convictions. Such a position was not that far removed from the opinion of many Catholics.[39]

The Pietist movement which sprang from orthodox Lutheranism in the 1670s was equally ambivalent. Pietists believed in the importance of a virtuous and moral life and were often highly critical of the extravagance and excesses of princely rule. However, they were more than quietist introverts as they strove for moral reform and sought an appropriate vehicle for their social activism. This could lead them into alliance with absolutism, particularly where they were opposed by the Lutheran church establishment as in Brandenburg-Prussia. Frederick III/I and particularly his son and successor, Frederick William I, were able to harness Pietism for their own objectives and helped its adherents to establish a training school in Halle from where they spread their beliefs across the monarchy. The alliance was potent because Frederick William I shared many of the Pietists' own convictions, especially their dedication to hard work and sense of obligation and duty. Considerable weight has been placed on this, with one scholar holding the Pietists responsible for a 'cultural revolution' in Prussia after 1713.[40] What is certain is that Pietism contributed far more than simple, passive obedience by encouraging active collaboration with state utilitarian policy and fostering a social conscience and work ethic.

The philosophy of Neostoicism provided another important contribution to absolutism's cult of obedience. Neostoicism was a product of late sixteenth-century humanism and particularly Justus Lipsius's reworking of the original Greek philosophy of the third century BC. Like many contemporaries, Lipsius was concerned by the violence that seemed endemic and a particular characteristic of aristocratic life. He believed that peace could be achieved if the nobility could suppress their constant warring and engage in a different kind of combat: self-conquest to master their unruly emotions and destructive passions. In place of the symbol of 'fortune' (*fortuna*) which was emblazoned on the banners of many aristocratic mercenary captains, Lipsius advocated the Neostoic ideals of virtue (*virtus*), discipline (*disciplina*) and obedience (*oboedientia*). Neostoicism thus stiffened the self-discipline increasingly expected of the prince and extended it to the aristocracy in the hope that it would be emulated by other groups to the eventual benefit of all society. Lipsius further underpinned his arguments by providing a new reading of the history of ancient Rome which emphasised the imperial rather than the republican phase and highlighted the seizure of power by Emperor Augustus (31 BC–AD 14) to end civil strife.[41]

Reformed Christianity and Neostoicism contributed to the model of the prince as the firm but kind 'father of the territory' (*Landesvater*). This ideal had its roots in the *pater patriae* of pagan antiquity, but underwent a transformation during the sixteenth and early seventeenth centuries to produce a particular amalgam of Christian and classical ideas that was a major characteristic of central European absolutism. What made it so significant was its coincidence with a new model of fatherhood which helped redefine the role of the subject and his duty to obey. Fatherly responsibility and authority were combined in the ideal of the morally upright, Christian 'house-father' (*Hausvater*) who, as patriarch, had personal supervision of the household economy and authority over its members. The concept of *Landesvater* transposed these ideas to the level of the state. As *Landesvater*, the prince had personal authority over the state and paternal responsibility for its subjects, who, as *Landeskinder* (literally, 'children of the territory'), were regarded as minors, incapable of acting or thinking without guidance from above. The duty to obey was reinforced, while opposition to princely rule was equated with the horrors of patricide. The gradual emergence of more impersonal conceptions of the state only partially displaced these ideas. German theorists clung to conservative patriarchicism throughout the eighteenth century and beyond, simply subsuming the *Landesvater*'s characteristics within a broader definition of an impersonal state.[42]

Natural Law added further arguments for obedience which it regarded as the subjects' part of the social contract. Pufendorf argued that 'the citizen owes respect, loyalty and obedience to the governors of his state. This entails that he be content with the actual state of things and not give his mind to revolution.'[43] However, Pufendorf was reticent on what to do if the sovereign broke his side of the bargain. This was not an oversight but deliberate, revealing a fundamental reluctance to prescribe precise limits to absolute power.

REASONS OF STATE

The obligation of the monarch to uphold the law posed a dilemma for absolutist theory by introducing the awkward issue of the limits to royal authority. The famous outburst of Frederick William I of Prussia that 'we are lord and master and can do what we like' has created the impression that central European absolutism knew no bounds. Certainly, some contemporaries believed this. Johann Jacob Moser, a prolific expert on imperial law, wrote of the German princes in 1773 that 'one does what one wants, and the territorial estates and subjects can howl'. Moser's own experience in Württemberg gave him good reason to say this as his opposition to Duke Carl Eugen had brought him five years in prison.[44] Many modern commentators have often taken this line and linked absolutism with arbitrary rule, either ignoring the legacy of medieval constitutionalism altogether or claiming that it was destroyed by the growth of royal power.[45] Matters have not been helped by the influence of English political theory, and particularly of John Locke who equated the two and described absolutism as an attempt to enslave the population.[46] The fact that apologists for absolutism went to great lengths to distinguish it from tyranny should give us pause for thought.[47]

German political theory dealt with this issue in its reception of the Italian ideology of the 'reasons of state' (*Ragione di stato*). This term was coined by Giovanni Botero in 1576 in an attempt to reconcile Machiavelli's ideas with Christian virtues. Significantly, when his book appeared in German translation in 1596 it was not entitled *Staatsräson* but *Gute Policey*, indicating the continued preoccupation with the moral elements present in territorial police regulation, rather than an interest in arguments for unrestrained royal power. Habsburg discussions of kingship written in the 1630s to 1650s made no mention of the concept at all and expected rulers to be morally upright in both their public and private dealings. However, there were signs that a distinctly baroque absolutist response to Machiavelli was emerging. It was Machiavelli's core argument that was so troubling to early modern minds. Since the world was sinful, a successful prince had to know how to be immoral as well as virtuous. The standard reply was to agree that the world was sinful, but to recommend a withdrawal into pious monasticism. Such a response was incompatible with the active role in worldly affairs now expected from the prince. Adam Contzen offered a solution by advancing more pragmatic arguments for virtue, claiming that God rewarded the good in this life as well as the next, and citing Ferdinand II's victory over the Protestants at White Mountain as proof of this.[48]

Nonetheless, the problems posed by the question of secrecy and deceit indicated that there was still a need for guidance as to what rulers could or could not do. Most responses centred on the role of imperial and territorial law, but there was no agreement on how far a ruler was bound by these. Apologists for absolutism tended to regard laws as guidelines for behaviour which the ruler should respect, but could disregard in emergencies. Far from being harmful restrictions on princely power, such laws strengthened the state by making it more efficient and encouraging loyalty to its ruler. This idea has been interpreted as the genesis of German conservatism by providing a model for the bureaucratic *Rechtstaat*, or state governed by the rule of law. It certainly encouraged a positivist sense of justice more to do with practical rights and the social regulation of them than with morals or metaphysical concepts of 'justice'. The development of the judicial system within the German territories mirrored that of the imperial courts in that it was primarily concerned with finding an efficient means to avert violence by setting boundaries on behaviour and arbitrating disputes. Most Germans were reluctant to accept a concept of justice based on verdicts identifying clear winners and losers. The complex network of overlapping jurisdictions, with its numerous opportunities for appeal, provided a practical mechanism to secure this by making it difficult to reach a clear-cut verdict at any stage and forcing decisions towards a common middle ground.[49]

This sense of justice was linked to the wider imperial political culture. The Reich was a complex structure with few large, compact territories. Both it and its components depended on the preservation of the internal status quo for their survival, particularly as inter-territorial conflict exposed them to foreign interference. The imperial equilibrium was defined and regulated by law, and while change was not impossible, it was certainly potentially dangerous since it threatened to disturb this balance. Alterations such as an exchange of territory or the elevation of a ruler's status had to adhere to recognised norms and were generally balanced by appropriate changes elsewhere. This process has been labelled the 'juridification' of imperial politics and had been under way since the late fifteenth century when the two imperial courts were established to resolve conflict peacefully. Though it was placed under severe strain during the Thirty Years War, the system of imperial justice revived after 1648, while the Treaty of Westphalia related the Reich's internal equilibrium to the wider effort to preserve peace within Europe.[50] The imperial political culture was received positively outside the Reich. Philosophers as diverse as Rousseau, Sully and St Pierre all considered the Reich as a constitutional state regulated by the rule of law that could provide a model for pan-European harmony and an inspiration for reforming France.[51]

However, absolutism's use of fundamental laws often seemed more concerned with efficiency than justice. The tacit understanding that an absolute prince could override the law in the interests of expediency during an emergency indicated a potential gap between theory and practice. The concern encouraged an alternative version of constitutionalism that posed a major threat to absolutist theory. The first major German theorist to tackle this problem was Gottlieb Samuel Treuer (1683–1743) in his 1719 critical edition of Schröder's apology for absolutism. Significantly, Treuer equated despotism with tyranny and thus made an important contribution to early German liberal thought. To prevent tyranny, fundamental laws must take precedence over all, including the monarch, who could be removed if he broke them. Moreover, Treuer assigned a more positive role to the territorial estates as guardians of the law to prevent monarchical power *degenerating* into absolutism, though it took until the early nineteenth century before these ideas gained ground.[52]

PRELIMINARY CONCLUSIONS

The theory of absolutism emerged in the early seventeenth century to delineate a distinct form of monarchy. Though many of its threads had been present before, it was only when they were woven with the practical experience of the Thirty Years War and advances in philosophy, science and theology that the picture of this new form of monarchy began to take shape. This image was never clearly defined

and was always refracted through a variety of confessional and territorial traditions. Other contemporary political forms also reflected
many of its elements and these remained in a constant state of evolution, preventing the portrayal of absolutism on a single canvas. Nonetheless, there was sufficient common ground to distinguish the new
style of central European princely rule from its sixteenth-century precursor, as well as from other institutions like the office of emperor
and the imperial free cities.

Ideas of territorial sovereignty had evolved to the point where they
departed from the late medieval conception of the princes' status
within the Reich and began to undermine the basis for early modern
mixed monarchy and the estates. This coincided with the flowering of
baroque piety and a new conception of the religious foundations of
political power as reflected, for instance, in changes in inheritance practices among Protestants and the inflated sense of majesty projected by
the princely court. The exclusion of others from executive authority
received further endorsement from the ideology of prudence and the
mysteries of state. Gradually, the basis of these beliefs shifted from
the theological to the secular and from the personal to the wider conception of the state, but it was not until the early nineteenth century
that this process went beyond what could be accommodated within
absolutist thought.

Throughout, all advocates of absolutism were already preoccupied
with the distinction between a necessary, beneficial exercise of power
and its arbitrary and despotic misuse. The belief that absolute princes
governed ultimately by consent was a constant underlying theme. All
were concerned that a prince should not alienate the love and affection
of his subjects, which remained a fundamental pillar of successful
government. The emphasis on leading a truly virtuous and Christian
life was one reflection of this concern. Another was the drive for efficiency since promotion of the common good was essential to retain
and foster support and loyalty.[53] Thus, though absolutism denied its
subjects a formal role in political action, it nonetheless remained
bound to bargain with them, devising sophisticated ways to convince
them of its continued legitimacy. These methods form the subject of
the next chapter, which also turns its attention to the key elements of
the 'absolutist state' and its relationship with important social groups.

3 Practice

THE COURT

The courts of the central European absolutist princes were once not thought worthy of serious attention. Their great expense seemed to corroborate the nineteenth-century bourgeois critique of them as a wasteful extravagance. Worse, they appeared politically irrelevant, merely a source of intrigue and gossip that could fill the pages of anecdotal popular history but provide nothing of interest to those who sought the true locus of political power. The Prussian example is important in this context. Frederick William dramatically cut back court spending after his succession in 1713 and concentrated all available resources on developing his monarchy's military potential; drawing the admiration from generations of nationalist historians who endorsed this policy as contributing to Prussia's subsequent rise to great power status.

It is only relatively recently that there has been a revival of interest in the court leading to a new appreciation of its significance under absolutism. Norbert Elias and Jürgen Freiherr von Krüdener provided the most important contributions to this, working independently, but publishing their findings at roughly the same time.[1] Elias based his study on France, but, like Krüdener, intended it for wider application. Both contributions have been well received within German-language scholarship and have established an influential model of the 'court society' which defines the basis of the absolutist state and its relation to society.[2]

Though they drew slightly different conclusions, both Elias and Krüdener argued that the court played a vital role in promoting the growth of absolutism, as well as sustaining it and defining the nature of its rule. They recognised that the monopolisation of taxation and coercion were significant elements in the emergence of absolutism, but merely provided the backdrop to the court society. To explain absolutism fully we need to go beyond such material factors and consider social behaviour and cultural attitudes.

The origins of absolutism are thus closely connected to the origins of the court. Elias and Krüdener drew on established arguments for the decline of the nobility in the sixteenth and seventeenth centuries following changes in military technology and economic practice. The monarch gained a degree of freedom from aristocratic restraint but was only able to become absolute through the development of a court to consolidate his power. Absolutism becomes a process of manipulation and socialisation, rather than one of direct coercion. The ruler's stronger position permitted the 'domestication of the nobility' by offering them the temptations of the court society. These inducements were social, rather than economic or material, reflecting the influence of Weber rather than Marx on these arguments. Once attracted to the royal residence, the nobles became ensnared in its honey trap of court ceremonial, unable to leave for fear of losing status and influence.

Of the two, Elias devoted the most space to discussing court ceremonial which he interpreted as part of a wider 'civilising process' transforming European society since the Middle Ages. The formation of a monopoly of violence identifying a single focus for political power was the first of four interrelated elements in this process. The second was modernisation in the sense of a growing functional differentiation within society and in overcoming distance and time obstacles to cement greater interdependency within society. Elias saw society in terms of 'figurations', or chains of individuals forming the complex social web. These grew more pronounced with the process of inner-group distinction which constituted the third, civilising element. Importantly for our study of absolutism, Elias thought this process began at the court and provided the 'origins' of civilised behaviour. Individuals competing within a group, in this case the social elite gathered at court, were forced to acknowledge behavioural norms, such as eating with a knife and fork or not urinating in public, because those who did so proved more successful in the scramble for rank and prestige.[3]

Elias used the analogy of the stock exchange to explain this. A courtier's prestige and status defined his social 'stock' and depended not on his own intrinsic worth, but on how others perceived him. Elias termed this 'court rationality' based on a 'rank ethos', distinguishing the courtly aristocratic society in the age of absolutism from the 'economic rationality' of nineteenth- and twentieth-century bourgeois-professional society. Prestige at court was thus rational by the standards of the age, and this explains why courtiers were prepared to sacrifice material gain to achieve it.[4]

Inner-group distinction encouraged a particular form of behaviour Elias dubbed 'restraint of affects' (*Affektbeherrschung*), involving the suppression of true emotions and passions behind the façade of politeness. This behaviour assumed an important part in his theory and underpinned the transition from social constraint (*Fremdzwang*) to self-restraint (*Selbstzwang*) which he borrowed from Freud and which he believed explained what he termed the 'courtization of warriors'.[5] Behind these forbidding terms are some simple arguments. The ruler's practical monopoly of violence was paralleled and underpinned by the emotional disarmament of the nobility who no longer vented their passions in violent competition for political influence and material wealth, but were drawn into courtly intrigue instead.

Court ceremonial played an important part by providing the etiquette of this new behaviour in such a way as to enhance the position of the monarch further. Though Elias did not claim that Louis XIV invented court ceremonial, he did believe that he transformed it for his own ends. The king now stood above and partly outside the ceremonial order as the one who determined its rules and the only one who could disregard them to favour or punish those he chose. The lifestyle prescribed by these rules was very expensive, further strengthening the king's hand. Conspicuous consumption became a distinguishing feature of the aristocratic court society and left nothing remaining for political or military competition, depriving the nobility of the material basis for independent action. It also reinforced the inter-group distinction which Elias identified as the fourth element of the civilising process. As other groups such as the bourgeoisie began aping aristocratic behaviour in an effort to share in their prestige and status, the nobles sought to affirm their own exclusivity by defining their behavioural norms still more sharply. In this sense the civilising process filtered down from the court to change lesser social groups, gradually transforming the whole of society.

Krüdener differed slightly from Elias when it came to defining crown–noble relations. He agreed that baroque ceremonial undermined the old warrior ideal and created opportunities for the king, who, as monopolist of the social and economic opportunities at the court, was well placed to offer them an alternative. However, Krüdener identified two distinct phases in this relationship. Drawing on Weber, he argued that initially crown–noble relations were characterised by a 'community of interest'. Though the monarch manipulated the nobles, he nonetheless shared with them a common domination over the rest of society. Court ceremonial thus cemented a symbiosis of ruler and nobility in place of their previous conflict. Far from being defeated, the nobles were transformed and given a new role in the absolutist–bureaucratic state. As this evolved, the nature of rule changed from government by aristocratic community of interest to that based on the state's impersonal domination over all society. By contrast, Elias's arguments are closer to Engels than Weber as he postulates the workings of a 'royal mechanism' whereby the crown exploited the impasse between nobility and bourgeoisie to emancipate itself from medieval constitutional restraints. The court provided the venue where this mechanism could operate through patronage and clientelism.[6]

The model of the court society is only now being subject to critical scrutiny and the remainder of this section examines the impact of this challenge and assesses what it reveals about the significance of the court to absolute monarchy.[7] The implications of the Elias–Krüdener model are that we should consider the court in its widest sense, encompassing not just the courtiers, but buildings and palace architecture, ancillary staff, guards, music, theatre, activities and the ritual of daily life. Changes in all these areas have been detected in the early to mid-seventeenth century and are associated with the rise of the central European baroque absolutist court. The shift is attributed to the impact of the Thirty Years War, which left the princes better placed than the nobles to assume the political and cultural initiative. Though often seen as a predominantly Catholic phenomenon, the baroque court also emerged in Protestant territories like Hanover, Saxony and Brandenburg.[8]

Its first distinguishing characteristic was its permanence and centralisation. The medieval model of the itinerant court of the royal progress was giving way to an institution permanently based in one location. The small scale of most German territories meant the many princes already only had one main residence, but they still travelled about, staying in other castles and hunting lodges. Numerous territorial partitions had also served to fragment and shift the focus of power. This was particularly pronounced in the Habsburg monarchy, which established several separate courts during the Renaissance, reflecting its decentralised political system and the dispersal of power among different branches of the dynasty. Emperor Rudolf II's decision to leave the previous residence in Vienna resulted in a new court at Prague between 1576 and 1612, while the creation of two junior lines resulted in further ones at Graz (1564–1619) and Innsbrück (1564–1665). Other relatives were entrusted with governing detached portions of the monarchy and set up their own establishments in Brussels, Milan, Naples, Pressburg (Bratislava) and elsewhere.[9] Though the Habsburgs persisted in this longer than most, a distinct trend was emerging by the mid-seventeenth century as rulers became increasingly identified with a single residence as the focal point for both their court and administration. Other residences continued to be used, but were now clearly secondary as 'summer palaces', hunting lodges and convenient places to shut up unwanted relatives. Moreover, this central court was now sited in a new building, often some distance from earlier palaces.

At first sight this is not so apparent as in France, where Louis XIV left the former royal palace of the Louvre in Paris in 1678 and moved permanently into the new residence at Versailles (built mainly 1661–82). The Habsburgs did not make this transition, retaining the Hofburg in the heart of Vienna as their main residence despite the construction of the Schönbrunn palace on the edge of the city after 1695. Their court took on a different, possibly grander character than that of the Sun King, especially as they had an entire city as a stage upon which to project their imperial image. The construction of numerous palaces for the high aristocracy that congregated at the imperial court served to magnify the general glory of the dynasty, encouraging a building boom that began with the relief of the city from its Turkish siege in 1683 and continued in the wake of further victories in Hungary and the Balkans.[10] Frederick III/I of Brandenburg-Prussia also continued work on his Berlin palaces despite the existence of a second residence at Potsdam which was favoured more by his son and grandson after 1713. The construction of Mannheim as a new capital for the Elector Palatine was also a lengthy process, dating back to its foundation as a fortress in 1606 and only really commencing with its reconstruction in 1699 after it had been destroyed by the French during the Nine Years War (1688–97). Even then it only became the elector's official residence in 1720.

Nonetheless, the new palaces represented a significant departure and were conspicuous, particularly in the lesser territories whose rulers had largely abstained from construction during the Renaissance and still lived in adapted medieval castles. The break was noticeable in Württemberg where the shift to the new residence at Ludwigsburg after 1704 coincided with the duke's deteriorating relations with his territorial estates who remained based in the old capital at Stuttgart. A second absolutist phase under Duke Carl Eugen was also marked by a move back to Ludwigsburg in 1757 which ended in 1775 following the estates' successful appeal to the imperial courts at the erosion of their privileges.[11] Such shifts indicate that the buildings were also important symbols of a new political direction, representing the concentration of power by housing more than simply the prince and his court. Württemberg government was moved to Ludwigsburg after 1718 as fast as it could be accommodated in the new town growing up around the palace. The prince of Waldeck also transferred his officials to his new palace at Arolsen by 1719, while Frederick III/I had the Berlin palace doubled between 1706 and 1716 to accommodate new administrative offices. Even the apparently old-fashioned Habsburgs built a new court chancery at the Hofburg after 1717 to house the Austrian central government, while a separate *Reichskanzlei* was constructed to house the officials dealing with imperial affairs in 1723.[12]

The expansion in the total size of the court also necessitated additional buildings. The Habsburg court had numbered 531 individuals in 1576, but totalled 1,966 in 1672 and over 2,000 for the period 1711–40. Other German courts were sometimes almost as numerous, particularly at times when the prince was engaged in political and military competition within the Reich. The Bavarian court numbered 1,360 at the time of Elector Carl Albrecht's bid for the imperial title in 1741 and that in Württemberg was larger still when Duke Carl Eugen hoped to obtain an electoral title during the Seven Years War (1756–63). Even 'small' courts could total several hundred, as in Hessen-Darmstadt between 1630 and 1710.[13]

The cost grew in proportion with the increased scale and magnificence, with spending on the Habsburg's court rising from 200,000 florins in 1574 to 1 million by 1672 and peaking at around 2.6 million by the 1730s. These totals represent an average of 5 to 8 per cent of total central government spending, or somewhat less than that in France where the court of Louis XIV consumed about 11 per cent of the budget and that of Louis XV between 8 and 12 per cent. Austrian spending declined somewhat under Maria Theresa's reign (1740–80), but still averaged 6 to 9 per cent of central spending. The lavish Berlin court under Frederick I cost 436,000 taler (654,000 florins) in 1706, or approximately 9 per cent of Prussian expenditure. The figure could go far higher in smaller territories which lacked the economies of scale to sustain courts on a truly international scale. Spending on the court in Bavaria and Württemberg took about a quarter of the central budget throughout the eighteenth century, rising to double that at times of acute political competition, as in Bavaria at the start of the War of Spanish Succession (1701–14).[14]

These sums suggest that Elias and Krüdener are right to stress the importance of the court to absolutism and that rulers thought it worth sacrificing scarce resources on it. The costs included the pay and allowances of servants and courtiers, food and clothing, as well as the construction and maintenance of buildings and gardens. The cost of special festivities could be considerable. The coronation of Frederick III/I in Königsberg in 1701 consumed no less than 6 million taler, with his wife's crown alone costing 300,000, or roughly what the entire court required in a normal year.[15] Carl Eugen spent 230,910 florins on his trip to the Venetian carnival in 1766, including 1,342 florins on chocolate, equivalent to twice the annual salary of a Württemberg university professor![16]

Such gross extravagance sparked a debate on the economic impact and utility of the court which began with contemporary criticism and developed into the nineteenth-century condemnation of it as wasteful and irrational. Max Weber represented the most considered example of this view, arguing that court spending retarded the development of capitalism by diverting money from investment and production. Krüdener incorporated this view within his interpretation, and while arguing that the court was politically important, he still regarded it as economically irrational.[17] By contrast, the German political sociologist Werner Sombart, writing at the start of the twentieth century, argued that the court did promote economic growth because the luxury goods industries were essential to early capitalism. Sombart drew similar conclusions for military spending which was almost invariably higher than that on the absolutist court.[18]

The utilitarian language used in this debate featured in some seventeenth-century discussions. The Austrian cameralists Schröder and Johann Joachim Becher (1625–82) claimed that the court provided valuable employment and boosted the circulation of money within the economy. There is some evidence that luxury expenditure did have a positive impact, with Berlin recovering faster from the effects of the Thirty Years War than other Brandenburg cities thanks to heavy court spending.[19] The transfer of a princely residence from one town to another could have serious consequences. The population of Ludwigsburg grew from nothing before 1704 to reach 5,028 by 1732. When Duke Carl Alexander temporarily moved the court back to Stuttgart, it fell by 60 per cent in a single year. The return to Ludwigsburg under Carl Eugen raised the number of inhabitants from 5,000 in 1763 to 11,607 by 1774, or only about 3,000 less than the much longer-established town of Stuttgart. The final move back to the original capital in 1775 cut Ludwigsburg's population by half and it still only

numbered 5,419 inhabitants in 1786.[20] It is also true that the grand
palaces were not entirely built on the backs of the poor: for example,
Frederick III/I introduced a tax on wigs and coaches in 1698 to help
pay for Berlin palace construction. Nonetheless, the arguments of
Schröder and Becher were more a retrospective justification for the
lavish outlay than a comment on the court's function. Elias's concept
of 'court rationality' is helpful here, highlighting that princes regarded
the maintenance of courts and armies as important elements of their
rule, while any positive economic impact was simply an unintended
bonus.

The court's primary role can be subdivided into four key functions
which operated on three distinct but related levels. Its general function
of symbolising absolute rule was present throughout, while its role in
outshining potential rivals was primarily intended for an international
audience. Its part in domesticating the nobility allotted it by Elias and
Krüdener took place within the level of the domestic elite, while that of
fostering a sense of absolutism's legitimacy and encouraging obedience
and loyalty interacted with the broad mass of subjects. A variety of
influences can be detected in shaping the style and purpose of the
court in these activities. The place of France – and especially Louis
XIV – is controversial, as we shall see, but other influences included
the Spanish and Burgundian legacy in court ceremonial and palace
design, the impact of baroque piety, inspiration from the world of
classical Greece and Rome, as well as new impulses from seventeenth-
century science and philosophy.

In its broadest sense the court symbolised absolutism and was
intended to encourage a belief in its power and legitimacy. The
construction of grand palaces was a direct attempt to put theory into
practice and to translate abstract political ideas into tangible substance.
The baroque emphasis on the importance of external appearances
encouraged a direct appeal to the senses through art and architecture.
The earlier Renaissance emphasis on order and symmetry was replaced
by deliberate disruption of lines to indicate boldness and movement
that was nonetheless tamed and rendered beautiful. The intention
was to express absolutism's claim to master disorder and could be
found not only in buildings and their interior decoration, but in the
music, festivities and ceremonial that accompanied and regulated
court life.

The construction of new buildings in the distinct baroque style
symbolised the innovatory element within absolutism and its claim to
represent a new dawn of tranquillity and calm after earlier crisis. By
siting these palaces apart from former capitals, princes also distanced

themselves from institutions like the estates which they frequently blamed for the earlier trouble. The sheer size of the buildings surpassed all previous construction and demonstrated absolutism's claim to be above ordinary mortals, especially the nobility, who lacked the resources to compete. The sense of distance was heightened by the new location of the palace and by the fact that it was often surrounded by walled gardens or parks. Order and harmony were implied by the coherent, connected and systematic designs which contrasted with the ad hoc and eclectic extensions previously tacked on to medieval castles. This practice has been dated to the Tuileries palace in Paris, built in 1564 to a new design of three wings arranged around an open courtyard intended to display the grandeur of the occupant instead of hiding it from view behind high walls. The palaces built in Germany after the Thirty Years War generally followed this design, but the architectural styles were far from uniform. The Habsburgs were notable in their rejection of baroque architecture before 1711, even declining plans from Balthasar Neumann to rebuild the Hofburg, and the palaces of their nobility were often more 'modern' than their own. The choice was deliberate. The Hofburg dated back to the thirteenth century and thus symbolised the dynasty's long heritage. The Habsburgs could safely leave the baroque to parvenus like the Prussian and Saxon monarchs and concentrate instead on demonstrating the religious foundations of their rule by endowing fine churches and monuments.[21]

The construction of massive palaces in the open country reflected the claims to political domination, while the carefully crafted gardens, with their clipped hedges and regimented bushes, indicated that even Nature could be bent by the royal will. The construction of the palace and new town of Karlsruhe in 1715 by Margrave Carl Wilhelm of Baden-Durlach is a dramatic example of this. The palace was built around a central tower from which radiated thirty-two roads like spokes from the hub of a wheel. At the same time, the margrave founded a chivalric 'Order of Loyalty' with thirty-two members, including himself. The order and the tower both symbolised the state to which all, including the margrave, were subordinate.[22]

The choice of interior decoration provided a further opportunity to convey the impression of absolute power. One example is the transformation through baroque decorative art of the image of the hero. The ideal of heroism was depersonalised and generalised so that few beyond the ruler were now capable of fulfilling a truly heroic role. Heroism became centralised in the person of the prince, often depicted larger than life, while others were reduced to bit players in his grand actions. Simultaneously, absolutism borrowed from classical antiquity to extend heroism beyond martial exploits to include other actions intended to promote the common good. Charles VI was depicted as a 'hero' protecting Austrian trade, for example.[23]

The use of the sun is well known from the court of Louis XIV where it was frequently used from the 1650s as the monarch's personal emblem. As the highest star, now accepted by science as the centre of the universe, the sun was an obvious choice to symbolise absolutism's claim to constitute the political centre of earthly life. The sun was both terrifying and awe inspiring, dazzling through its brightness, yet also warming and beneficent, and without its presence all life would whither away. The sun was also related to appropriate classical images, notably the Greek god Apollo who symbolised the rational and civilised side of human nature, as well as male physical beauty and the guardian role of shepherd. Not surprisingly, Louis XIV appeared personally in a royal ballet dressed as Apollo and the image was repeated in statues, paintings and medals. However, the sun image was not a registered trademark and Emperor Leopold I chose the same symbol for his son Joseph at his birth in 1678. The choice seemed singularly appropriate for the Habsburgs who triumphed over the Turkish half-moon throughout the 1680s–1710s. Leopold himself preferred the image of Jupiter who, as father of the gods, was naturally superior to Apollo and hence the Sun King, while Habsburg propaganda sometimes used the god Helios, whose association with the sun was believed to predate that of Apollo.[24]

Pagan symbols often jostled for position with those from Christianity, and the fusion of political and religious imagery was a defining feature of baroque Catholicism. The famous Pillar of the Holy Trinity in Vienna symbolised the unity of the Habsburg monarchy by combining the coats of arms of the three key territories of Austria, Bohemia and Hungary with images of their patron saints. The Plague Column of 1687 also conveyed a political message by placing the statue of the emperor in the position normally reserved for the Virgin Mary as mediator between heaven and humanity.

The baroque court was further distinguished by a more prominent role assigned to secular music. This was a time of musical innovation with the development of the modern orchestra and greater use of strings and woodwind instruments. Opera was first performed in public in Vienna in 1637 and spread to other parts of the Reich after 1648. Most large and medium territories had their own court orchestras by 1670, averaging around twenty permanent players, but that of the Habsburgs reached 134 by 1723. Court music was a status symbol, indicating wealth, power and good taste and was particularly popular because it provided a cheaper field of competition than palace construction. Opera was also a medium peculiarly suited to conveying an absolutist message. Its performance mirrored the idealised, hierarchical social order, with its stylised staging and segregated and multilayered seating. As it had a plot and a libretto, it could transmit a direct message, and titles and themes were often carefully chosen in response to political events.[25]

Music was also chosen to accompany the elaborate baroque court festivals that celebrated royal births, marriages and other events important to the dynasty. No such celebration could be without its appropriate elements, such as fountains flowing with wine, roasted oxen, bread distributed to the masses and coins minted for the occasion. Their presence was important and indicated the original purpose of such festivities, which had been to demonstrate the common ties between ruler and ruled through the symbolic sharing of a meal. Under absolutism this symbolism was transformed to distance the ruler from his subjects by displaying his magnificence and largesse. One such set piece was staged at the marriage of the Saxon crown prince to the emperor's daughter in Dresden in 1719. In addition to fitting out existing palaces and building new ones, there was a parade of a hundred decorated coaches and a flotilla of boats on the River Elbe, as well as the usual music, theatre, sports, triumphal arches and general excess.[26]

France has often been regarded as the main influence on the development of these activities, particularly in the lesser German principalities. 'Taken as a whole, the German courts remained droll caricatures of Versailles' as their 'boorish despots' failed to imitate the virtues of French culture and acquired only the vices. It is perhaps not surprising that these lines were penned by a Frenchman, but this interpretation is not merely a case of national prejudice, but is echoed in other works and has contributed profoundly to the myth of German petty despotism.[27] There is substantial evidence for the influence of French court culture in central Europe. Frederick III/I was known as 'Louis XIV's monkey' (*le singe de Louis XIV*) because of his aping of the French court and, as a dedicated follower of fashion, he reputedly ordered the Prussian envoy in Paris to obtain the exact measurements of the king's wig so that he could have a copy made.[28] Many courts employed French musicians, actors and dancing masters to teach their own staff the latest skills or simply to perform in the absence of suitable local talent. France also contributed the fashion for hunting on horseback with packs of hounds to add to the already impressive array of cruel sports practised by the German nobility. In short

Louis XIV was the proverbial legend in his own lifetime and it would be wrong to underestimate his international influence.

He was not, however, the only source for central European baroque court culture. The importance of classical imagery has already been noted, as has the strength of *pietas* and Christian morality. The latter was taken seriously as a guide to what was acceptable, rather than merely fashionable. Margrave Christian Ernst of Bayreuth (1661–1712) asked his consistory whether dancing was sinful and should be banned, while both Catholics and Protestants (especially Pietists) condemned opera as the 'devil's music'.[29] Moreover, central European absolutism had its own cultural heritage to draw upon and adapt. Apart from Bonn, no German palace followed the same internal layout of rooms as Versailles. Leopold I spoke Latin, German, Spanish and Italian, but not French. Italian was the preferred language for most opera librettos and it was to Italy that Elector Johann Georg III turned in 1685 when he established a court opera company in Dresden – and this was at the height of Louis XIV's grandeur and that of his court composer Jean-Baptiste Lully (1632–87), himself an Italian![30]

One final note of caution needs to be sounded before we leave the general projection of absolutism through the court. There is a danger of overestimating the political intent behind the court's external appearance and activities. The symbols were carefully chosen to convey a message, but they also reflected individual taste. For example, many princes patronised music from personal inclination and it was not just Frederick the Great who was a royal composer. The Bavarian elector Max Emanuel was considered an above-average musical talent and especially skilled at playing the viola da gamba. His son, Carl Albrecht, appeared at eighteen as a dancer in an opera and later directed rehearsals in the court theatre. Several of the Habsburgs were also noted as performers or composers. Moreover, the Church remained an important influence throughout the period, both as a direct contractor for some of central Europe's finest baroque buildings, and as patron of musicians and artists. Some of the most important and innovatory German composers were to be found not at court but in the employ of the imperial cities or important territorial towns: notably, Georg Philipp Telemann (1681–1767) who worked in Hamburg after 1721, Dieterin Buxtehude (1637–1707) who was in Lübeck from 1668, and J.S. Bach (1685–1750) who served as composer for the Saxon city of Leipzig after 1721. In this respect Elias's model of the court society is flawed. The court was certainly a trend setter, but it did not have an exclusive cultural monopoly. Both it and absolutism were open to more general norms, particularly religion, which Elias tended to underestimate. Moreover, although the court functioned as a forum to display absolutist rule, it cannot be understood solely on those terms. Elias's model has been rightly criticised as an exclusively 'functionalist' explanation which rationalises the court in terms of its utility to absolutism. The court was always more than simply a propaganda tool and, as we shall see shortly, it could serve the interests of those other than the monarch.[31]

The external arena of cultural competition provided the first level for a more specific projection of absolutism. This is an area of some debate and a number of historians have argued that the lesser princes were squeezed out of political competition after 1648 by the rise of two German great powers in Austria and Prussia and the general shift towards a European system of fully sovereign states. They took refuge behind the protective framework of the Reich and diverted their energies into cultural competition, attempting to outshine their rivals by the brilliance of their courts and artistic achievements.[32] The lesser territories were certainly overshadowed by the growth of Austria and Prussia, though it was not until after the Seven Years War that a number of them significantly reduced their armies. Courtly display remained for all central European absolute rulers an important part of the general projection of their power, and the efforts of the lesser princes in this area were closely connected to the pursuit of their political ambitions, however illusory these may appear in retrospect.[33]

There is a direct correlation between palace construction and periods of intense political competition. Duke Maximilian of Bavaria supported his efforts to secure an electoral title during the Thirty Years War by remodelling Munich as the 'German Rome'. Leopold I began major new work on the Hofburg in 1660 – the first since 1575 – so as not to be outdone by the Wittelsbachs. Further extensions by Charles VI after 1717 coincided with his efforts to secure international recognition of the Pragmatic Sanction. More work was considered during the mid-eighteenth century at a time when Habsburg imperial and international power was under threat, and construction began again in the early nineteenth century to consolidate the establishment of a distinct Austrian imperial title. Frederick III/I supported his bid to secure an independent royal title for Prussia by a major programme after 1688, including some of northern Europe's finest baroque buildings: the Marstall (stables) of 1690, the Zeughaus (arsenal) of 1695 and the remodelled Berlin palace of 1698. The message was clear: by making the city a capital of European importance, Frederick intended to prove he was worthy of a royal crown. Similarly, the dramatic expansion in Dresden under Elector Augustus the Strong (1697–1733) was connected to his efforts to secure and retain the Polish crown amid fierce competition. His son's chief minister, Count Brühl, continued this programme to bolster Saxony's faltering international prestige after 1733, and it has been suggested that Frederick the Great's remodelling of Berlin was in part a response to this.[34] Even minor princes who could ill afford such an expense considered it nonetheless vital to maintain their prestige. Christian Ernst feared a loss of his reputation if he stopped work on his palace in Bayreuth in good weather on the grounds of economy.[35]

The external projection of absolutism also made use of more subtle practices. The fragmentation of the medieval international hierarchy and the collapse of Catholic unity in the Reformation had disrupted established methods of communication. Alongside the emergence of international law in the seventeenth century, baroque court ceremony offered a substitute by providing a new etiquette to determine the prestige and standing of a rule and the appropriate respect due to his or her representatives. It offered a measure a security in an unpredictable international order by drawing on established symbols and accepted beliefs to create a new language of diplomacy. These foundations are important since they not only underpinned the etiquette of international relations, but all ceremonial at the absolutist court. According to Johann Christian Lünig, ceremony was necessary to display the differences stemming from the Fall from Grace which had destroyed original social equality. Princes and nobles maintained large staffs and needed practical guidelines to ensure their servants knew their place and duties. Neostoicism and the baroque obsession with rational systems and the science of geometry provided further impulses. Finally, there was the belief that humans reacted more to stimulation of the senses than to abstract ideas. Ceremony and ritual provided the outward show needed to reinforce social distinctions and guide behaviour.[36]

The importance of baroque ceremony to the external projection of absolutism is acknowledged even by those who dispute its significance in other areas.[37] It was particularly important in central Europe given the territorial complexity within the Reich where approximately 25 major and medium princes jostled for influence with 260 or so minor rulers, counts and prelates, a further 50-odd imperial cities and 1,500 imperial knights. Projecting the right image was vital in this environment where status had to be constantly reaffirmed, political demands backed by appropriate display and where a grand court could disguise a lack of real resources.

The Elias–Krüdener model of the domestication of the nobility forms the second level of the court's activity. This thesis has been well received and appears to explain not only why absolutism emerged, but how it functioned. The experience of central Europe provides considerable evidence to support this interpretation. Life at court was certainly expensive, costing twice as much as that on a country estate by the mid-seventeenth century. Becher and other cameralists had great difficult convincing princes and nobles of the utilitarian value of economic as opposed to personal credit, and were themselves obsessively concerned with their own status and 'standing' at court. Numerous court ordinances (*Hofordnungen*) and unofficial handbooks on polite behaviour spelt out in precise detail the role and function of each courtier and servant, even to the point of specifying appropriate facial expressions during a dance.[38] The role of court ritual has also been related to contemporary developments in military affairs, where the imposition of new forms of discipline and drill instilled subordination in previously unruly mercenaries in the seventeenth century. Elias's 'courtization of warriors' can be detected in parallel efforts to foster new concepts of honour and loyalty among aristocratic officers and cement a new bond between them and their prince and paymaster.[39] As usual, this is regarded as having been most extreme in Prussia, where collective obedience is supposed to have replaced individual aristocratic personal honour and, in so doing, laid a key foundation of later Prusso-German militarism.[40]

Princes certainly went to great lengths to integrate aristocratic social life into court routine. For instance, the Saxon electors made a habit of attending noble weddings from 1638 and Johann Georg II was present or represented at no less than 120 marriages in two years alone.[41] However, as this example also shows, rulers were enmeshed within the same courtly system. Rulers such as Leopold I considered ceremony a duty and clearly felt constrained by it. It consumed much of their time, fixing their daily routine and often placing a considerable physical burden upon them, although this was often less so than in France where Louis XIV's court etiquette made even the king's personal hygiene the subject of elaborate public ritual. By contrast, German rulers dressed and undressed in private and only ate in public on formal occasions.[42] Nonetheless, it remained a strain because princes still depended on everyone else playing their part. Those courtiers who did not know the rules – which varied from court to court – or made mistakes were liable to destroy the whole performance. A prince could waive ceremony to elevate a favourite, acquire titles for a mistress, or legitimise bastard children, but this involved considerable effort and was frequently dependent on the consent of outsiders, particularly the emperor, who reserved the right to approve new imperial titles. The underlying rules could not be changed since to tamper with aristocratic pedigree would be to undermine the entire hierarchy of the social elite.[43]

In addition to restricting the monarch's freedom of action, court ceremonial brought considerable benefits for the nobility. It reinforced their sense of collective social superiority and regulated access to their ranks from below, while also requiring the prince to dispense liberal rewards in the form of patronage, offices, titles and gifts. It did not, however, guarantee the smooth running of the court. Nor did it prove a barrier to faction and intrigue, or eliminate the separate aristocratic patronage and clientele networks. Indeed, there is little evidence to support Elias's supposed transition from social constraint to self-restraint as the court was as much a place of excess as politeness and reserve, as the numerous reports of scandals and misdemeanours indicate.[44] The absolutist standing army exhibited the same mix of discipline and disorder, and its soldiers were noted for their excess, drunkenness and brawling, as well as for clockwork precision in drill and exercises. The inability to eradicate duelling among officers also indicates limits to the courtisation of the warriors.[45]

The changes in aristocratic behaviour that did take place owed much to influences beyond the court. For example, many German nobles submitted themselves to the discipline of study at one of the exclusive knights academies (*Ritterakademien*) that were founded in the later sixteenth century, especially in the Protestant territories. Education was increasingly seen as essential to noble advancement and the passport to a career in princely service. Though princes encouraged this and indeed founded most of the academies, these cannot be simply regarded as evidence of 'domestication'. The most famous of the academies, the High School (*Hohe Schule*) established at Herborn by the count of Nassau in 1584, employed Althusius, that noted opponent of unfettered royal rule, as one of its teachers. Rather than functioning as an instrument to domesticate the nobility, the court provided the forum for the social bargaining process at the heart of absolutism. Though the prince remained a pivotal figure in a venue which served to display and reinforce his authority, it also rendered him accessible to factions within the nobility and to others in society who jostled for influence.

Similar problems were encountered in the last level of the court's activity where it functioned to subordinate the wider population. Its role was to invoke respect and compliancy, and to sustain the myth of power behind the hierarchical social order. The court was a glittering stage which magnified the cult of a charismatic monarch, both distant from earthly restraints and elevated far above the subjects. The beliefs behind baroque ceremonial underpinned this role. The divinely ordained social hierarchy placed the masses closest to the world of beasts, incapable of rational thought and so more likely to be swayed by external appearances. Unable to appreciate the intellectual arguments for absolutism, they would only believe in its legitimacy if convinced by courtly display. For this reason, court ritual accentuated the distance between ruler and ruled. The fact that most of its symbolism and classical allusions would have been incomprehensible to the majority of onlookers would have only reinforced the general sense of mystery and omnipotence.

However, this course of action was inherently dangerous as the prince could seem too remote and detached from the responsibilities of rule. The chances of failure were even greater than with aristocratic court ritual because, unlike the courtiers, most subjects were not initiated in the purpose of the performance. Not even an absolute monarch could command the weather, while scenery could break, or the crowd laugh at the wrong moment and the whole effect be ruined. In practice, the small scale of most German territories mitigated against this by reducing the physical distance between ruler and ruled, while the rhetoric of the morally upright territorial patriarch (*Landesvater*) made such proximity actually desirable.

Nonetheless, the ambivalence inherent in these relationships engendered the growth of court criticism which had been present since the sixteenth century and developed in parallel with the rise of the baroque court. It drew on the earlier anti-Machiavellian critique of deceit, as well as the moral–Christian tradition and the emergence of secular individualism. German critics tended to be circumspect, often remaining anonymous and choosing to attack France rather than their own rulers. Criticism became more pronounced during the 1690s at the height of the baroque court and exposed the discrepancy between the excesses of court society and absolutism's claim to promote the common good. The concept of baroque prudence and the general secrecy surrounding the arcane ritual of the court particularly incensed the Pietists as it contradicted their belief in openness and honesty. However, some criticism was intended as constructive, arguing that the court was simply a wasteful extravagance which detracted from absolutism's purpose. Rather than hiding behind this façade, princes should let their true majesty be judged by their moral rectitude and the social value of their actions. Significantly, most critics came from outside the nobility, indicating the validity of Krüdener's claim that the crown and aristocracy shared a certain community of interest.[46]

It is difficult to assess the overall impact of such criticism, but it is certainly possible to detect a significant change in central European courts from the 1710s. This move to a more restrained, less ostentatious style can be labelled the rococo court and encompassed more than just artistic and architectural fashion. As with the earlier baroque court, developments were far from uniform. Courtly restraint was most apparent in Berlin where Frederick William I completed his father's town palace, but left the ceilings whitewashed rather than gilded. The accession of Frederick II in 1740 initially appeared to herald a return to past extravagance as the new king planned to remodel the city centre as the Forum Friderizianum, complete with a new town palace. Very little of this was ultimately undertaken, and Frederick broke with the past by pulling down military buildings in the city to make way for a new theatre in 1774 and demolishing most of Berlin's fortifications. His brother's new palace was later converted to house the Humboldt University, while the landgrave of Hessen-Kassel also rebuilt his capital after 1762 as a centre for the arts and learning. Palace construction could still perform a representative role, as indicated by the Neues Palais in Potsdam built by Frederick in 1763–9 to demonstrate that his monarchy had not been bankrupted by the Seven Years War. Nonetheless, it is significant that the building was reserved for his guests, while he preferred to live in the more modest Sans Souci palace near by. Other princes also chose to withdraw into smaller, though still palatial, retreats, and it is no coincidence that Carl Eugen chose the name Solitude for his new residence, built 1763–7.[47]

In addition to their more intimate scale, these palaces were built to a different design. Frederick II surrounded his palaces in Potsdam with colonnades rather than walls, symbolising a less aloof form of monarchy, while the Habsburgs allowed limited public access to their gardens and others opened court libraries, theatres and opera houses. Ceremonial was also loosened and by the later eighteenth century it drew a greater distinction between person and function, in keeping with the growth of the impersonal state. Monarchs like Joseph II took to travelling incognito to avoid diplomatic protocol, and save time and expense. These changes were often most pronounced in the smallest courts which are sometimes mistakenly regarded as lagging behind, and by the late eighteenth century Dessau, Karlsruhe, Bückeburg and Weimar had all become leading centres of refinement and learning. For example, Franz of Anhalt-Dessau (1758–1817) was not content simply to impress his subjects, wanting them instead to be active participants in his schemes to improve his small territory. The public was invited into his new garden at Wörlitz to see the agricultural and cultural activity which he hoped they would emulate.[48]

The new intellectual climate of the Enlightenment certainly influenced these developments, as did a desire for economy after prolonged warfare in 1672–1714. However, absolutism was also more secure, both domestically and internationally, and it is notable that both the Hanoverian and Prussian courts were scaled down once their monarchs had gained European recognition for their new royal titles. The new uncertainties posed by the French Revolution and collapse of the Reich coincided with a revival of the court's representational role under the influence of the new classical style.[49]

The preceding indicates that the Elias–Krüdener model needs modification. Though their thesis of the domestication of the nobility cannot be entirely upheld, they are right to stress the importance of the court in sustaining absolutism's 'myth of power'. The image it projected was indeed a façade, but no less potent for that and indicates the extent to which absolute rule rested on persuasion rather than coercion.

POLITICAL COMMUNICATION AND PUBLIC OPINION

In their efforts to persuade others of their grandeur and legitimacy the princes employed a variety of media and needed to be constantly sensitive to public opinion. The orthodox view of absolutism denies the existence of this dialogue prior to the Age of Enlightenment and the French Revolution. This view rests on the work of Reinhart Koselleck and especially the Frankfurt critical theorist Jürgen Habermas who called the growth of 'modern' public opinion the 'structural transformation of the public sphere'.[50]

Both argue that a stark division between public and private emerged in the early modern period with the rise of the absolutist state. As this concentrated 'public' powers in the hands of the prince and a few high aristocrats, all other inhabitants were reduced to 'private' individuals. The emphasis on the mysteries of state suppressed public discussion of political affairs, forcing individuals into a neutral private sphere. Political communication became a one-way process of a 'representative public sphere' in which only the absolute monarch and his officials were active participants, projecting a carefully constructed message to be received by a passive, uninformed audience of subjects. The growth of commerce and new markets fostered alternative channels of private communication based on mutual exchange and understanding. As these clashed with state intervention in the economy, they produced a new 'bourgeois public sphere' critical of absolute monarchy. Strengthened by the growth of enlightened philosophy, this successfully challenged the absolutist monopoly over political discourse in the late eighteenth century, producing Habermas's structural transformation.

The influence of this model can be detected in those who have studied the absolutist state and the spread of enlightened philosophy,[51] while a recent study has unearthed considerable evidence suggesting that it can be applied to eighteenth-century France.[52] However, the theory has a number of significant flaws. It employs a neo-Marxist economistic argument relating the growth of new forms of communication to the rise of capitalism and the middle class which ignores the importance of specialist groups like educated officials and other factors that can account for the fragmentation of early modern discourse. The schematic relationship between 'bourgeois criticism' and the end of absolutism misses the earlier critique of princely rule we have already encountered in our discussion of the court. Finally, the model concentrates on verbal and written discourse, underplaying the significance of other forms of communication in the early modern world. Absolutism did seek to monopolise political discussion and to suppress certain forms of communication, but it also expected an active response from its audience, while its efforts at control were far from successful.[53]

Official communication under absolutism was highly sophisticated and used a variety of different forms to target specific audiences. We have already met many of these during our examination of the court's general projection of the image of absolute power to fellow-monarchs, the nobility and the masses. Within the latter we can also single out the elitist world of the educated commoners (*Gelehrten*) who emerged as a potentially far more dangerous and critical group than the 'bourgeois' merchants. Some forms of communication were specific to a single target group, such as formal diplomacy which only involved fellow-princes and their advisers. Others, such as the design and decoration of palaces, or the elaborate court festivals, were intended to speak on different levels to particular sections of their audience. Even public executions were stage-managed to convey an impression of the state's omnipotence and its triumph over crime and disorder.[54] In addition, we must remember that, as with the court in general, absolutism's audience included posterity. The construction of magnificent palaces, the collection of wondrous and precious objects and the recording of the ruler's actions in texts and images were all intended to speak as much to future generations as to address the present.

Habermas was nonetheless correct in stressing the significance of written forms of communication which began to displace the verbal, though not the symbolic or allegorical, during the eighteenth century. Since the Reformation, the territorial state had made considerable use of the Church to convey its announcements through the weekly Sunday service, but began replacing the oral recitation of its message by the parish priest with printed placards for public display. Many German territories also instituted their own state-owned or state-funded papers which published decrees and other pronouncements starting with the Prussian weekly based in Halle from 1727.

However, attempts to censor the commercial press proved unsuccessful, particularly given the fragmented nature of the Reich and its ease of access to the relatively free Dutch papers. Recent research on the growth of the regular press has dispelled the belief that the German public was primarily interested in literature and that intellectual discussion was restricted prior to the Enlightenment and the establishment of reading societies (*Lesergesellschaften*) and spread of freemasonry in the late eighteenth century. There were already at least sixty newspaper publishers in the Reich by 1700, and though their papers generally had limited print runs, each copy was read by ten or more people. A separate journal literature had been growing since 1682 and by 1720 about 1,000 new journals and books were published each year, rising to 3,200 by 1791. Individual library holdings could be substantial, with that opened to the public in Ludwigsburg in 1765 containing 120,000 volumes by 1787 (or ten times the number at the nearby Tübingen university!). Though an estimated 3.5 million Germans (about 15 per cent of the total) could read by 1700, the main markets for these publications were the 80,000 educated intellectuals and 100,000 aristocrats.[55] Though small, these were influential groups and territorial governments expended considerable effort trying to convince them of the legitimacy and efficacy of their policies.

The flow of information to the rest of the population was even harder to control, despite the fact that the bulk could not read. Rumour remained rife under absolutism given the tensions between concern for the mysteries of state, the rudimentary forms of popular communication and the growing appetite for information. Itinerants formed a significant minority of the population and were often welcomed as a source of news from distant places. They formed a distinct subculture with their own argot (*Rotwelsch*) and signs (*Zinken*) that were often indecipherable to the authorities. Rumour was always regarded as the first step to sedition and was frequently blamed for trouble, as in the case of the mutiny of the Württemberg army in 1757.[56] It was often linked to the circulation of printed broadsheets which had developed during the Reformation and been used for propaganda in the Thirty Years War. These generally displayed a striking visual image with an appropriate rhymed verse underneath and could be sung out for a fee by travelling pedlars. Unlike the regular press, the news content of these broadsheets declined after 1648 because they were abandoned as an official form of state communication and they became marginally less threatening as they concentrated on gossip and scandal. Folk songs remained an alternative source of potential criticism but they tended to be restricted to particular localities and the more widely popular ones were often panegyrics on such notable figures as Prince Eugene of Savoy.[57] Popular theatre offered a fourth arena for topical commentary, but was easier to control by threatening to expel any performers who overstepped the mark.

Even where the state could restrict the forms of communication it never completely controlled the response. The Habermas–Koselleck model of public communication corresponds only to the official view under absolutism. Rulers and intellectuals certainly believed that the masses were incapable of rational thought or the articulation of political ideas, were susceptible to external display and so could be duped by appearances. However, this communication was never intended to be exclusively one-way. The masses were required to remain subordinate, unequal partners in this dialogue, but they were also expected to respond with appropriate gestures such as cries of '*vivat!*' as the prince passed by. As the discussion of court festivals has suggested, the chance of mishap or misunderstanding was ever present. Despite the attempt at secrecy, princes were, in the opinion of Frederick the Great, 'more exposed than any other men to the reflections and judgements of the world'.[58] The emergence of court criticism, as well as discussions of reform and state policy within universities and cameralist bureaucratic circles, also indicates that several overlapping spheres of public discourse emerged well before the alleged structural transformation associated with the commercial bourgeoisie.

ESTATES AND INTERMEDIARY BODIES

The presence or absence of territorial estates has long been regarded as a vital factor determining the extent of absolute rule. Absolutism is deemed strong where estates were weak or non-existent, and German princely rule is usually regarded as having crushed or neutralised all formally incorporated bodies between it and its subjects. The Prussian example is frequently cited where the Great Elector turned his new standing army on the estates in Cleve and Mark, and later against those in East Prussia. The decline of the estates is dated to the Thirty Years War, which damaged their former financial credit and witnessed the introduction of taxes without their consent. Continued warfare after 1655 in northern Europe and 1672 in western Europe permitted rulers to continue their new fiscal and military arrangements.[59]

A variety of reasons have been advanced as to why the German estates were unable to resist these developments. One lies in the nature of their representation which emphasised the corporate rights of distinct groups such as the nobility, clergy and urban burghers. Though these often elected their representatives, each group sat in a separate chamber and so could be played against the others by skilful princes. By contrast, areas outside the Reich had geographically based estates representation where deputies from the same social background often sat in different chambers. This was the case in Hungary where nobles were represented in both chambers, a fact which clearly helps explain the prolonged resistance of the Hungarian diet to Habsburg absolutism. Hungarian resolve was further stiffened by ethnicity since all Magyars, regardless of social origin, were faced by imported Austrian rule.[60]

Less convincing arguments were proposed by Francis Carsten, to whom we otherwise owe much for our current understanding of these institutions. In addition to the personal example of Louis XIV which is supposed to have animated German princes towards more absolute rule, Carsten noted an ingrained attitude of obedience in the estates, particularly those dominated by the nobility, as well as the 'enfeeblement of the Empire' which failed to prevent the erosion of estates' rights during the seventeenth century.[61] Carsten did note the significance of the estates' survival in Württemberg, where they continued throughout the eighteenth century to contest moves towards absolutism, while the post-1945 interest in earlier German democratic institutions encouraged further research which detected similar situations in Mecklenburg, East Frisia and several other territories.[62] Though this research modified the detail, its basic conclusions remained much the same. Territorial politics were presented as a dualism between ruler and estates, suggesting a stark alternative between absolutism and constitutional representative government.

More recent studies have corroborated these findings on the persistence of the estates, but have provided a more rounded explanation for their survival. One reason was structural, since those estates which covered the entire territory and developed such permanent institutions as standing committees and archives clearly faired better than those whose organisation lagged behind that of the princely administration. Weakness in the ruling house provided a second reason, particularly where the conversion of the dynasty to another faith left the estates as constitutional guardians of the subjects' religion, as in Württemberg, Hessen-Kassel and Saxony, or where acquisition of a separate kingdom resulted in long-term absence from the territory, as in Hanover, Holstein and Saxony. Moreover, far from being left enfeebled by the Thirty Years War, imperial institutions experienced a revival after 1670 that enabled the two supreme courts to interfere in ruler–estate disputes, frequently to the benefit of the latter. Finally, several princes appreciated that by working together with their estates they could enhance the effectiveness of their rule and so continued to collaborate with at least a select standing committee or with officials connected with their institutions, as in the case of the Landräte in Brandenburg-Prussia.[63]

This last point raises the question whether ruler–estate relations were characterised more by conflict or cooperation. This is best explored through the recent controversial thesis of Peter Blickle, which postulates the existence of a distinctly democratic tradition that was suppressed by absolutism. Blickle bases his arguments on a reappraisal of early modern German rural and urban communities and the claim that they fostered a popular representative tradition he labels 'communalism'. He is careful not to resurrect the old, folksy-patriotic notion of ancient German fellowship as the basis of a distinctly superior way of life. Instead, he argues that communalism was a relatively recent development stemming from a major shift in German settlement patterns from the early fourteenth century. The medieval manorial system had constituted a direct form of lordship relying on large demesne worked by unfree labour. It was gradually replaced by a new form of indirect lordship whereby previously servile farm workers were transformed into peasants commanding their own labour, but paying a rent to their landlord. Simultaneously, the lord delegated much of the local government to the peasant heads of household who became collectively responsible for the management of the village's internal affairs and increasingly represented it in dealings with outsiders. Blickle believes the formation of this associative principle of neighbourhood provided the basis for the growth of communalism and argues a similar process took place in urban communities where government devolved to recognised citizens (*Bürgers*) and their elected representatives.[64]

Whereas others relate the growth of German territorial estates in the fourteenth century to the surrounding fiscal crises and public order problems, Blickle regards them as products of the growth of communalism. The need for territorial authorities to cope with their new responsibilities could only be met by fiscal and administrative innovation which, in turn, was only possible with the consent of the governed. The estates provided the forum for securing this and emerged *from below* as key groups demanded representation. The influence of communalism was strongest where the peasants obtained a voice in these assemblies, since their representation was based on the same principle of enfranchising heads of households that existed in the villages and many towns. Peasants sent deputies to estates in Austria, the Tirol, the Voralberg, Salzburg, Basel, Württemberg, Baden, Trier, Kempten, the Palatinate (briefly) and many small south-western territories.[65] Their presence determined what Blickle terms the 'age of the common man' between 1300 and 1650 when the territorial state could only achieve its objectives with the help of its estates and enfranchised peasants. The growth of communalism within this period offered a powerful alternative route to state formation, as exemplified by the Swiss Confederation dating back to 1291, the autonomous peasant community of Ditmarschen in north Germany (1283–1550) and, most spectacularly of all, the Peasants' War which Blickle dubs the 'revolution of 1525'.[66]

The basis of communalism was eroded after the defeat of the peasants in 1525, paving the way for the authoritarian, absolutist state by 1650. The power of the estates withered as the princes were joined by the nobles and created their own bureaucracy. The influence of 'foreign' court culture assisted this process, as did the impact of the Reformation, which propagated the model of a patriarchal 'house father' (*Hausvater*) as an authority figure at local level. The state endorsed this ideal, which was further disseminated through popular manuals on household management between 1670 and 1750, and by sanctioning male parental authority co-opted the village headmen into the lower echelons of its own administration. Meanwhile, communalism had failed to take root east of the Elbe because agrarian settlement had departed from the Western pattern and remained dominated by direct feudal lordship. Though crushed by the 'feudal state', communalism was not entirely extinguished. 'Peasant parliamentary estates' survived in many small territories thanks to the protection of the imperial courts, while communalism persisted as a 'German national tradition' of freedom that offered a 'third way' between the imperial and absolutist traditions, on the one hand, and French revolutionary ideas, on the other.[67]

Blickle's interpretation fits the dualist model of ruler–estate relations as primarily conflictual and as a struggle between mutually hostile traditions of absolutism and authoritarianism versus constitutionalism and democracy. His arguments are at times deliberately polemical and are intended as a challenge to what he perceives as a conservative distortion of the German past. They are far from uncontroversial and can be rebutted on a number of points. Some of these are comparatively minor, such as his claims for 'foreign' court culture, or his exaggeration of the effectiveness of militia systems associated with some communal institutions, like those in the Tirol. Others are more substantial and merit fuller treatment.

The link between communalism and later parliaments is implied throughout, but never satisfactorily explained. What Blickle refers to are not so much the estates, but the lesser *Landschaften*, or representative institutions that did genuinely emerge from below as assemblies of non-noble urban and rural subjects. That in Kempten is the most famous and forms Blickle's primary example. It appeared briefly in 1496 and again in 1525–7 during the Peasants' War, before being revived in the 1660s following a severe financial crisis. However, Kempten was only a minor ecclesiastical principality encompassing no more than 880 square kilometres and 36,000 inhabitants even in the eighteenth century, and virtually all the other examples are in equally tiny territories.[68] Peasant representation elsewhere was largely a happy by-product of the nobility's self-emancipation from princely jurisdiction, as in Württemberg and Trier where they joined the imperial knights in the fifteenth and sixteenth centuries. Blickle is right to stress the desire for *Landschaften* and others have found evidence from the eighteenth century that many peasants regarded the estates as unrepresentative and sought active participation for themselves.[69] Such desires were rarely realised even before 1650, while there is no clear correlation between the presence of peasant representatives and opposition to absolutism. The East Frisian estates were almost entirely composed of peasant deputies and continually resisted the imposition of absolute rule between about 1660 and the duchy's eventual incorporation into Prussia in 1744. However, the Mecklenburg estates did precisely the same but were dominated by an extremely reactionary, archetypal feudal nobility, while their would-be absolute dukes were allied to the free peasants and urban burghers.[70]

The second substantial problem concerns the contested nature of 'community' and 'common good' in early modern central Europe. Blickle concentrates on the horizontal elements within German communes and misses many of the vertical. Villagers and townspeople were not simply bound together by common ties but were integrated into a wider hierarchy. The term 'common' (*gemein*) and its derivatives were all ambiguous and could be exclusive as well as inclusive: every community contained outsiders as well as insiders, while gender, wealth and property relations always hindered rigid solidarity among its members. The householders who were enfranchised in both town and village were almost invariably male and rarely numbered above 20 per cent of the total population, so that every community contained a strong element of oligarchy.[71] There was indeed a strong communal basis to popular revolts indicating that solidarity could override local tensions, but equally communities were themselves often riven by conflict, providing opportunities for both the territorial state and imperial institutions to intervene in their affairs.[72]

Blickle's location of communalism in the western half of the Reich is also problematic and unintentionally echoes the post-1945 partition of Germany and the historiographical divisions of the Cold War. Whereas western villages provide a communal basis from which to resist authoritarianism, those in the east allegedly succumbed to a 'refeudalisation', especially where princes surrendered jurisdiction over them in a compromise with their nobility.[73] Recent research provides a very different picture of rural life east of the Elbe, detecting communal elements similar to those found by Blickle in the west, but without losing sight of the continued presence of hierarchical, authoritarian factors like the landlords' jurisdiction and the intrusion of the state.[74]

Finally, Blickle has been accused of present-mindedness by some of his critics who regard his thesis as an attempt to trace the origins of a liberal tradition for the Federal Republic back into the German past. An example is his claim that Althusius was an advocate of communally based republicanism. Far from being a far-sighted vision of a liberal-democratic future, Althusius's discussion of estates simply reflected a contemporary faith in mixed monarchy and he only appears radical when set against the subsequent growth of absolutism.[75]

Though clearly exaggerated, Blickle's conclusions do demonstrate the power of popular action prior to the formation of modern representative institutions. Communalism was present as a political force in the *Landschaften* and could provide an alternative to princely state formation, as the emergence of Switzerland from an alliance of mountain cantons demonstrates. His arguments also reinforce Carsten's earlier claim for the estates' positive contribution, and serve as a timely reminder when historians persist in writing out the popular representative tradition from German history.[76] However, closer investigation reveals the complexity of ruler–estate relations. These cannot be encompassed within the dualist model. Tensions at local level could be pronounced, and created opportunities for princes to seek popular support by favouring particular groups or areas. This is important, because it indicates that the bargaining process underpinning absolutism extended beyond negotiations with the nobility in the formal forum of a territorial assembly or the confines of the court. The co-option of the heads of peasant households through the image of the patriarchal house father indicates that it also stretched deep into peasant communities.

The impact of war on these relations was also ambiguous. War did not automatically favour the growth of absolutism and could also undermine it. It is significant that most estates became institutionalised by holding regular diets during the later fifteenth century precisely because their rulers' constant demands for cash necessitated further meetings. They extracted further concessions in return for tax grants into the seventeenth century and often continued to do so even after their prince had established additional sources of revenue outside their control. Military defeat could strengthen their position, as is illustrated by the example of the Habsburgs. The Turkish victory in 1526 left the Habsburgs dependent on their estates for resources to defend the exposed eastern frontier. However, the absence of a single central diet denied the estates a central coordinating role and permitted the dynasty to assume greater prominence as the only institution transcending provincial boundaries. The same could be said of the Hohenzollerns in the seventeenth century and provided an advantage on which absolutism could be built. Nonetheless, though the crown secured executive control, its infrastructional power remained far from centralised, particularly in the Habsburg monarchy, which continued to depend heavily on negotiated tax grants into the mid-eighteenth century.[77]

Though the estates retained a reduced presence under absolutism and even a formal existence into the early nineteenth century, there is no easy link between them and later parliaments. Even peasant *Landschaften* were far from fully representative, while the tendency towards oligarchy grew more pronounced under absolutism since princes preferred to deal with the more manageable small standing committees than with full diets. More fundamentally, the ideas on which estates representation was based were not those of nineteenth-century liberalism, let alone modern parliamentary democracy, although the estates did provide a precedent for early nineteenth-century liberals seeking to limit the post-revolutionary neo-absolutist state. Article 13 of the Founding Act of the German Confederation in 1815 obliged all its members to establish estates (*Landständen*) as part of their new constitutions. These were established in the south-western states and evolved as parliaments, but they incorporated political arrangements absent before 1806. Despite the desire for broader representation, most estates had remained reactionary in the sense that they surrendered the initiative to their ruler and simply responded to his demands. Frustration with this can be detected even before 1789 and prompted some progressive thinkers to distinguish between estates and popular sovereignty, breaking the bounds of the old debate on limited monarchy by arguing that the constitutional limits to monarchical power should be put on a new basis of common rights.[78]

BUREAUCRACY

The development of a strong bureaucracy is regarded as integral to the emergence of absolutism and a particular characteristic of its central European variant. Unlike absolutism, 'bureaucracy' at least dates from the period and was derived from the French word *bureaux* (offices) by Vincent de Gournay (1712–59), an opponent of 'big government'.[79] However, it is Prussia that exemplifies for many the emergence of a modern bureaucracy.[80] There is a widespread view that it was the only German territory to develop a fully integrated and rational administrative structure, though other territories followed this general trend.[81] Prussian bureaucracy is also held to have been more efficient than that in France, which was hamstrung by the continued presence of an office-holding *noblesse de robe* and failed to foster the modern ethos of a professional civil service. The peculiarities of the Prussian system accounts for its prominence in distinctive models of 'bureaucratic absolutism' or 'military–bureaucratic absolutism'.[82]

These interpretations support the general theory of absolutism as a key stage in the formation of the modern state. The centralisation of executive authority required an appropriate infrastructure to make it effective. Late medieval institutions could not provide this because they were too deeply rooted in the networks of power that bound early modern monarchs to consult their estates and nobility. A separate corps of expert princely servants was recruited to staff new institutions which gradually displaced existing structures. Related to this process was a switch from a spatial division of responsibility to one organised along functional lines. Instead of separate officials or institutions carrying out a wide range of tasks for each locality, responsibility for key functions like tax collection, justice and military affairs was centralised in specialist departments. This encouraged a drive to uniformity as the same rules began to be applied across the entire territory, while staff became more professional as experience and qualifications replaced connection and birth as requirements for appointment, and as salaries and conditions of service were placed on a more regular footing. Professionalisation transformed administrative personnel from servants of an individual prince (*Fürstendiener*) to those of an impersonal state (*Staatsdiener*), while a collective sense of their own status and responsibility engendered a potent group consciousness and made bureaucrats a social force.

These developments have been subjected to widely differing interpretations. The myth of absolutism as a positive historical force regarded the formation of a modern bureaucracy as one of its major achievements, providing the foundation of the Prusso-German power state and acting as an impartial but benevolent force for social improvement. More recently, it has been interpreted as a socially partisan alliance of reactionary aristocrats and the authoritarian state that held back the emergence of democratic institutions by managing change from above.[83] Subsequent research has tended to follow the latter line, further relativising earlier claims for the rationality and efficiency of absolutist bureaucracy in general and the Prussian in particular. Older forms of administration persisted even in Prussia, where the transition to a functionally based structure was far from complete by the end of the eighteenth century, while the Habsburg monarchy lacked a single central coordinating body before 1761 and continued to be administered on the basis of its historic provinces long after that. These delays retarded absolutism's development and undermined its ability to deal with the problems posed by the mounting cost and scale of international conflict. Non-absolutist states proved more effective at mobilising resources and it has been argued that the continued participation of representative institutions in Britain and the Dutch Republic sustained the legitimacy of their governments and made it possible for them to raise credit and levy higher taxes.[84] Paradoxically, absolutism's drive for centralisation was counter-productive since the concentration of executive authority placed too great a burden on a monarch of even the calibre and dedication of Frederick the Great. The sheer impossibility of personally overseeing all business left scope for dissension, inefficiency and corruption at all levels.[85] The practice of deferring to the king could paralyse the administration if the monarch was unwell or incompetent. It also encouraged an unhealthy jockeying for position in the 'ante-chamber of power' as the senior figures sought to bend the king's ear and exclude their rivals, something which has recently been identified as a cause of Prussia's diplomatic miscalculations between 1795 and 1806.[86]

As this suggests, ministers were rarely impartial and one theorist has rightly disputed the overreliance on Weber's model of bureaucracy to explain administrative developments under absolutism. According to Weber, the process of rationalisation alienated state servants from the 'means of administration' since they no longer had a direct stake in the institutions they served, but instead depended on salaries paid from central funds. Though office-holding (ownership) was unusual in the German states, and personal fees were gradually eliminated, administrators continued to see their office as a means of individual and collective advancement. Informal patronage continued, while officials at all levels were not immune to ideas and pressures emanating from the rest of society.[87]

The overall impact of such work is to highlight the persistence of the old alongside the new, as well as to modify earlier claims for absolutism's administrative efficiency. As with absolutism in general, there is a danger of judging developments against an ideal, abstract model that never existed in practice and so of losing sight of what was different. One important change was the erosion of the local and social autonomy of the previous administrative structures and the establishment of a greater degree of uniformity and centralised supervision. Much of this took place during the Thirty Years War, but was also dependent on the long-term expansion of German higher education. There were twenty-six universities in the late medieval Reich; a number roughly comparable in proportion to that in France and elsewhere. However, a further 24 institutions were founded after 1600, bringing the total to 50, compared with 22 in France and only 2 in England. Significantly, only two of the new universities were based in imperial cities, indicating the significance of princely patronage and the general role of higher education as a training ground for state administration. This cut across the social divide as nobles also regarded a degree as the proper foundation for a career. The political fragmentation within the Reich widened the choice of potential recruits, and despite the formal presence in many territories of laws restricting employment to natives or co-religionists (*Indigenatsrecht*), princes hired specialists from outside their lands. Territorial administrations also expanded downwards by co-opting parish priests, village headmen and municipal officials into their wider networks, and by imposing standardised rules on previously diverse local management.

Nonetheless, these networks functioned largely through persuasion and the state administration should be regarded as another arena of the wider bargaining process under absolutism. Not only did the prince rely on his officials to convey the image of his power to his other subjects, he had to convince them of the legitimacy of his rule. There are signs that, by the later eighteenth century at least, the concept of personal loyalty to the prince was conflicting with a wider collective duty to the impersonal state. Some officials also began to see monarchy as a hindrance, rather than a help, to reforms they believed necessary. However, such criticisms were expressed only rarely and most officials remained loyal to the concept of monarchical rule, and often to the dynasty itself, throughout the revolutionary and Napoleonic eras.[88]

FINANCE AND WAR

Discussions of absolutism's relationship to war generally rest on two key assumptions: that political and military organisation are related and that certain types of state engage in specific sorts of warmaking. Absolutism is thus related both to the mercenary standing army and external wars of aggression. Executive authority was concentrated in the monopoly of violence, eliminating the nobility's feuds and private armies. Infrastructional power was secured through the professional administration of the 'fiscal–military state' which provided both the general means to wage war and the specific institutional support for permanent military forces.[89]

The monopoly of violence and the fiscal–military state were identified by contemporaries as interrelated and integral to absolutism. Hermann Conring regarded absolutism as entirely dependent on an army of paid henchmen and saw its origins in the spread of mercenaries through the Reich in the late fifteenth century which had undermined the previous collective forms of warmaking. Subsequent commentators have continued this emphasis on mercenaries as the basis of princely military power and a major example of the coercive element inherent in absolutism. Beginning with the professional infantry (*Landsknechte*) hired to defeat the peasants in 1525, German princely rule has been widely interpreted as resting on armed might deployed to crush internal opposition and defeat external rivals. The correlation between foreign military expertise and the consolidation of monarchical power has been identified elsewhere, notably in France where moves towards greater centralisation are related to the employment of Swiss mercenaries in the late fifteenth century. (The Swiss Guards became part of the royal household troops (*Maison du roi*) and a key pillar of the French monarchy until massacred by the revolutionaries in 1792.) Such conclusions have led Marxist historians to term the standing army the 'pillar of feudal reaction'.[90]

The Saxon and Brandenburg electors briefly maintained similar household units, ironically composed of *French* Huguenot refugees in the 1680s, but otherwise the existence of such guard units was rare in central Europe and the almost complete absence of any elite units in the Habsburg army set it even further apart from those of the Western monarchies.[91] Nevertheless, the mercenary component is regarded as fundamental to all central European armies and is combined with references to the Historic Compromise to explain the basis of their military power. Though they did not group them into distinct units, German princes nonetheless relied heavily on 'foreign' soldiers who supposedly would not sympathise with any rebellious subjects. The army's loyalty was further secured by regularising pay and conditions funded by permanent war taxes introduced during the Thirty Years War and retained thereafter. The territorial nobility initially opposed these new standing forces, but they are thought to have been reconciled through the general compromise with the crown and by the subsequent expansion of employment opportunities provided by the officer corps.

It is no surprise that Prussia appears as the most prominent example in this context, as it does for the compromise theory in general.[92] In an influential thesis, Otto Büsch argued that the compromise was strengthened by the expansion of Prussian military power after 1713. The demands of the crown were balanced with the Junkers' agrarian interests by the canton system of limited conscription introduced by 1733. This inducted serf labourers as recruits for a period of basic training before releasing them for most of each year to work on their landlords' fields. Since the Junker landlord was often the recruits' company commander as well, military jurisdiction reinforced feudal agrarian powers and further cemented the crown–noble alliance. The rest of the army was composed of 'foreign' professionals who could number half the total strength and, particularly under Frederick the Great, served as cannon fodder to relieve the burden on Prussia's limited population. This system militarised Prussian society and eventually that of the other German states which allegedly copied it following Prussia's victories over Austria in 1740–5 and 1756–63. However, this structure was inherently flawed. Its only motivation was fear, and soldiers, especially foreigners, deserted at the first opportunity. The numerous exemptions to conscription on social and economic grounds prevented the monarchy from maximising its full potential, while continued reliance on aristocratic officers stifled talent and inhibited a flexible promotions policy. These flaws were exposed when the Prussian and other 'old regime' armies met those of dynamic revolutionary France, and their defeats explain the wider demise of absolutism itself.[93]

However, these arguments are also riddled with contradictions, some of which we have already touched on during our examination of the Historic Compromise theory in Chapter 1. Nobles displaced commoners from officer positions from the late seventeenth century, but many were 'foreign' in the sense that they came from outside the territory they served. This practice continued throughout the eighteenth century, especially as most territories reduced their armies at the end of wars in 1714, 1735, 1748 and 1763, forcing discharged officers to seek employment elsewhere. These changes affected the Prussian army as well and it was rare that officers came from the same part of the monarchy as the conscripts in their company. Indeed, the proportion of foreigners has been greatly exaggerated and most princes recruited their forces from their own subjects using variations on a militia system whereby men were enrolled in their parishes and expected to do minimal annual training, but remained liable for service in regular units in wartime if selected by drawing lots or rolling dice. Most 'foreigners' came from neighbouring territories or from other Germans enlisted by parties sent to recruit in the imperial cities. Natives were clearly preferred and many princes took the opportunity to rid their ranks of the more unreliable outsiders when hiring regiments to serve as auxiliaries elsewhere. Desertion was a problem, but one which has also been exaggerated; rates were much lower than was once thought and often below those of the later French revolutionary forces.[94]

What we have here are two definitions of a 'foreigner'. One encompassed those recruited outside the Reich and corresponds more closely to the cliché of the rootless adventurer willing to fight for whoever paid the most. Such individuals never accounted for more than a minority of any army. The other 'foreigners' were subjects of the Reich, generally serving with the permission of their own rulers in the forces of neighbouring territories. Such remarks are not intended to imply that soldiering was just another trade (*Kriegshandwerk*), but rather to stress that early modern military recruitment cannot be interpreted through the lens of later nationalism and the nation state. Confessional allegiance frequently proved a stronger bond than ties of a common language, as the example of the Huguenots serving Protestant Brandenburg illustrates. Moreover, though the German princes supplied most of the auxiliaries serving other powers, it was the British and Dutch constitutional regimes rather than the French, Spanish, Danish and Swedish monarchies which hired the majority of them. In short, there is no simple correlation between the cliché of the foreign mercenary (or recruiting systems in general) and early modern forms of government (or absolutism in particular).

It was fortunate that princes rarely needed to deploy their soldiers against their subjects as they were neither trained nor equipped to deal effectively with popular protest. The juridification of conflict within the Reich reduced the occasions when troops were deployed and made it unwise to do so without explicit imperial approval or obvious cause. The Württemberg estates appealed successfully to the imperial courts after Carl Eugen deployed soldiers to collect taxes in 1764, while similar actions in Nassau-Siegen and Mecklenburg even resulted in the formal deposition of the ruler.[95] Bishop Galen of Münster finally suppressed the autonomy of his territorial capital once he received imperial backing and international military support in 1661. The elector of Mainz forced the town of Erfurt into submission on the second attempt in 1664, but only after he received considerable assistance from other princes. The entire Guelph dynasty combined to bombard the city of Brunswick into accepting its authority in 1671 and did so only after a sustained propaganda campaign to justify its action. In all three cases civic autonomy rested on insecure legal foundations and each time the victorious prince confirmed most municipal privileges once his authority had been recognised. The Austrians also granted concessions after they suppressed the popular uprising against their occupation of Bavaria in 1705 during the War of the Spanish Succession.[96] There were no formal constraints on the Habsburgs in Hungary, which lay outside the Reich altogether, but their experience there shows that open repression was counterproductive. Leopold I's deployment of troops after 1671 only exacerbated an already tense situation and the subsequent Ten Dark Years of repression failed to break the resistance of the Hungarian diet to absolute rule. Habsburg forces encountered grave difficulties in suppressing the open revolt of Prince Rákóczi in 1703–11 and only succeeded once skilful negotiation split the rebel leadership.[97]

Despite these problems, princes were determined to maintain powerful forces as symbols of their authority and political autonomy. The emergence of absolutism coincided with the establishment and growth of permanent forces in the German principalities and Habsburg monarchy from the 1650s. These peaked in size around 1710, except for Prussia and Austria, which continued to expand their armies throughout the eighteenth century.[98] The administrative infrastructure underpinning this expansion has already been considered. Contemporaries were convinced that absolute rule was more efficient at mobilising resources than mixed monarchy or republican government. However, John Brewer and others have demonstrated the superiority of British and Dutch administration and methods of finance, and a comparison of tax burdens indicates a higher per capita level in these states than in absolute monarchies. The more advanced state of the British and Dutch economies accounts for this in part, particularly as they were able to tax goods in circulation, while the agrarian base of central European states forced their governments to rely primarily on cumbersome direct taxes. However, the more active role of British and Dutch representative institutions in managing as well as funding war is clearly another important factor.[99]

It is widely believed that these forces were assembled to pursue wars of aggression and that bellicosity was inherent in absolutism. The idea that centralised states had a natural tendency to expand was already deeply rooted in seventeenth-century thought and appeared corroborated by the contemporary experience of Louis XIV who embarked on a series of aggressive conflicts shortly after assuming personal rule. Many Marxist and non-Marxist interpretations have also regarded absolutism as inherently violent and usually include one or both of the following points. First, there is the socio-economic explanation which interprets absolutist warfare as an extension of extra-economic coercion, in short a means to find plunder for the native nobility. There is some evidence to support this, such as the redistribution of Hungarian land to Habsburg generals and army contractors during the reconquest from the Turks in 1683–99. Second, there is the socio-cultural interpretation that the nobility had a natural tendency to violence which had caused the civil and religious strife of the sixteenth and early seventeenth centuries. Absolutism rested on its claim to guarantee domestic tranquillity and so had to redirect aristocratic energies into external wars. Moreover, standing armies were symbols of prestige which had to be constantly reaffirmed to uphold the crown–noble compromise and the elite's general sense of its own worth.[100]

Absolutism was structurally prone to certain wars, but not on these grounds. The emphasis on hereditary right engendered claims to territory based on dynastic relationship and the clashes over rights of succession that were behind all the major continental wars from 1655 to 1778.[101] However, there is little evidence for aristocratic pressure as a cause for conflict, or that princes went to war in order to give unruly nobles something to do. Far from being the 'sport of kings', war was embarked upon with great reluctance. Absolutism glorified conflict and martial exploits, but only as means to an end. That purpose was peace and the preservation of order, not the satisfaction of personal vanity or the pursuit of glory. The ideological foundations of absolutism were all pacific: the claim to preserve peace and order, to adhere to Christian principles and to promote the common good. War threatened all these objectives and was only to be started as a matter of last resort. Individual monarchs may have plunged their countries into disastrous conflicts and war throughout this period brought misery to millions, but absolutism did not have a monopoly on bellicosity.

The actions of Frederick the Great – perhaps central Europe's most famous absolute monarch – appear to contradict this. Only seven months after his accession Frederick invaded the almost defenceless Austrian province of Silesia in December 1740, beginning two Silesian Wars (1740–2 and 1744–5) which merged with a wider struggle over the disputed Habsburg succession (1740–8). Having secured Silesia by 1745, Frederick later launched a fresh attack on Saxony in August 1756 when he feared that Austria was preparing a war of revenge in concert with France, Russia and Sweden. This precipitated the Seven Years War (1756–63) which compelled Austria to renounce Silesia for ever, but only after heavy Prussian losses. Nonetheless, Frederick was not deterred from using force a third time in 1778 when he invaded Bohemia, this time with Saxon support, in order to force Joseph II to abandon his plans to swap part of the Austrian Netherlands for Bavaria.

To many historians in the nineteenth and early twentieth centuries, Frederick exemplified the virtues of successful power politics and in some respects he does represent a break with earlier absolutism. He was far more prepared to settle disputes by force than either his grandfather Frederick III/I, or his father Frederick William I, whose soubriquet the 'Soldier King' belies his hesitant and pacific foreign policy. Further, the acquisition of Silesia and especially the opposition to Joseph's Bavarian plans were discussed in the materialist language of geopolitics, economic potential and human resources belonging to the future of nineteenth-century *Realpolitik*, rather than the past of absolutist arguments based on dynastic claims and hereditary right. Nonetheless, Frederick's own attempts to justify his actions were far from half-hearted. The Dresden archives were ransacked in 1757 for evidence that Saxony had been conspiring with Austria, while the dispute over Bavaria in 1778 generated an unprecedented pamphlet war to sway public opinion. Frederick himself seems to have regretted acting too rashly in 1740 and certainly subsequently sought to avoid conflict by forming alliances to counterbalance perceived threats to Prussia. Above all, neither Frederick nor his fellow-rulers embarked on war lightly or, as Michael Howard puts it, simply as 'a seasonal variation on hunting'. However inadequate the reasons may seem to later generations, the causes of absolutism's conflicts were not trivial to contemporaries.[102]

War and foreign policy was one area where rulers came closest to establishing a genuine personal monopoly of executive authority.[103] This has fostered the image of conflict under absolutism as 'cabinet wars' (*Kabinettskriege*), fought for limited objectives by professionals with little popular involvement or even impact on the population.[104] Absolutism waged narrow wars in the sense that military objectives were determined by the prince and his immediate advisers, but the geographical scope and human and material cost of these struggles can scarcely be termed limited. War and the preparations for it consumed the lion's share of all state budgets, while princes and their advisers concocted schemes for massive territorial redistributions which their forces were thankfully rarely able to put into effect. However, the underlying emphasis on peaceful resolution of conflict and the need to legitimise war aims restricted the scale of international disputes. The emphasis on domestic tranquillity also deterred princes from radically altering social and economic relations within their territories and so restricted their ability to maximise the military potential of their subjects. These factors inhibited an effective response to the French revolutionary armies after 1792 as the central European princes were not prepared to be as ruthless as their opponents.[105]

SOCIAL DISCIPLINE

The study of state formation in central Europe provides an ideal opportunity to consider the question of absolutism's social consequences, which has been unduly neglected because of the general preference for French and British history. The prevailing convention regards social transformation in Britain and France as the product of capitalism and the French Revolution, while German historiography attributes the creation of modern society to the role of the absolutist state. These claims are best explored through an examination of the concept of 'social discipline', which sets out to explain the social consequences of political centralisation.

The term was coined by Gerhard Oestreich in an attempt to render comprehensible European-wide trends from the fifteenth to the nineteenth century.[106] Oestreich was influenced by Marx, Weber and Elias, but rejected their explanations for emphasising only one strand of what he regarded as an interrelated set of cultural processes transforming European society. The first of these was the process of rationalisation already identified by Weber and which had human reason as its impulse. Elias's civilising process formed the second strand and focused on social behaviour. Social discipline was the last current and was Oestreich's own theoretical contribution. Though he did not ignore economic factors, Oestreich rejected the Marxist emphasis on capitalism as *the* disciplining force in modern society, arguing instead that the moral force behind early modern social discipline was a precondition for capitalism's emergence. The final source was provided by Hintze and others who had studied the state, since Oestreich argued that social discipline was propelled by the state's response to wider change. He saw this process progressing through a series of distinct changes, of which absolutism was the most important.

In the initial stage of 'social regulation' (*Sozialregulierung*) the state was constantly confronted with new problems – increasing population density, improved communications, the growth of new social and economic groups, the advent of different forms of production, distribution and consumption, the disintegration of face-to-face society and the erosion of political organisation based on personal (feudal) ties and obligations. The state responded by trying to render these changes comprehensible and manageable through regulation and definition. These attempts took place within the culture of the High Renaissance at the end of the fifteenth century and so were infused with its search for order, measurement and harmony. The practical product was the growing volume of regulatory measures we have already encountered in Chapter 2 in the discussion of *Polizei* and included attempts to proscribe certain styles of dress for particular social groups through sumptuary ordinances, and fix work practices in guild legislation. Such measures tried to define society as well as simply order it, but in doing so proved a force for change and, according to Oestreich, a modernising force. One example would be the way in which efforts to standardise weights and measures encouraged the integration of previously disparate localities within a common network. Regulation favoured centralisation and standardisation, but not necessarily absolutism since it could take place within the existing social and political framework where corporate groups and institutions such as the clergy, guilds and municipal governments largely regulated themselves, or provided the instruments through which overarching institutions such as the Reichstag managed social affairs.

As the internal dynamic inherent in social regulation began to break its original constraints, it placed these institutions under growing strain. The impact of the Reformation posed new problems of communication and coordination which only the territorial state could master. It was assisted by the new intellectual climate of late humanism in general and the ideology of Neostoicism in particular. The recharged emphasis on discipline and hierarchical order elaborated by Justus Lipsius provided a new language with which to make sense of the world and, even more than before, acted as a force for change, transforming regulation into social disciplining (*Sozialdisziplinierung*). The intention of the new 'cameralist' ordinances was not simply to regulate society but to improve it through better discipline and rationalisation. The decline of the Church hastened this by reducing the earlier emphasis on theology and morals and clearing the way for more utilitarian and secular concepts.

The political direction of social discipline was thus authoritarian and hierarchical and Oestreich identified two further phases in its transformation of state and society. The first was the disciplining of the state infrastructure (*Stabsdisziplinierung*) whereby the structures of the army, bureaucracy and court were rationalised and their personnel brought under tighter surveillance and control. Here, Oestreich borrowed from Elias in his arguments that the new military drill and Neostoic values enabled a switch from external coercion (threat of punishment) to internalised self-discipline.[107] As rationalisation rendered the state infrastructure more reliable and effective, the process broadened into 'fundamental disciplining' (*Fundamentaldisziplinierung*) in the eighteenth century, affecting all aspects of individual lives and even taming Nature itself in the formal baroque garden. Oestreich believed this process to be the essential prerequisite for modern citizenship since it broke up the corporate social order and encouraged a society of individuals.

Like all grand historical explanations, social disciplining is problematic, though this was not entirely Oestreich's fault since he died before he could complete his theory. His ideas nonetheless were welcomed by historians studying the Reformation because they appeared to explain its relationship to secular and moral social regulation.[108] Social discipline also has certain advantages over its better-known rival concept proposed by the French philosopher Michel Foucault.[109]

Whereas Oestreich identifies motive forces and explains change, Foucault describes patterns of disciplining between 1650 and 1800 without a sense of longer-term transformation. Unlike Oestreich, Foucault's discipline concept is not related to a single discourse (Neo-stoicism), but has multiple origins in both discourses (especially the Enlightenment, medical science and philosophy) and environment (school, prison, barracks, hospital, factory). For his champions,[110] this is an advantage, but for his critics it is a serious flaw. Foucault's 'carceral network' is all pervasive, yet elusive, with no particular locus or driving force(s), a fragmentary, a-historical and bleak vision of mankind trapped in the prison of modernity.[111]

If Foucault can be accused of being overly pessimistic, Oestreich has been criticised for being too positive about growing state power and his concept appears to some to be a thinly disguised revival of the older tradition of beneficial state-building and especially of absolutism as a positive force in human development. These critics have identified a number of substantive points: he overemphasised the effectiveness of social discipline, his concept perpetuates a myth of authority, and it only makes sense within a particular 'master narrative' of the past.

Taking these in turn, it is clear that Oestreich intended to broaden the existing interpretation of absolutism with its preoccupation with ruling dynasties, diplomacy and military affairs. However, his approach remained both top-down and macro in that it looked at official state regulation and the ideas behind it, rather than its effects. Empirically based studies following this route have tended to analyse what those in power *intended* rather than what they *achieved* with their regulatory measures.[112] The fact that the ordinances had to be repeated indicates that they were not being observed, while the scope of government action was comparatively limited. Official welfare measures, along with economic intervention, penal reform and education initiatives are all well documented and appear impressive until put into perspective.[113] For example, there were no less than 115 workhouses in the Reich, Prussia and Austria by the late eighteenth century, but their total capacity was under 10,000 inmates. Police forces were spread equally thinly, while economic intervention had only a limited impact outside a few state-sponsored concerns and is unlikely to have contributed much to the already slow rate of German indus-trialisation.[114] Appreciation of the state's limitations has encouraged a recent trend for micro historical studies to reveal more about indi-vidual lives and how the poor coped under these conditions.[115]

Second, social discipline perpetuates a myth of authority by implying that Germans were natural subjects who submitted meekly to state regulation. As we have seen, Blickle's communalism thesis is one attempt to rebut this. Carsten Küther and others have tried to rediscover the forgotten histories of those who fell outside the well-regulated society of the absolute police state, such as bandits and itinerants. Even if Küther's figures are exaggerated, at least 3 per cent of the total population had no fixed abode, while many more lived precariously on the margins of settled society.[116] Further research since the 1980s has also revised earlier assumptions that Germans were crushed into passivity by absolutism. The absence of large-scale rebellions after the Peasants' War of 1525 appeared to prove this point, and the few major revolts, such as that in Upper Austria in 1626, or those in Bavaria 1633–4 and 1705, were dismissed as largely isolated and hopeless attacks on an increasingly powerful state. The lack of a workable ideal after the defeat of 'Christian Liberty' in 1525 deprived the masses of an inspiring ideology prior to socialism, while the absence of 'bourgeois leadership' forced the uneducated peasants back on 'lower forms of class struggle' instead. Anti-fiscal protest replaced anti-seigneurial, until the example of the French Revolution encouraged more general attacks on the late feudal order.

This interpretation has now been revised following the discovery of numerous small-scale protests throughout the smaller territories of the south and west of the Reich, plus even more widespread passive resistance to the demands of both landlords and state.[117] Such findings corroborate Blickle's assertion of an active popular political tradition and dispels the myth that the poor were powerless to help themselves and could only act when led by their social superiors or socialist revolutionaries. It is clear that they were quite capable of formulating their own aims, including demands for political representation.

However, it is also clear that the state's response was equally sophisticated. The preceding section has indicated that the standing army was a crude, blunt instrument ill suited to combating civil unrest. It was rarely required, not because Germans were cowed into submission, but because the state channelled their protest along controllable lines. This is an important part of the wider disciplining process which Oestreich neglected, but which stemmed from the same sources. The social regulation which Oestreich analysed included the codification of law and legal procedure, while the expansion of the territorial state extended to the formation of a (partial) judicial monopoly as the previously exclusive jurisdictions of the clergy, landlords and other groups were breached and incorporated within a single system. This was related to the parallel juridification within the Reich which also sought to defuse conflict by peaceful arbitration, while later cameralism encouraged bureaucratic review, intervention and reform to address 'abuses'.

It is important to realise that this was not exclusively a top-down process, but was also shaped by pressure from below. It was not a benevolent, impartial system of justice, but indeed highly partisan, corrupt and cumbersome. Nonetheless, it could prove responsive to popular demands, because it was usually in the interests of at least one influential prince to ensure that it functioned. Peasants and towns-folk saw advantages in judicial and bureaucratic review and became adept at manipulating it, notably through appeals to the imperial courts which proved a far more effective means to limit tax increases than violent protest. There is considerable evidence of rural com-munities exchanging experience of court cases and of maintaining their own lawyers and lobbyists to press their demands with some success.[118] In this sense juridification both reinforced absolutism by defusing and deflecting violent protest, and limited it by subjecting at least the lesser princes to external moderation and constraint. This balance made German absolutism more effective by reducing the friction caused by protest, even if it did not necessarily make it more benign. The absence of a comparable system for Bohemia and outside the Reich in Hungary left the Habsburgs more reliant on direct coercion and reduced their ability to prevent unrest from escalating into open revolt.

The third charge against social discipline as an explanatory concept is levelled by Hermann Rebel, who argues that it 'overcontextualises' absolutism and especially cameralism as parts of a single 'master narrative' of European history ending happily in modernity and the unitary state.[119] Rebel claims that Oestreich only identifies the positive, forward-looking elements in cameralist discourse, such as liberal economic ideas, and weaves these into his story of progressive moder-nisation. Rebel seeks to explode this modernisation narrative by being deliberately provocative, replacing Oestreich's largely positive story with its 'happy end' with an alternative 'Holocaust master narrative' to prove that historical endings are multiple and an account of abso-lutism could just as easily be concluded with the horrors of National Socialism. This exercise in postmodernism is inherently dangerous as it risks reviving the equally biased interpretation of the German past following a 'special path' leading inevitably towards totalitarianism and the gas chambers. Nonetheless, Rebel makes an important point that Neostoicism, cameralism and police regulation were not all inherently 'rational' or 'modern', but complex ideas, the applications of which were often contradictory and counterproductive. In short, social discipline created disorder as well as order, by disrupting previously natural social relations and patterns of behaviour. By drawing on extensive Austrian evidence, Rebel indicates how Habsburg officials displaced problems downwards, worsening the situation for ordinary people and thus flatly contradicting the stated intention of furthering the common good. The primary examples were the fiscal problems arising from the state's involvement in military competition – itself disordering and disrupting. To meet the growing demand for ready cash, officials sought to make peasant households more productive so that tax levels could be raised, but their interference in established customs simply disordered family life and may even have reduced agrarian output. The cameralist rhetoric of the absolutist state was then an attempt to ignore or displace these 'costs' by denying their existence and instead rewrite order and stigmatise those who fell outside it as criminals, deviants or simply naturally ignorant and lazy.

There is considerable further evidence to support this. The codification begun by sixteenth-century police regulation disrupted existing social and economic relations through a process of expropriation to benefit the state. For example, the rationalisation of forestry laws narrowed the range of those who could exploit them and criminalised previously accepted behaviour such as foraging for firewood. Similarly, codification of village customs disrupted the social relations these had previously sustained.[120]

From the preceding, we can see that the state's social disciplining measures were not entirely effective, provoked opposition and often proved counterproductive. However, we should not discount their impact altogether, while Oestreich's model is very helpful in drawing attention to cultural factors, social regulation and discipline should be seen within the wider process by which absolutism sought to legitimise itself and retain popular consent. As Oestreich suggested, this process was dialectical in that absolutism was itself transformed as it took on wider functions and as the more professional ethos of its officials was increasingly at odds with dynastic notions of personal service. However, Foucault's model also provides a valuable insight by suggesting that the state was not the only agent of social control. Detailed micro studies of life in small communities reveals that some of the harshest disciplinary measures came from within and that state regulation was sometimes simply a response to pressure from parents, employers and householders.[121]

PRELIMINARY CONCLUSIONS

Central European absolutism existed in practice in four overlapping spheres of activity. Overall, there was the general effort to convey the myth of power underpinning its system of rule. Its relations with other powers within the networks of imperial and international politics provided a second sphere, while the connections between the crown and the nobility and between the state and all social groups constituted the other two.

The image of power conveyed by the court and official political communication was indeed a façade, but one which nonetheless constituted a reality of its own. The symbolic and ideological articulation of absolutism and its constant effort to encourage acceptance helped distinguish it from other early modern forms of rule. Style *was* important as it guided personal behaviour, shaped the range of options open to absolute princes and encouraged them to seek certain allies and follow particular courses of action. Other people had courts, including the republican Dutch, but their rulers were not absolute monarchs. Subtle though they might be, such differences were significant.

External relations was one area where executive authority was genuinely concentrated in princely hands and where personal dynastic ambition had a significant impact. The expansion of state administration along with social regulation and discipline were primarily propelled by the demands of resource mobilisation and warmaking. Though this does support the primacy of foreign policy theory encountered in Chapter 2, we should remember that domestic considerations also affected these processes. In particular the need to retain legitimacy added to the practical constraints on policy-making imposed by limited resources and relatively inflexible agrarian economies.

Analysis of these considerations has produced a bewildering range of terms and concepts: Historic Compromise, the captured state, rule by community of interest, court society, domestication of the nobility, and the royal mechanism. All attempt to encapsulate crown–noble relations with varying degrees of success. The absolutist state was clearly not captured by a single class, nor did the nobility enter into a wholesale compromise with the crown. The growth of a court society magnified the power of the prince, but it also placed constraints that inhibited the exercise of a royal mechanism of divide and rule. There was always a vacuum between the formal claim to power and an individual's ability to exercise it, a gap that was filled by 'first ministers', favourites, mistresses and factions. The last were not defined exclusively by social class, but by a variety of criteria varying from court to court but often including confession, place of origin and generation, as in the case of the 'Young Court' around Archduke Joseph during the last years of the elderly Leopold I.[122] The presence of these factions indicates that the nobility was not entirely domesticated, but retained some room for manoeuvre both in formal fora like the court and estates and through informal patronage networks that could stretch across territorial boundaries in the relatively cosmopolitan world of central European aristocracy. Absolutism brought benefits for the nobility, or at least sections of it, whose privileged social position it sustained and enhanced, but it must be remembered that this was in a constant state of flux. Individuals were disgraced for political or social transgressions, such as Count Plettenberg who was banished from Cologne in 1734, while others rose to fame and fortune, like Count Georg Friedrich of Waldeck who eventually acquired princely status in 1682.[123] Such change also affected larger groups, as is illustrated by the fates of those who opposed or supported Habsburg rule in the early seventeenth century. These findings suggest that absolutism resembled rule by community of interest, provided we remember that 'community' was a contested term that excluded as well as included. They also indicate that we should not ignore the force of individual personality, as some rulers were clearly more adept at seizing opportunities than others who became enmeshed in the elaborate world of baroque ceremony.[124]

These conclusions can be extended to the sphere of absolutism's relations with wider society. The inhabitants of the central European monarchies and principalities were not cowed into silence, nor did they meekly submit to authoritarian social discipline. Their behaviour was certainly disrupted by growing interference in their personal lives, while fiscal and military burdens caused widespread hardship and misery. The response to this outside the Reich was often violent, but the lack of large-scale protest within the German territories is misleading. Though communities were riven with tension and conflict, they nonetheless provided a basis for sustained opposition to the demands of those in higher authority. This opposition was not straightforward rejection of absolutism, but grasped what opportunities it offered to advance individual and popular goals and, in doing so, also helped sustain absolute rule.

4 Enlightened absolutism

ENLIGHTENED ABSOLUTISM OR ENLIGHTENED DESPOTISM?

It remains to be seen whether anything changed to mark eighteenth-century absolutism as a distinct and 'final' phase, and whether it contained elements that can explain the preservation of monarchical rule into the nineteenth century. Unlike absolutism, the term 'enlightened despotism' (*despotisme éclairé*) dates to the period it purports to describe, having been coined in 1767 by the French liberal economists known as physiocrats. Though rejected by Rousseau and other contemporaries, it was resurrected as 'enlightened absolutism' in 1847 to describe the last part of Roscher's three-stage developmental model encountered in Chapter 1. The new term did not displace despotism entirely and both provide convenient labels for two contrasting interpretations of later absolute monarchy.

Enlightened absolutism implies monarchical rule tempered by enlightened rationality. In the classic model proposed by Roscher this occurred in the later eighteenth century and was a particular feature of central and eastern European absolutism. Its leading exponents were Frederick II, Joseph II and Catherine II, who sought to translate enlightened ideals into practice in a systematic attempt to rationalise government and improve conditions for their subjects. Monarchy was no longer to be about the pursuit of dynastic ambition, but to serve humanity by engaging in a wide range of beneficial reforms. These activities assume considerable importance in this interpretation as the list of reforms itself often defines enlightened absolutism: education reforms, religious toleration, legal codification, penal reform, abolition of serfdom and improvement of social conditions. Most early assessments of these reforms conclude they were remarkably successful, given the difficult circumstances in which the three leading enlightened absolutists worked. Nineteenth-century historians regarded such activity as further evidence of the growth of the state and its role in promoting progress. An influential school of thought developed that regarded enlightened absolutism as a form of benevolent authoritarianism that had genuinely existed and which distinguished an entire age. Reinhold Koser summed it up by borrowing a phrase from the cameralist writer Johann Heinrich Gottlob Justi (1717–71) that enlightened absolutism represented 'everything for the people, nothing by the people'.[1]

Implicit in this interpretation was an appreciation that enlightened absolutism had limitations which prevented its further development and caused some of its reforms to fail. According to Fritz Hartung, monarchs like Joseph II and Frederick II did not 'have the courage' to follow the logic of their enlightened convictions and fully rationalise the socio-political structure of their states since this would have necessitated reforming themselves out of existence.[2]

This largely German view was displaced somewhat by the findings of the 1928 Oslo International Commission of Historical Sciences and notably its 1937 report which shifted the emphasis on to France. French physiocratic ideas now received greater attention, as did the reforms of Louis XVI's minister Turgot and his correspondence with Catherine II, while the new explanation was located in the context of the dissemination of enlightened thought by Voltaire and other leading French philosophers. Anglo-Saxon historians took up this interpretation along with the unfortunate term 'enlightened despotism' which had been reintroduced into the debates in Oslo.

The French bias has proved unsustainable. There is little evidence of the practical application of enlightened thought by the late eighteenth-century French monarchy and Louis XVI hardly fits the archetype of an enlightened absolutist. The general influence of French thought within the Enlightenment has been downplayed thanks to a better understanding of intellectual development elsewhere in Europe.[3] Within this, greater prominence has been given to the contribution of German cameralists and their role in transmitting both French and other ideas to Russia.[4] Finally, like the earlier German variant, the French historiographical model of enlightened absolutism failed to demonstrate convincingly how ideas were translated into practice, or explain why supposedly enlightened monarchs like Frederick II, Joseph II and Catherine II engaged in aggressive wars and partitioned defenceless Poland between them.

Use of the term despotism contributed to another, contradictory school of thought which held that, far from being moderated by the enlightenment, absolutism became even more extreme. While the philosophers thought the kings served them, the reverse was true, as monarchs exploited enlightened ideas to stabilise royal rule and maximise military and economic efficiency. Far from being humanitarian, the reforms were simply intended to strengthen the state and make it more successful in international competition. A quotation, again from Justi, can be found to support this view that the 'subjects' happiness' was only a 'secondary consideration'.[5] The 'marriage of absolutism and *Aufklärung* [enlightenment] was more of convenience than mutual love' and monarchs like Frederick, Joseph and Catherine competed with one another by introducing 'cheap . . . headline-grabbing' measures like the abolition of witchcraft prosecutions to win applause from philosophers.[6]

This is close to the Marxist interpretation which believes enlightened absolutism applies only in the 'underdeveloped' eastern half of the continent. The partial adoption of enlightened ideas by Frederick II and his fellow monarchs thus represented a continuation of earlier attempts to close the gap with more advanced Western states. However, the ideas were applied only selectively and half-heartedly in an attempt to bolster the 'old regime' by taking some account of bourgeois interests without fundamentally altering the class basis of the state.[7] This fits the broader scheme of absolutism as a transitional stage and of the state facing growing pressure *from below* for change. The idea that monarchs introduced reforms simply to deflect mounting criticism is voiced by non-Marxists and reflects the general assumptions underpinning Habermas's 'structural transformation of the public sphere' that the critique only developed with the rise of a commercial bourgeoisie.[8] Such attempts were doomed to failure because of the contradiction between (feudal) absolutism and (bourgeois) enlightenment.

Yet, Marxist scholars are well aware that central European monarchies did not collapse like that of France in 1789 and have posed the question why they survived into the next century along with other elements of the 'old regime', including serfdom east of the Elbe. One answer came from West German historians sympathetic to Marxist analysis while rejecting its dogmatic application. Hans-Ulrich Wehler elaborated a model of 'defensive modernisation' to explain the persistence of aristocratic and princely power throughout nineteenth-century Germany. Wehler's concept is a sophisticated version of the idea of reform from above to avoid revolution from below. He maintains that by managing change monarchs and bureaucrats recruited new allies, broadening their social base and so defusing tension and heading off threats of revolution.[9] The Prussian minister

Struensee observed in 1799 that the revolution being introduced violently from below in France was proceeding peacefully from above in the Hohenzollern monarchy.[10]

By the 1960s it was clear that some historians were becoming frustrated by these discussions and doubted whether the terms had any utility at all. Enlightened absolutism became the first part of the wider concept to be dismissed as a myth, particularly after Derek Beales proved the untrustworthiness of some of the documents on which it was based.[11] Almost simultaneously, a string of monographs appeared reaffirming the term, suggesting that the rush to abandon it had been premature, and by the mid-1980s several of the earlier critics recanted and re-embraced enlightened absolutism as a valuable model.[12] These dramatic shifts reveal a problem that has concerned us throughout our study. Many of the difficulties encountered in explaining absolutism in general, and its enlightened variety in particular, are caused by the use of misleading abstract definitions and anachronistic models. The Enlightenment was interpreted as the precursor to modern liberalism and when measured against liberal ideals eighteenth-century monarchs naturally fell short.[13] To arrive at a more appropriate definition of enlightened absolutism, we need to examine the nature of enlightened thought and the extent to which rulers and officials were influenced by it.

THE INTELLECTUAL CLIMATE

Enlightened philosophy was far from monolithic or unambiguous and it is possible to find elements that seem reactionary, while others are progressive. The same is true for its proponents and followers, who came from backgrounds as diverse as their interests. Count Rumford (1753–1814), who reformed the Bavarian army and founded the Munich workhouse in the 1790s, had been born Benjamin Thompson, an American who fancied himself as scientist and inventor.[14] The self-styled philosophes did not see themselves as a vanguard for a new socio-economic order, but as the inheritors of the earlier achievements of the scientific revolution. They believed their ideas transcended social forces and they looked down on the mass of society as inherently hostile, mired in superstition, tradition and aristocratic prejudice. They were interested in social improvement, but did not see this in class terms. Some of the most radical statements were made by scions of the existing order, like Joseph II, whose views on careers open to talent were far more progressive than those expressed in the famous enlightened *Encyclopedie*.[15] Even those who were hostile to many enlightened ideas were not necessarily against change. Joseph's mother, Maria Theresa, disliked the secular tone of much enlightened thought, but introduced some changes that seem more radical than those of her son. In short, the Enlightenment cannot simply be labelled a bourgeois ideology inherently at odds with absolutism.

Enlightened ideas appeared particularly compatible with central European absolutism because they were largely filtered through existing cameralist thought. Cameralism emphasised strong government, which many philosophes also thought necessary to implement their vision of a better future. There was a further similarity in the concern for social issues and the stress on the legitimate aims of government rather than the personal ambitions of the prince. Like much early enlightened thought, cameralism also had strong roots in late seventeenth-century Natural Law and shared its emphasis on secular rationality as opposed to divinely revealed truth.

This raises the question as to what was novel about the ideas that supposedly made enlightened absolutism a distinct phase of political development. Many point to an enlightened model of constitutional government, where the law was superior to the monarch, that distinguished late eighteenth-century rule from the unrestrained classical absolutism which preceded it. Some princes made such a distinction themselves. Elector Max Franz of Cologne criticised other princes in 1798 for forgetting their duty to their subjects and argued that fundamental territorial laws alone determined right from wrong.[16] These arguments were not new, but represented a development on earlier concepts of limited monarchy. Similarly, the idea of the prince as the state's servant rather than master had been expressed before, while the idea of a monarchical social contract was already there in Natural Law. However, the way these ideas were conveyed was rather different, as we have seen in the discussion of the transition from the baroque to the rococo court. To cite one further example: the subsumption of the monarch within the state was expressed by the fashion for military uniform rather than court or aristocratic dress. Even civil officials began to wear uniforms, while Joseph II insisted on changing into his field marshal's uniform when he realised he was dying because he wanted to depart the earth in nothing else.[17]

The other aspect generally highlighted as distinctive for enlightened political thought is its wider definition of the common good. Baroque or 'classical' absolutism is regarded as resting on a pessimistic, Hobbesian view of humanity where a natural tendency to anarchy could only be held in check by a powerful monarch. The enlightened outlook was optimistic, and its belief that humanity possessed the ability to determine its own fate provided the intellectual foundation for the idea of progress. The earlier emphasis on order and security could therefore be widened to embrace positive change and the pursuit of happiness. Such a distinction is broadly valid, but the actual contrast was often more apparent than real. As we saw in Chapter 2, late seventeenth-century advocates of absolutism also expected it to do far more than preserve order, while even many enlightened thinkers still saw human happiness as collective rather than individual.

As with the ideology of absolutism in general, what we are really dealing with here is a range of comparatively diverse and even partially contradictory ideas, and it is as pointless to construct a single definition of enlightened thought as it is to manufacture a single model of absolute monarchy. It is equally impossible to identify a linear relationship between enlightened thought and absolutist action because none such connection existed. Ideas were taken on selectively and often put to uses unintended by those who had originally conceived them. What is important is that the general intellectual climate was gradually changing and that this provided the context within which late eighteenth-century policy took shape.

THE IMPETUS FOR REFORM

We can get closer to discovering whether late eighteenth-century absolute monarchy was distinctive when we explore the background to its policies. There is a general assumption that enlightened rationality encouraged rulers and officials to devise systematic, well-planned programmes of reform rather than simply react to circumstances with piecemeal, ad hoc improvisation. This is misleading. The baroque world was also one of rational systems and elaborate schemes to render chaos into order. Similarly, the pressures of war and international crisis which had disrupted the plans of late seventeenth-century ministers also taxed the minds of their successors a hundred years later. What was different was a heightened sense of self-criticism and a growing awareness of the relative position of states and of the interaction between ideas, people and material resources.

This can be illustrated by the example of the Habsburg monarchy which underwent successive periods of internal reform from 1703. The wars against France and the Turks had placed a mounting burden on the creaky Habsburg administration since 1672, but official action had been limited to necessary repairs rather than fundamental reform. The Young Court around Joseph I had grown impatient with the elderly Leopold I, who appeared incapable of taking decisive action. Near collapse in 1703 prompted significant changes in senior personnel and the introduction of some fiscal reforms. Further modest initiatives were adopted during Charles VI's reign (1711–40), but none of these seriously departed from existing norms. However, the monarchy suffered a string of serious political and military defeats between 1733 and 1745 which appeared at times to place its entire future in question and have conventionally been regarded as the impetus for the reforms of Maria Theresa after 1748.[18]

However, more had changed than Austria's international position. There was a growing awareness of the varied nature of European development that forced Habsburg officials to reflect on their own assumptions. Cameralists including Becher, Schröder and Hörnigk had already criticised the confessional bias of the Habsburg monarchy during Leopold I's reign. There was a gradual appreciation that *pietas* and the religious foundation of the monarchy might not represent timeless values, but outdated ideas that were retarding beneficial development. The dynamism of the Protestant Dutch Republic was already apparent to all by the mid-seventeenth century. The emergence of England as a second Protestant power after 1688 was also striking, and the fact that both these states bankrolled the Habsburg war effort from 1689 to 1712 only reinforced the sense that they were overtaking the monarchy. Such change could also be perceived closer to home. The Protestant dynasties in Hanover and Brandenburg-Prussia emerged as significant powers in their own right after 1688, securing additional territory at Sweden's expense, as well as royal titles by 1714. The apparent superiority of Protestant states received further dramatic confirmation when Prussia invaded Austrian Silesia in 1740. All these states were considerably smaller than the Habsburg monarchy, suggesting that size did not guarantee pre-eminence and that more attention should be paid to internal structures. A shift away from genealogy and hagiographic dynastic history encouraged this new sense of the past and implied that those in the present need not be bound by what their predecessors had done.[19]

Such reflection generated an internal debate that persisted after the failure of Austria's attempts to recover Silesia in the Seven Years War. These discussions were never simply a clash between conservatives and progressives, but involved a wide spectrum of opinion. Conservatism and religious sensibilities were not the only barriers to change. The Leopoldine recovery of Habsburg authority in the Reich after the Thirty Years War had been based on working within the traditional framework of imperial politics with its respect for corporate rights and innate hostility to sudden or radical change.[20] Change within the monarchy had also been kept within bounds and had been directed at removing recalcitrant nobles rather than abolishing their collective rights or institutions. The death of Charles VI in 1740 proved a significant turning point as the failure to get Maria Theresa's husband elected as his successor deprived the dynasty of the imperial crown for the first time in 300 years. The monarchy was now less bound to respect traditional values and corporatist sensibilities, and the proponents of change became more influential.

Their leading advocate was Friedrich Wilhem Haugwitz (1700–65), who represented the culmination of cameralist thinking present in the monarchy since the late seventeenth century. His ideas found support from those Catholics who were prepared to abandon the earlier emphasis on *pietas* and embrace a more secular promotion of the common good. Collectively, they formed a second group opposed to those wishing to preserve traditional values, corporate rights and provincial particularism. A third group coalesced around more radical secularists and enthusiasts for more recent enlightened ideals.[21] Haugwitz and the cameralists won the initial arguments and the monarchy belatedly embarked on a large-scale reform programme after 1744.

The reforms have been described as 'nothing short of a revolution',[22] but if so were only a narrow political one. Haugwitz's bible was neither Christian theology nor enlightened thought, but Schröder's cameralist manual with its calculating cost–benefit analysis and emphasis on fiscal–military power.[23] Though more systematic and ambitious than previous reformers, Haugwitz did not attempt anything new. He renegotiated the tax grants with the estates to provide larger annual sums for the army and intervened in the economy to divert surplus extraction from the landlords' pockets into the state treasury. Schemes to reduce peasant tax burdens and make the landlords' pay more had already been advanced by Gundaker Starhemberg who headed the Austrian treasury in 1703–15, while others had also advocated consolidating peasant holdings and reducing labour service as ways to boost overall productivity. Joseph I and Charles VI had implemented these latter suggestions on their royal estates before 1740.[24] However, the scale of Haugwitz's programme established its own inner momentum as other officials began proposing more radical changes. The Seven Years War lent greater urgency to these calls as it became clear that Haugwitz's system had not narrowed the efficiency gap between the Habsburg and Hohenzollern monarchies.

Franz Szabo has detected two directions for this new radicalism. One was represented by Maria Theresa's son Joseph II who succeeded his father as emperor in 1765 and became sole ruler of the Habsburg monarchy after his mother's death in 1780. Joseph looked directly to Prussia and advocated introducing its methods of military recruitment into his own lands. His ideas essentially represented a more radical extension of those of Haugwitz as he was even less concerned to respect corporate and provincial privilege. Wenzel Anton von Kaunitz (1711–94), the foreign minister, represented the alternative, more genuinely enlightened view which regarded individual human dignity as both a better foundation for the state and the proper goal for its policy. Others have been more sympathetic towards Joseph and believe he was genuinely inspired by enlightened ideals of human happiness.[25] Whatever their true intent, it is clear that the direction of Habsburg policy moved away from benevolent paternalism, with its emphasis on protecting peasants from rapacious landlords, to emancipating them from feudal obligations altogether as the means to raise agrarian productivity.

THE SMALLER TERRITORIES

Similar changes have been detected in Prussia after 1740 and are associated with a parallel debate as to how far they and their promoter Frederick II were genuinely influenced by the Enlightenment.[26] This focus on Austria and Prussia is common in most discussions of central Europe and reflects a longstanding belief that enlightened absolutism was only a feature of the two German great powers, while the lesser territories remained rooted in the attitudes of the previous century. Karl Otmar Freiherr von Aretin offers a sophisticated version of this view, arguing that the Reich inhibited not only enlightened change, but absolute rule. Austria and Prussia escaped these restrictions because of their scale and the fact that their monarchies grew out of the Reich by acquiring large territories beyond its frontiers. These lands offered a field for enlightened and administrative experiments, especially the Habsurg's Italian possessions, which lacked the internal barrier of German- or Hungarian-style estates.[27] Others have been rather more sympathetic to the lesser princes' efforts, but still see them trailing behind the lead blazed by Frederick II and Joseph II.[28]

Recently, this view has been challenged by those who argue that enlightened absolutism in fact worked better in the smaller territories within the Reich.[29] Though several of the petty princes dabbled in militarism, the Reich generally insulated them from power politics and left them free to concentrate on promoting the common good. They also ruled more compact and manageable dominions with fewer inter-mediary bodies to oppose change, while the centralisation of executive authority had not been pursued to the extent that it provoked serious opposition. Finally, 'the lesser German princes were never too proud to learn from others' and borrowed and exchanged novel and innova-tive ideas.[30]

Though the Reich provided a protective framework, this was within a system of collective security that obliged even the smallest territory to contribute money and men to the common imperial army (*Reichs-armee*). Uncertainty over their status in the post-Westphalian states system encouraged many lesser territories to raise forces that were pro-portionately far larger than those of the two German great powers, necessitating an even greater degree of fiscal–military effort.[31] The reduction of these forces after 1763 reflected not so much a response to enlightened criticism, but the dawning realisation that they had been decisively outclassed by the growth of Prussia and Austria. Far from removing external pressure, this merely intensified it, since the experience of what amounted to two German civil wars in 1740–5 and 1756–63 showed that neither the Habsburgs nor the Hohenzollerns could be trusted to respect rights and territorial integrity. Such fears grew after Frederick and Joseph collaborated in the first partition of Poland in 1772 and intensified after 1780 when the emperor trampled on the rights of the ecclesiastical principalities which extended into his own lands. The Enlightenment had introduced a new language of utility that could be used to justify such action as necessary to remove barriers to progress and Voltaire himself praised the partition of Poland as paving the way for beneficial reform.

The ecclesiastical princes looked most vulnerable, given the trunca-tion of the Imperial Church during the waves of secularisation in the sixteenth and early to mid-seventeenth centuries. It was particularly alarming that Catholic dynasties such as the Habsburgs and Wittels-bachs which had traditionally supported them now perceived them as potential territorial acquisitions. Leading princes of the Church such as the three ecclesiastical electors in Mainz, Cologne and Trier now embraced the wider spirit of reform in an effort that was strongly motivated by the desire to prove their territories were not backward despotisms ripe for annexation. Rulers of smaller secular territories also saw public opinion as a potential bulwark against annexation and endeavoured to win support by exemplary reforms. In particular they promoted the view that regional diversity rather than standardisation was more conducive to progress since it promoted beneficial change through emulation and example. Franz of Anhalt-Dessau expressed this philosophy in his 'composite garden' at Wörlitz where the juxta-position of varied landscape features mirrored the political patchwork of the small territories in the Reich in contrast to the regimented formality of the large-scale baroque royal garden.[32]

However, reform in the smaller territories often encountered greater problems than those facing Frederick or Joseph. There were no econo-mies of scale and the scramble for scarce resources caused long-running disputes between rulers and estates, notably in Württemberg, Mecklen-burg and East Frisia, but there were also lesser-known cases such as that in Lippe-Detmold.[33] Those territories that genuinely lacked inter-mediary bodies were often worse off as opposition to taxation lacked constitutional or legal channels and could explode into violent protest, as in Sayn-Wittgenstein or Nassau-Siegen.[34] In this sense Aretin is correct when he stresses that the Reich inhibited change in the smaller territories. Reform, whether enlightened or otherwise, always meant change and almost invariably required money. Both stirred opposition and prompted those who felt threatened to appeal to the imperial courts and other external assistance. For example, it was Carl Eugen's attempt to introduce a new, more progressive form of taxation that prompted his estates to lodge their case against him in 1764.

The differences between the lesser territories and the two great powers are least in the question of openness to new ideas. Much depended on the personal inclinations of the prince and the relative degree of support given by his officials to cameralist and enlightened arguments. Both Carl August of Weimar and Carl Theodor of the Palatinate were clearly more concerned with the cultural and artistic dimension of current culture than the world of practical reform. The interests of Friedrich II of Hessen-Kassel were broader, and while Carl Eugen's engagement with enlightened ideas remained somewhat superficial, he nonetheless founded one of the most progressive higher education establishments of the late eighteenth century. As in the Habsburg monarchy, change could develop its own momentum and Carl Eugen found himself at odds with the staff and students of his Hohe Karlsschule whose enthusiasm for new ideas outstripped his own.[35]

The tenor of the changes in the lesser territories was increasingly at odds with the broader imperial structure. Whereas princely govern-ments were becoming more innovative, reform proposals for the Reich aimed essentially at restoring what had ceased to function or reviving initiatives from the previous century.[36] However, few contemporaries perceived an incompatibility between territorial flexibility and imperial immobility, and the majority still regarded the Reich as the ideal constitution for central Europe. It was the growth of Austro-Prussian rivalry and the experience of military defeat that caused the collapse of the Reich by 1806, not the emergence of new political ideas. Many of the former imperial institutions were revived in modified form in the German Confederation established after Napoleon's defeat in 1814/15.

REVOLUTION

The tensions we have perceived in the previous section are often thought to have placed absolutism under an intolerable strain. Reinhart Koselleck argued that the contradictions grew more pronounced as the reforms progressed until they prevented further development altogether. This paralysis occurred about the time of the French Revolution, which offered the only solution to break the deadlock and permit the growth of the modern state.[37]

Such arguments appear convincing only with the benefit of hindsight. Change was forced on the central European monarchies from outside with military defeat, not from below through popular pressure or the paralysis of reform. It was resistance to change rather than the dangers of it that concerned most officials before the mid-1790s. The collapse of the French monarchy was thought the result of its inability to reform itself, not the product of revolution, and it was only after the execution of the royal family in 1793 that most Germans became seriously alarmed at its implications. The famous reversal of the Josephine reforms in the Habsburg monarchy by his two successors, Leopold II and Francis II, was more than simply a reaction to the threat of revolution. The anti-clerical and anti-seigneurial character of many of Joseph's policies had provoked a popular and conservative backlash after 1787. However, it was also clear that many peasants expected the state to go further and introduce full emancipation. The dangers of these conflicting popular pressures grew as Austria proceeded to annex further Polish territory in the third partition of 1795 amid massive unrest and armed resistance to the invading forces.[38] Opinion was already divided within the administration, while Joseph himself had hardly been consistent. In his censorship policy, for example, he first permitted all Catholics to read the Bible in August 1781, but then reversed this decision the very next year while tightening central control of other publications. Those who proposed a further change of course after 1790 were far from uniformly reactionary and included many sympathetic to the Enlightenment.[39] The break was neither sudden nor solely a response to revolution.

Whereas the Habsburg reform programme largely stopped, those elsewhere continued and have been held responsible for preserving most of the central European dynasties. The changes introduced since 1763 had made many territorial governments more flexible, while the tradition of judicial and bureaucratic review was already well established as a means of responding to popular demands. Unlike those in France, few German intellectuals believed that a fundamental change in government was necessary since their state was already 'modern'.[40] Precedent for change was already established and influenced many of the changes that accompanied Napoleon's territorial reorganisation of the Reich after 1802, including those of the Reform Era in Prussia between 1806 and 1813.[41]

Significantly, the absolutist principalities survived the collapse of the Reich whereas the imperial cities, counts, prelates, knights and institutions all disappeared. Despite the upheavals and prolonged warfare after 1792, the same dynasties were still in place in 1815, not only in Austria and Prussia, but in lesser states like Bavaria, Württemberg, Baden and Hessen-Darmstadt. However, it was monarchy that had survived, not absolutism. Management of the territorial reorganisation and the reforms introduced to stabilise the social base of these states transformed the nature of their governments. The process of codification and rationalisation already under way was greatly accelerated from the 1790s, unintentionally challenging the foundations upon which absolutism rested. Precision replaced ambiguity, undermining the aura of omnipotence and furthering the secularisation of state ideology. Written constitutions, however limited, still defined the extent of royal power more clearly than before, while also establishing more formal channels of consultation that displayed absolutism's informal bargaining practice. Monarchy shifted its basis to a new combination of ideas claiming legitimacy. These included elements like hereditary rule that had been present under absolutism, but also new conceptions of nationalism which had been absent. Enlightened absolutism can stand as a distinct phase, but one which was more of a transition from the 'new regime' of seventeenth-century absolute monarchy to the final 'old regime' stage of European royal rule in the nineteenth century.[42]

5 Conclusions

It has been the contention of this work that absolutism was a reality which characterised central European political development between the mid-seventeenth and very late eighteenth centuries. Though it drew on ideas and practices already in place, it pushed monarchical rule in a significantly new direction; one which justifies the use of a specific term to distinguish it. It was neither monolithic nor excluded the persistence and development of other political traditions. Nonetheless, it was the predominant form of rule for a century and a half and it left an important legacy which helped sustain central European monarchy after 1800.

In one sense it remains a myth. As it has been used and understood, the term 'absolutism' is clearly far from neutral. It originated in the political disputes of the early nineteenth century, but failed to acquire a uniform, universally accepted definition. Nicholas Henshall is quite correct when he states that it 'means whatever historians want it to mean'.[1] There has been little agreement as to when it started, why it developed, when it finished, or whether it was a positive or negative force in human development. At the root of this confusion is a failure to reach a satisfactory definition of what absolutism was, leading to the recent rejection of the term altogether.

Much of the controversy centres on the misleading myth of absolute royal power. Those who still use the term tend to regard absolutism as 'always striving but never victorious' and believe that it was 'not so much a form of government as a tendency, a direction which the exercise of power always seems to take'.[2] There are two problems inherent in such a position. One is that absolutism simply becomes a meaningless byword for centralisation, something which is apparent in its indiscriminate application to large sections of European and world history. Second, it measures monarchical rule against an abstract model with little foundation in the thought and practice of the seventeenth century.

Such models miss the fine distinctions drawn by contemporaries between despotism, absolutism and other forms of monarchy and assess the actual extent of royal power against a standard no ruler sought to achieve. As this book has shown, what we can call absolutism emerged from the debate on the ideal form of limited monarchy during the early seventeenth century. It drew on a variety of sources and was never expressed in a single, coherent form, remaining instead a shifting amalgam of ideas which changed over time in response to events and new intellectual currents. The Enlightenment was one of these and influenced the thought and practice of princely rule sufficiently to justify identifying the later eighteenth century as a distinct phase of absolutism. However, the limits to authority demanded by the Enlightenment were already placed there by earlier writers and the theory of absolutism never called for totally unrestricted royal power. What makes absolute rule distinctive, at least in its central European form, is the specific way it sought to legitimise princely authority. It rejected most forms of formal consultation with corporate institutions, and relied instead on informal bargaining with different power groups to foster a wider sense of its grandeur and worth based on a revitalised image of monarchy and its moral, social and religious purpose. How this process worked in practice determined the specific character of each absolute monarchy and, despite the emphasis on centralised executive authority, pressure from below played a significant role in moulding it. The image conveyed by absolutism was a myth of power, but the process of projecting and sustaining this myth constituted a tangible reality and helped shape the practice of political authority.

Absolutism was definitely a force for change, but whether this can be labelled 'progressive' depends very much on how this is defined. It certainly did not eliminate other political traditions in central Europe, and both the territorial estates and popular pressure influenced policy-making and helped shape the state. As the predominant form of political organisation, absolutism qualifies as a distinct phase in state formation, but it was simply the particular course that developments in central Europe and elsewhere followed and did not constitute a 'necessary' stage. The warnings posed in the discussion of the myth should be heeded: historical endings are multiple and absolutism was not the only outcome, and nor were its consequences necessarily beneficial.

Consideration of central Europe has allowed us to consider a fourth dimension to the myth of absolutism in the issue of the lesser principalities. There were significant differences in scale between the majority

of these and what became the two German great powers of A⟩
Prussia. It was also important that these territories remair
within the Reich while the Habsburg and Hohenzollern ⟩
grew out of it by the mid-eighteenth century. Nonetheles⟩,
many similarities suggesting that the lesser territories were neɪtnⱼ
backward petty despotisms nor models of enlightened rule, but instead
likewise faced problems of external military and political pressures,
internal bargaining with social groups and the constant need to
reaffirm the legitimacy of absolute rule.

Absolutism came to an end in the political transformations wrought
by the French Revolutionary and Napoleonic Wars and by the
dramatic reorganisation of eastern Europe through the partitions of
Poland and the retreat of Ottoman Turkey. These international shifts
were associated with the adoption of new definitions of legitimacy,
which borrowed heavily from the past, suggesting that it may be appropriate to use the term 'neo-absolutism' for some Napoleonic and post-
Napoleonic monarchical regimes. However, other ideas received
greater prominence, shifting the emphasis decisively away from the
Christian and moral arguments previously underpinning absolutism
and encouraging new perceptions of state–individual relations.
Absolutism is now long gone and no right-thinking person would
support it as a model of government, but its influence on European
history should not be forgotten.

Chronology

1517–30	Lutheran Reformation, followed by Catholic reform from 1540 and the growth of Calvinism in central Europe after 1550. Start of 'confessionalisation' and intensification of police legislation (*Polizei*).
1524–6	German Peasants' War.
1526	Habsburg acquisition of Bohemia and Hungary. The Ottoman Turks nonetheless ruled two-thirds of Hungary following their victory at Mohacs in 1526 until their defeats in the Great Turkish War after 1683 (q.v.).
1531	Schmalkaldic League of Protestant German princes. Defeated by Emperor Charles V in 1547.
1555	Religious Peace of Augsburg formally recognised Lutheranism within the Reich. Calvinism was recognised officially in 1648.
1556	Abdication of Charles V and division of the Habsburg monarchy into Austrian (until 1918) and Spanish (until 1700) branches.
1562–98	French Wars of Religion: civil strife and monarchical weakness in France.
1568	Start of the Dutch Revolt against the Spanish Habsburgs which ended with the formation of the Dutch Republic as an independent state by 1648, leaving Spain with only the southern Low Countries (Spanish Netherlands).
1576	Jean Bodin articulated his new concept of sovereignty.
1589	Publication of Justus Lipsius's major work on the philosophy of Neostoicism.
1593–1606	Thirteen Years War between the Austrian Habsburgs and the Ottoman Turks. Onset of political strife within the Habsburg monarchy and growing tension within the Reich.

1618	Bohemian Revolt against Habsburg rule. Start of the Thirty Years War which lasted till the Peace of Westphalia (1648) and was linked to wider international struggles: Franco-Spanish War 1635–59, and intermittent conflict in the Baltic between Poland, Sweden and Russia 1600–34. The revival of Habsburg power after 1620 was checked first by Swedish (1630–52) and then French (1635–48) intervention in the Reich. Consolidation of princely power and its articulation as absolutism.
1640–88	Reign of Frederick William, the Great Elector of Brandenburg-Prussia.
1643–1715	Reign of Louis XIV in France. His minority was marked by civil unrest during the Fronde (1648–53). His 'personal rule' began in 1661.
1648	Peace of Westphalia. Start of the post-war economic and demographic recovery which continued into the eighteenth century and witnessed the transition from traditional *Polizei* to more innovative 'cameralist' regulatory measures in the German territories.
1653	The 'Historic Compromise' of the Brandenburg Recess between the Great Elector and the Brandenburg nobility.
1654	The Reichstag confirmed and extended princely powers of taxation and military recruitment (the 'Latest Imperial Recess').
1658–1705	Reign of Emperor Leopold I, which was marked by a recovery of the emperor's influence within the Reich and a revival of imperial institutions, like the imperial courts.
1660	Sovereignty of East Prussia recognised after successful Brandenburg intervention in the Northern War (1655–60) between Poland and Sweden. Great Elector acted forcefully to curb the East Prussia estates in 1663.
1662–4	Habsburg–Turkish war over Transylvania. Leopold I's attempts to enforce his authority in Hungary aroused discontent among the nobility who resisted Habsburg repression during the 'Ten Dark Years' 1671–81.
1664	Suppression of Erfurt by the elector of Mainz.
1667	French attack on the Spanish Netherlands. Start of prolonged warfare on the western frontiers of the Reich: Franco-Spanish War 1667–8; Dutch War 1672–9; Nine Years War 1688–97; War of the Spanish Succession 1701–14.

1678	Louis XIV moved into Versailles (built 1661–82). German baroque palace construction peaked *c*.1690–1710.
1683–99	Great Turkish War. Habsburg conquest of Turkish Hungary as well as Transylvania. Imposition of hereditary rule in Hungary (1687).
1686	Publication of Wilhelm von Schröder's *Fürstliche Schatz- und Rentkammer*. Height of influence of other cameralists like Becher and Hornigk.
1697	Start of Saxon (Wettin) rule in Poland (until 1763).
1700–21	Great Northern War: Sweden eventually defeated by Russia, Saxony and Denmark. Russia emerged as a major power.
1701	Prussian royal title.
1713	Pragmatic Sanction revised Habsburg right of succession.
1713/14	Utrecht–Rastatt peace settlement ended the prolonged conflicts on the Reich's western frontier. Among other territorial gains, the Austrian Habsburg monarchy acquired the former Spanish Netherlands.
1714	Start of Hanoverian (Guelph) rule in Britain.
1716–40	Intermittent international conflict weakened the Habsburg monarchy: Turkish War (1716–18), conflict with Spain (1718–20), War of the Polish Succession (1733–5), Turkish War (1735–40).
1719/25	Height of ruler–estate disputes in Mecklenburg and East Frisia.
1740	Accession of Frederick the Great in Prussia. Prussian invasion of Austrian Silesia starting two Silesian Wars (1740–2, 1744–5). War of the Austrian Succession (1740–8) between Austria, supported by Hanover–Britain, against France, Spain and Bavaria.
1744/48	Start of political and military reforms in the Habsburg monarchy associated with Friedrich Wilhelm von Haugwitz (1700–65).
1756–63	Seven Years War between Prussia, supported by Hanover–Britain, against Austria, France, Russia, Sweden and most of the German territories.
1764–70	Ruler–estate dispute in Württemberg.
1765	Joseph II became emperor and co-regent of the Habsburg monarchy with his mother, Maria Theresa (1717–80). New reform impulses within the Habsburg monarchy since the early 1760s are paralleled by similar activity in

the smaller and ecclesiastical territories which continue into the early nineteenth century.

1772	First partition of Poland between Prussia, Austria and Russia.
1778–9	War of the Bavarian Succession: Prussia successfully blocked Joseph II's plans to exchange part of the Austrian Netherlands for Bavaria.
1780	Death of Maria Theresa leaving Joseph II as sole ruler of the Habsburg monarchy. Intensification of the Josephine reforms triggers popular and conservative protests: Bohemia (1775), Transylvania (1787), Austrian Netherlands (1787).
1787–92	Turkish War: Austria and Russia inflicted further defeats on the Ottoman Empire.
1789	French Revolution
1792	Start of the French Revolutionary Wars (until 1801).
1793	Second partition of Poland between Prussia and Russia.
1795	Third (final) partition of Poland between Austria, Prussia and Russia.
1802–3	Annexation of most of the smaller German territories and cities by their larger neighbours in a major reorganisation of the Reich.
1805	Napoleon defeated Austria at Austerlitz.
1806	Abdication of Francis II as Holy Roman Emperor signalled the formal dissolution of the Reich. Napoleon defeated Prussia at Jena. Reorganisation of central Europe into Prussia, Austria and the German Confederation of the Rhine. Wide-ranging reforms in Prussia and the German states (the Reform Era) help refound the social and political basis of central European states. New arguments replace those associated with absolutism as the basis of political legitimacy.
1815	Final defeat of Napoleon. Vienna peace settlement. Establishment of the German Confederation.
1823	The term 'absolutism' emerges from the debate between liberals and conservatives in France and Spain.
1847	Publication of Wilhelm Roscher's historical analysis of absolutism.
1866–71	The German Second Reich replaced the Confederation following the Austro-Prussian War (1866) and Franco-Prussian War (1871).

Appendix

Major rulers

EMPERORS

Note: All were from the Habsburg dynasty until 1740 and simultaneously rulers of the Habsburg monarchy, including Hungary and Bohemia. Francis I was formerly duke of Lorraine and married to the Austrian archduchess and queen of Hungary, Maria Theresa, who was co-regent and ruler of the Habsburg monarchy from 1740. After her death, her son Emperor Joseph II became sole ruler of the monarchy, as were his successors.

1519–56	Charles V
1556–64	Ferdinand I
1564–76	Maximilian II
1576–1612	Rudolf II
1612–19	Matthias
1619–37	Ferdinand II
1637–57	Ferdinand III
1657–8	interregnum
1658–1705	Leopold I
1705–11	Joseph I
1711–40	Charles VI
1740–2	interregnum
1742–5	Charles VII (the Wittelsbach Carl Albrecht of Bavaria)
1745–65	Francis I
1765–90	Joseph II
1790–2	Leopold II
1792–1806	Francis II (assumed a distinct Austrian imperial title in 1804 and ruled until 1835)

BRANDENBURG-PRUSSIA (HOHENZOLLERN DYNASTY)

Note: The rulers of Brandenburg-Prussia took their titles from their electorate of Brandenburg until 1701 when their sovereign duchy of East Prussia was raised to a kingdom and they assumed a royal title.

1640–88   Frederick William, the Great Elector
1688–1713 Frederick III; from 18 January 1701 King Frederick I
1713–40   Frederick William I, the Soldier King
1740–86   Frederick II, the Great
1786–97   Frederick William II
1797–1840 Frederick William III

BAVARIA (WITTELSBACH DYNASTY)

Note: Bavaria was a duchy until 1623 when it was raised to an electorate.

1598–1651 Maximilian I (elector from 1623)
1651–79   Ferdinand Maria
1679–1726 Max II Emanuel
1726–45   Carl Albracht (Emperor Charles VII 1742–5)
1745–77   Max III Joseph
Passed to the Palatinate (q.v.)

THE PALATINATE (WITTELSBACH DYNASTY)

Note: An electorate, joined to Bavaria in 1777. Raised as the kingdom of Bavaria in 1805.

1610–23   Friedrich V (died 1632)
1623–48   under Bavarian rule
1648–80   Carl Ludwig
1680–5   Carl (the last of the Simmern line of the Palatine Wittelsbachs)
1685–90   Philipp Wilhelm (Pfalz-Neuburg line)
1690–1716 Johann Wilhelm
1716–42   Carl Philipp (last of the Pfal-Neuburg line)
1742–99   Carl Theodor (Sulzbach line, inherited Bavaria in 1777)

1799–1825   Maximilian IV Joseph (Birkenfeld line, king from December 1805)

SAXONY (WETTIN DYNASTY)

Note: An electorate, linked by dynastic union to the kingdom of Poland 1697–1763. Raised to a kingdom in 1806.

1611–56   Johann Georg I
1656–80   Johann Georg II
1680–91   Johann Georg III
1691–4   Johann Georg IV
1694–1733 Friedrich August I (Augustus II 'the Strong' of Poland from 1697)
1733–63   Friedrich August II (Augustus III of Poland)
1763   Friedrich Christian
1763–1827 Friedrich August III (king from 1806)

HANOVER (GUELPH DYNASTY)

Note: Originally the duchy of Calenberg, but raised to an electorate in 1692 and known generally as Hanover. Its rulers became kings of Great Britain 1714–1837.

1641–8   Christian Ludwig
1648–65   Georg II Wilhelm (became duke of Celle)
1665–79   Johann Friedrich
1679–98   Ernst August (also prince-bishop of Osnabrück since 1662; elector from 1692)
1698–1727 Georg Ludwig (King George I of Great Britain from 1714)
1727–60   George II
1760–1802 George III (died 1820)

MAINZ

Note: An ecclesiastical electorate.

1647–73   Johann Philipp von Schönborn
1673–5   Lothar Friedrich von Metternich

1675–8	Damian Hartard von der Leyen
1679	Carl Heinrich von Metternich
1679–95	Anselm Franz von Ingelheim
1695–1729	Lothar Franz von Schönborn
1729–32	Franz Ludwig von Pfalz-Neuburg
1732–43	Philipp Carl von Eltz
1743–63	Johann Friedrich Carl von Ostein
1763–74	Emreich Carl Joseph von Breidbach zu Bürresheim
1774–1802	Friedrich Carl Joseph zu Erthal
1802–3	Carl Theodor von Dalberg

WÜRTTEMBERG

Note: A duchy until 1803 when it became an electorate, and then a kingdom from 1806.

1628–74	Eberhard III (under Austrian occupation 1634–48)
1674–7	Wilhelm Ludwig
1677–93	Friedrich Carl, regent
1693–1733	Eberhard Ludwig
1733–7	Carl Alexander
1737–8	Carl Rudolph, regent
1738–44	Carl Friedrich, regent
1744–93	Carl Eugen
1793–5	Ludwig Eugen
1795–7	Friedrich Eugen
1797–1816	Friedrich (elector from 1803; king from 1806)

Notes

Introduction

1 N. Henshall, *The myth of absolutism. Change and continuity in early modern European monarchy* (London, 1992).

2 H. Duchhardt, 'Absolutismus – Abschied von einem Epochenbegriff?', *Historische Zeitschrift*, 258 (1994), 113–22; R.G. Asch and H. Duchhardt (eds), *Der Absolutismus – ein Mythos? Strukturwandel monarchischer Herrschaft* (Cologne, 1996); J.B. Collins, *The state in early modern France* (Cambridge, 1995), pp. 1–3, 185.

3 W.F. Church (ed.), *The greatness of Louis XIV. Myth or reality?* (Lexington, 1959); D. Parker, *The making of French absolutism* (London, 1983); J.B. Collins, *Fiscal limits of absolutism: direct taxation in seventeenth-century France* (Berkeley, 1988); R. Mettam, *Power and faction in Louis XIV's France* (New York, 1988).

4 In addition to the book cited in n.1 above, see his 'Early modern absolutism 1550–1700: political reality or propaganda?' in Asch and Duchhardt (eds), *Absolutismus*, pp. 25–53.

5 R. Southard, *Droysen and the Prussian school of history* (Lexington, 1995), pp. 42–52, 126–8, 142–3. See also L. Krieger, *Ranke. The meaning of history* (Chicago, 1977).

6 W. Mommsen, 'Zur Beurteilung des Absolutismus', *Historische Zeitschrift*, 158 (1938), 52–76, esp. 54–7.

7 This section draws on the views of F.L. Carsten, P. Blickle, P. Anderson and H.-U. Wehler, all of whom receive further attention in Chapters 1 and 3.

8 C. Tilly, *Coercion, capital and European states AD 990–1992* (Oxford, 1992); B.M. Downing, *The military revolution and political change in early modern Europe* (Princeton, 1991); T. Ertman, *Birth of the Leviathan. Building states and regimes in medieval and early modern Europe* (Cambridge, 1997); A. Giddens, *The nation-state and violence* (Berkeley, 1985). These views receive fuller treatment in Chapter 1.

9 For a fuller response to the postmodernist challenge see A. Callinicos, *Theories and narratives. Reflections on the philosophy of history* (Cambridge, 1995).

10 The now extensive recent literature on the old Reich is surveyed by P.H. Wilson, *The Holy Roman Empire 1495–1806* (London, 1999) and

H. Neuhaus, *Das Reich in der frühen Neuzeit* (Munich, 1997). An example of the persistence of the older interpretation of the Reich is provided by a recent article in the *Independent*, 26 October 1999. My thanks to Clarissa Campbell-Orr for drawing this to my attention. For further detail on the size and population of the German territories see E. Wallner, 'Die kreissägigen Reichsterritorien am Vorabend des Lunéviller Friedens', *Mitteilungen des Instituts für Österreichische Geschichtsforschung*, Supplement 11, (1929), 681–716, and P.C. Hartmann, 'Bevölkerungszahlen und Konfessionsverhältnisse des Heiligen Römischen Reiches deutscher Nation under der Reichskreise am Ende des 18. Jahrhunderts', *Zeitschrift für Historische Forschung*, 22 (1995), 345–69.

11 Ertman, *Birth of the Leviathan*, pp. 264–305; Downing, *Military revolution and political change*, pp. 140–56. For fuller coverage of Poland in this period see J.T. Lukowski, *Liberty's folly. The Polish–Lithuanian Commonwealth in the eighteenth century, 1697–1795* (London, 1991).

12 Examples of this Prusso-centric focus include: Downing, *Military revolution and political change*, pp. 84–112; Ertman, *Birth of the Leviathan*, pp. 224–63; C. Mooers, *The making of bourgeois Europe. Absolutism, revolution and the rise of capitalism in England, France and Germany* (London, 1991), pp. 103–53.

13 Frederick II, *Anti-Machiavel* (transl. and ed. P. Sonnino, Athens, 1981), pp. 77–8.

14 The historiography of this phenomenon is dealt with in P.H. Wilson, 'The German "soldier trade" of the seventeenth and eighteenth century: a reassessment', *International History Review*, 18 (1996), 757–92.

15 A. Fauchier-Magnan, *The small German courts in the eighteenth century* (London, 1958; first published Paris, 1947), pp. 21, 43 and ibid. pp. 42–50 generally. Comments in roughly similar vein can be found in B. Engelmann, *Wir Untertanen. Ein deutsches Anti-Geschichtsbuch* (Frankfurt/M., 1976); W.H. Bruford, *Germany in the eighteenth century* (Cambridge, 1935); K. Biedermann, *Deutschland im achtzehnten Jahrhundert* (5 vols, Leipzig, 1880); and the editorial remarks in P. Lahnstein (ed.), *Das Leben im Barock* (Stuttgart, 1974), and *Report einer 'guten alten Zeit'* (Stuttgart, 1970).

1 Emergence

1 H. Dreitzel, *Absolutismus und ständische Verfassung in Deutschland* (Mainz, 1992), esp. pp. 127–9. See also Henshall, *Myth of absolutism*, pp. 208–9, who notes that the first use of the term dates from debates in Spain in 1823.

2 J. Kunisch, *Absolutismus. Europäische Geschichte vom Westfälischen Frieden bis zur Krise des Ancien Regime* (Göttingen, 1986), esp. p. 179; H. Duchhardt, *Das Zeitalter des Absolutismus* (Munich, 1989).

3 R. Koser, 'Die Epochen der absoluten Monarchie in der neueren Geschichte', *Historische Zeitschrift*, 61 (1889), 246–88 at 251–64; K. Epstein, *The genesis of German conservatism* (Princeton, 1966), p. 254; R.J. Holton, *The transition from feudalism to capitalism* (London, 1984), p. 186.

4 S. Beller, *Francis Joseph* (London, 1996), esp. pp. 54–64, 71–3, 160–1, 172–3.

5 For examples see F. Hartung, 'Der aufgeklärte Absolutismus', *Historische Zeitschrift*, 180 (1955), 15–42 at 17 and further discussion in his 'Die Epochen der absoluten Monarchie in der neueren Geschichte', *Historische Zeitschrift*, 145 (1932), 46–52.

6 J. Anderson and S. Hall, 'Absolutism and other ancestors', in J. Anderson (ed.), *The rise of the modern state* (Brighton, 1986), pp. 21–40 at 21.

7 For a good summary of this perspective, see H. Boldt, *Deutsche Verfassungsgeschichte*, vol. I (3rd edn, Munich, 1994), pp. 196–242. Whilst this broad periodisation can be accepted, the dualistic character of ruler–estate relations is open to criticism: see Chapter 3 below.

8 Roscher's model is neatly summarised in H.M. Scott (ed.), *Enlightened absolutism. Reform and reformers in later eighteenth century Europe* (London, 1990), pp. 4–6.

9 Koser, 'Epochen der absoluten Monarchie', pp. 247–8. For problems with Roscher's model see also Kunisch, *Absolutismus*, pp. 180–8, and Hartung, 'Aufgeklärter Absolutismus', p. 50.

10 W. te Brake, *Shaping history. Ordinary people in European politics, 1500–1700* (Berkeley, 1998), esp. pp. 17–18.

11 Epstein, *Genesis of German conservatism*, p. 254; G. Poggi, *The development of the modern state. A sociological introduction* (London, 1978), pp. 61–77.

12 P. Geyl, *Napoleon for and against* (London, 1949).

13 Further discussions in G. Parker, *Europe in crisis 1598–1648* (London, 1982); T. K. Rabb, *The struggle for stability in early modern Europe* (New York, 1975).

14 W. Reinhard, 'Zwang zur Konfessionalisierung? Prologemena zu einer Theorie des konfessionellen Zeitalters', *Zeitschrift für Historische Forschung*, 10 (1983), 257–77 now available in English translation in C.S. Dixon (ed.), *The German Reformation* (Oxford, 1999), pp. 169–92; J.F. Harrington and H.W. Smith, 'Confessionalization, community, and state building in Germany 1555–1870', *Journal of Modern History*, 69 (1997), 77–101.

15 P.K. Monod, *The power of kings. Monarchy and religion in Europe, 1589–1715* (New Haven, 1999); J.Q. Whitman, *The legacy of Roman law in the German Romantic era* (Princeton, 1990), p. 12. For the general context see J. Overfield, 'Germany', in R. Porter and M. Teich (eds), *The Renaissance in national context* (Cambridge, 1992), pp. 92–122, and W. Clark, 'The scientific revolution in the German nations', in R. Porter and M. Teich (eds), *The scientific revolution in national context* (Cambridge, 1992), pp. 90–114.

16 G. Oestreich, *Neostoicism and the early modern state* (Cambridge, 1982), esp. pp. 155–65. Oesteich's ideas are discussed at length in Chapter 3 below.

17 P.M. Kennedy, *The rise and fall of the great powers: economic change and military conflict from 1500 to 2000* (New York, 1987).

18 O. Hintze, *The historical essays of Otto Hintze* (ed. F. Gilbert, Oxford, 1975), pp. 159–215.

19 E. Hinrichs, 'Abschied vom Absolutismus? Eine Antwort auf Nicholas Henshall', in Asch and Duchhardt (eds), *Absolutismus*, pp. 353–71 at 363–5.

20 For the debate on the military revolution see G. Parker, *The military revolution. Military innovation and the rise of the West 1500–1800* (Cambridge, 1988); C.J. Rogers (ed.), *The military revolution debate* (Boulder, 1995);

P.H. Wilson, 'European warfare 1450–1815', in J. Black (ed.), *War in the early modern world 1450–1815* (London, 1999), pp. 177–206.

21 N. Elias, *The civilising process* (Oxford, 1994), esp. pp. 270–2.

22 Downing, *Military revolution and political change*, pp. 56–83; Giddens, *Nation-state and violence*, pp. 105–14; B.D. Porter, *War and the rise of the state. The military foundations of modern politics* (New York, 1994), pp. 64–7; M. Mann, *The sources of social power* (2 vols, Cambridge, 1986–93); Ertman, *Birth of the Leviathan*; Tilly, *Coercion, capital and European states* and his 'War making and state making as organised crime', in P. Evans *et al.* (eds), *Bringing the state back in* (Cambridge, 1985), pp. 169–91.

23 Anderson and Hall, 'Absolutism and other ancestors', pp. 29–36.

24 H. Kamen, *European society 1500–1700* (London, 1984), pp. 93–119, 292–305.

25 M.S. Kimmel, *Absolutism and its discontents. State and society in seventeenth-century France and England* (New Brunswick, 1988).

26 Downing, *Military revolution and political change*, pp. 9–15; Ertman, *Birth of the Leviathan*, pp. 4–10. Michael Mann and Charles Tilly also identify different patterns of state formation: see n. 22 above.

27 This is a feature of R.A. Dorwart, *The administrative reforms of Frederick William I of Prussia* (Westport, 1953).

28 For example, Holton, *Transition*, p. 181, and Ertman, *Birth of the Leviathan*, p. 245. For a good overview of Frederick William's role see J. Arndt, 'Der Große Kurfürst, ein Herrscher des Absolutismus?', in Asch and Duchhardt (eds), *Absolutismus*, pp. 249–73.

29 For an introduction to the Annales perspective see P. Burke, 'The Annales in global context', *International Review of Social History*, 35 (1990), 421–32.

30 For an introduction to this substantial field see W. Doyle, *Origins of the French Revolution* (2nd edn, Oxford, 1988).

31 Overviews in A. Dorpalen, *German history in Marxist perspective. The East German approach* (London, 1985), pp. 138–47; Kunisch, *Absolutismus*, pp. 193–202.

32 H. Schnitter and T. Schmidt, *Absolutismus und Heer* (Berlin, 1987), pp. 29–34, 46.

33 P. Anderson, *Lineages of the absolutist state* (London, 1974); R. Brenner, 'Agrarian class structure and economic development in pre-industrial Europe', and 'The agrarian roots of European capitalism', both reprinted in T.H. Aston and C.H.E. Philpin (eds), *The Brenner debate* (Cambridge, 1985), pp. 10–63, 213–328; Mooers, *Making of bourgeois Europe*.

34 Anderson, *Lineages*, pp. 403–4, italics in the original. See also ibid. p. 197.

35 P. Anderson, *Passages from antiquity to feudalism* (London, 1974).

36 Anderson, *Lineages*, pp. 19, 195. See also ibid. p. 429.

37 D. Parker, *Class and state in ancien régime France. The road to modernity?* (London, 1996), pp. 19–22. See also J. Miller (ed.), *Absolutism in seventeenth century Europe* (Basingstoke, 1990), pp. 8–13.

38 Anderson, *Lineages*, p. 195. See also ibid. pp. 195–220 passim.

39 Anderson and Hall, 'Absolutism and other ancestors', p. 33.

40 Parker, *Class and state*, pp. 273–8.

41 J. Peters (ed.), *Gutsherrschaft als soziales Modell. Vergleichende Betrachtungen zur Funktionsweise frühneuzeitlicher Agrargesellschaften* (Munich,

1995); W.W. Hagen, 'Working for the Junker. The standard of living of manorial labourers in Brandenburg 1584–1810', *Journal of Modern History*, 58 (1986), 143–58; E. Melton, 'Population structure, the market economy, and the transformation of *Gutsherrschaft* in east central Europe, 1650–1800: the cases of Brandenburg and Bohemia', *German History*, 16 (1999), 297–327.

42 Anderson, *Lineages*, pp. 272–4, 278. For an interpretation emphasising Prussian agrarian capitalism see Holton, *Transition*, pp. 183–5.

43 Aston and Philpin (eds), *Brenner debate*, pp. 55–6, 236–42; Mooers, *Making of bourgeois Europe*, pp. 34–6, 55–6.

44 See the criticisms raised by H. Wunder, 'Peasant organisation and class conflict in eastern and western Germany', in Aston and Philpin (eds), *Brenner debate*, pp. 91–100.

45 This is something which has clearly exasperated those who have tried to understand it; see the review by G. Dalles in *Journal of Social History*, 20 (1987), 832–4. Chapter 3 provides further discussion of the social basis of absolutist foreign policy.

46 Anderson, *Lineages*, p. 260.

47 Part printed in English translation in C.A. Macartney (ed.), *The Habsburg and Hohenzollern dynasties in the seventeenth and eighteenth centuries* (London, 1970), pp. 228–41. Otto Hintze provided the classic formulation for the Historic Compromise of 1653 in his *Die Hohenzollern und ihr Werke* (Berlin, 1915), esp. pp. 202–5.

48 F.L. Carsten, *The origins of Prussia* (Oxford, 1954), pp. 179–277; L. Hüttl, *Friedrich Wilhelm von Brandenburg, der Große Kurfürst, 1620–88* (Munich, 1981).

49 F.L. Carsten, *Princes and parliaments in Germany from the fifteenth to the eighteenth century* (Oxford, 1959), pp. 240–1.

50 Anderson, *Lineages*, pp. 240–1; P. Bachmann and K. Zeisler, *Der deutsche Militarismus* (2nd edn, Cologne, 1986), p. 33; E. Willems, *A way of life and death: three centuries of Prussian–German militarism – an anthropological approach* (Nashville, 1986), pp. 19–23.

51 For example, O. Mörke, 'Social structure', in S. Ogilvie (ed.), *Germany. A new social and economic history 1630–1800* (London, 1996), pp. 134–63 at 140–5; H. Schilling, *Höfe und Allianzen. Deutschland 1648–1763* (Berlin, 1989), pp. 404–14. For a fuller discussion of the concept of a service nobility see H.M. Scott (ed.), *The European nobilities in the seventeenth and eighteenth centuries*, vol. II (London, 1995).

52 The implications of the canton system of recruitment are explored in Chapter 3 below.

53 P. Wick, *Versuche zur Einrichtung des Absolutismus in Mecklenburg in der ersten Hälfte des 18. Jahrhunderts* (Berlin, 1964). See also R.G. Asch, 'Estates and princes after 1648: the consequence of the Thirty Years War', *German History*, 6 (1988), 113–32 at 119–23.

54 W.W. Hagen, 'Seventeenth century crisis in Brandenburg. The Thirty Years War, the destabilization of serfdom and the rise of absolutism', *American Historical Review*, 94 (1989), 302–35, and his 'Village life in East-Elbian Germany and Poland, 1400–1800', in T. Scott (ed.), *The peasantries of Europe from the fourteenth to the eighteenth century* (Harlow, 1998),

pp. 145–90; E. Melton, 'The Prussian Junkers, 1600–1786', in Scott (ed.), *European nobilities*, pp. 71–109; and the literature cited in n. 41 above.
55 Hagen, 'Seventeenth century crisis', p. 334; A. Corvisier, *Armies and societies in Europe 1494–1789* (Bloomington, 1979), p. 115.
56 R.G. Asch, *The Thirty Years War: the Holy Roman Empire and Europe, 1618–1648* (London, 1997); R.J.W. Evans, *The making of the Habsburg monarchy, 1550–1700* (Oxford, 1979); J. Bérenger, *A history of the Habsburg empire 1273–1700* (Harlow, 1994), pp. 261–317; and the pieces on the Austrian and Hungarian nobility by J. Van Horn Melton and P. Schimert in Scott (ed.), *European nobilities*.
57 This point is discussed further in Chapter 4.
58 J.E. Thompson, *Mercenaries, pirates and sovereigns. State-building and extraterritorial violence in early modern Europe* (Princeton, 1994).

2 Theory

1 J. Althusius, *Politica* (transl. and ed. F.S. Carney, Indianapolis, 1995); H. Dreitzel, *Absolutismus und ständische Verfassung* and his 'Ständestaat und absolute Monarchie in der politischen Theorie des Reiches in der frühen Neuzeit', in G. Schmidt (ed.), *Stände und Gesellschaft im alten Reich* (Stuttgart, 1989), pp. 19–50. For political representation in imperial institutions see H. Neuhaus, 'Zwänge und Entwicklungsmöglichkeiten reichsständischer Beratungsformen in der zweiten Hälfte des 16. Jahrhundert', *Zeitschrift für Historische Forschung*, 10 (1983), 279–98. For a good introduction to seventeenth-century political thought see W.M. Spellman, *European political thought 1600–1700* (Basingstoke, 1998).
2 L. Krieger, *The German idea of freedom* (Chicago, 1957). The current debate on the existence of an alternative, democratic tradition is covered in Chapter 3.
3 A. Vincent, *Theories of the state* (Oxford, 1987), p. 50.
4 J. Bodin, *On sovereignty* (ed. J.H. Franklin, Cambridge, 1992; first published 1576).
5 This process is analysed by B. Arnold, *Princes and territories in medieval Germany* (Cambridge, 1991), and his *Medieval Germany, 500–1300* (Basingstoke, 1997).
6 C. Kampmann, *Reichsrebellion und kaiserliche Acht. Politische Strafjustiz im Dreißigjährigen Krieg und das Verfahren gegen Wallenstein 1634* (Münster, 1992), pp. 211–14; F. Bosbach, *Monarchia universalis. Ein politischer Leitbegriff der frühen Neuzeit* (Göttingen, 1988).
7 Two good collections of these charters are K. Zeumer (ed.), *Quellensammlung zur Geschichte der deutschen Reichsverfassung in Mittelalter und Neuzeit* (2 vols, Tübingen, 1913), and J.J. Schmauss and H.C. Senckenberg (eds), *Neue und vollständige Sammlung der Reichs-Abschiede* (4 parts in 2 vols, Frankfurt, 1747; reprint Osnabrück, 1967). For the emergence of territorial lordship see O. Brunner, *Land and lordship. Structures of governance in medieval Austria* (Philadelphia, 1992; German original 1939).
8 The treaty is printed in Zeumer (ed.), *Quellensammlung*, pp. 395–443. The key passage is in Article VIII, section 1. Further discussion is provided by an important recent article by D. Croxton, 'The Peace of Westphalia

of 1648 and the origins of sovereignty', *International History Review*, 21 (1999), 569–91.

9 J.-B. Bossuet, *Politics drawn from the very words of Holy Scripture* (Cambridge, 1990), pp. 48–51.

10 P. Sutter-Fichtner, *Protestantism and primogeniture in early modern Germany* (New Haven, 1989).

11 A. Kraus, 'Das katholische Herrscherbild im Reich, dargestellt am Beispiel Kaiser Ferdinands II. und Kurfürst Maximilians I. von Bayern', in K. Repgen (ed.), *Das Herrscherbild im 17. Jahrhundert* (Münster, 1991), pp. 1–25 at 10–16.

12 Frederick II, *Anti-Machiavel*, p. 37.

13 D. Albrecht, *Maximilian I. von Bayern 1573–1651* (Munich, 1998), pp. 277–83.

14 W. Brauneder, 'Die Pragmatische Sanction – das Grundgesetz der Monarchia Austriaca', in K. Gutkas (ed.), *Prinz Eugen und das barocke Österreich* (Salzburg, 1985), pp. 141–50; H. v. Zwiedeneck-Südenhorst, 'Die Anerkenung der Pragmatischen Sanction Karls VI. durch das deutsche Reich', *Mitteilungen des Instituts für Österreichische Geschichtsforschung*, 16 (1895), 276–341; M. S. Anderson, *The War of the Austrian Succession 1740–1748* (London, 1995).

15 For Hungary see E. Pamlényi, *A history of Hungary* (London, 1975); Ertman, *Birth of the Leviathan*, pp. 286–92.

16 Bossuet, *Politics*, pp. 57–9.

17 H.J. Berbig, 'Der Krönungsritus im alten Reich (1648–1806)', *Zeitschrift für Bayerische Landesgeschichte*, 38 (1975), 639–700. See Wilson, *Holy Roman Empire*, pp. 38–9 for the progressive desacralisation of the imperial title.

18 Monod, *Power of kings*, pp. 37–54.

19 For example, the *Princeps in Compedio*, allegedly written by Emperor Ferdinand II in 1632 was probably composed by a lawyer and not published until 1668. For the following see Kraus, 'Katholisches Herrscherbild', pp. 3–6, and R. Bireley, 'Antimachiavellianism, the baroque and Maximilian of Bavaria', *Archivum Historicum Societatis Jesu*, 103 (1984), 137–59.

20 P.H. Wilson, *German armies. War and German politics 1648–1806* (London, 1998), esp. pp. 84–6. For examples of Wittelsbach piety see Albrecht, *Maximilian I.*, pp. 285–337.

21 M. Tanner, *The last descendant of Aeneas. The Hapsburgs and the mythic image of the emperor* (New Haven, 1993), pp. 183–222; Evans, *Habsburg monarchy*, pp. 216–28, 252–7.

22 Kraus, 'Katholisches Herrscherbild', pp. 7–21; A. Schindling and W. Ziegler (eds), *Die Kaiser der Neuzeit 1519–1918* (Munich, 1990), pp. 142–9.

23 H. Duchhardt, 'Das protestantische Herrscherbild des 17. Jahrhunderts im Reich', in Repgen (ed.), *Herrscherbild*, pp. 26–42; L. Frey and M. Frey, *Frederick I. The man and his times* (New York, 1984), pp. 60–5. A contemporary description of the ceremony is printed in Macartney (ed.), *Habsburg and Hohenzollern dynasties*, pp. 275–92.

24 R. Po-Chia Hsia, 'The structure of belief: confessionalism and society, 1500–1600', in R. Scribner (ed.), *Germany. A new social and economic history 1450–1630* (London, 1996), pp. 355–77 at 361, 365; M. Fulbrook,

Piety and politics. Religion and the rise of absolutism in England, Württemberg and Prussia (Cambridge, 1983).

25 Bossuet, *Politics*, pp. 160–2.

26 For example, S. Pufendorf, *On the duty of man and citizen* (transl. and ed. J. Tully, Cambridge, 1991; first published 1673), p. 151. See also Frederick II, *Anti-Machiavel*, pp. 138–41, 149–55.

27 A. Gestrich, *Absolutismus und Öffentlichkeit. Politische Kommunikation in Deutschland zu Beginn des 18. Jahrhunderts* (Göttingen, 1994), esp. pp. 34–48.

28 Ibid., pp. 57–74; Bireley, 'Antimachiavellianism', pp. 146–7.

29 Pufendorf, *On the duty*, pp. 132–4; G.W. Frhr. v. Leibniz, *Political writings* (transl. and ed. P. Riley, Cambridge, 1988), p. 29; Bossuet, *Politics*, pp. 8–15.

30 A. Lossky, 'Maxims of state in Louis XIV's foreign policy in the 1680s', in R. Hatton and J.S. Bromley (eds), *William III and Louis XIV. Essays 1680–1720* (Liverpool, 1968), pp. 7–23.

31 Pufendorf, *On the duty*, pp. 151–4. See ibid. pp. 132–50 for his social contract.

32 Leibniz, *Political writings*, pp. 23, 25–6.

33 K.G.A. Jeserich *et al.*, *Deutsche Verwaltungsgeschichte*, vol. I (Stuttgart, 1983), pp. 389–98; Oestreich, *Neostoicism*, pp. 155–65.

34 Bossuet, *Politics*, pp. 64, 68, 167; F. Bluche, *Louis XIV* (Oxford, 1990), p. 608.

35 Cited in R. Endres, 'Markgraf Christian Ernst von Bayreuth', *Fränkische Lebensbilder*, 2 (1968), 260–90 at 260.

36 Pufendorf, *On the duty*, p. 151.

37 Dreitzel, *Absolutismus und ständische Verfassung*, pp. 82–3; Bossuet, *Politics*, pp. 173–5 and ibid. pp. 59–61, 167–89; Leibniz, *Political writings*, p. 29.

38 H. Duchhardt, *Protestantisches Kaisertum und altes Reich* (Wiesbaden, 1977).

39 'Subjects have nothing to oppose to the violence of princes but respectful remonstrances, without mutiny and without murmuring, together with prayers for their conversion' (Bossuet, *Politics*, p. 181).

40 R.L. Gawthrop, *Pietism and the making of eighteenth-century Prussia* (Cambridge, 1993), p. 12. See also E. Hinrichs, *Preussentum und Pietismus. Der Pietismus in Brandenburg-Preussen als religiös-soziale Reformbewegung* (Göttingen, 1971), and the works in n. 24 above.

41 Oestreich, *Neostoicism*, pp. 13–131.

42 P. Münch, 'Die "Obrigkeit im Vaterstand". Zu Definition und Kritik des "Landesvaters" während der Frühen Neuzeit', *Daphnis*, 11 (1982), 15–40.

43 Pufendorf, *On the duty*, p. 175.

44 M. Walker, *Johann Jakob Moser and the Holy Roman Empire of the German Nation* (Chapel Hill, 1981); R. Rürup, *Johann Jakob Moser. Pietismus und Reform* (Wiesbaden, 1965).

45 Anderson and Hall, 'Absolutism and other ancestors', pp. 32, 36; Downing, *Military revolution and political change*, esp. p. 93; Vincent, *Theories of the state*, pp. 45–6.

46 J. Locke, *Two treatises on government* (ed. P. Laslett, Cambridge, 1988), esp. II, paras 17 (p. 279), 23–4 (pp. 284–5), 172 (pp. 382–3).

47 Bossuet's arguments in this respect are flawed; see his *Politics*, pp. 61–2, 85, 262–4.
48 H. Münkler, *Im Namen des Staates. Die Begründung der Staatsraison in der frühen Neuzeit* (Frankfurt/M., 1987); Bireley, 'Antimachiavellianism', p. 144; Monod, *Power of kings*, pp. 90–4.
49 Epstein, *Genesis of German conservatism*, p. 273; M. Walker, 'Rights and functions: the social categories of eighteenth-century German jurists and cameralists', *Journal of Modern History*, 50 (1978), 234–51; W. Schmale, 'Das Heilige Römische Reich und die Herrschaft des Rechts', in Asch and Duchhardt (eds), *Absolutismus*, pp. 229–48.
50 H. Duchhardt, 'International relations, the law of nations and the Germanies', in C. Ingrao (ed.), *The state and society in early modern Austria* (West Lafayette, 1994), pp. 286–97; B. Diestelkamp (ed.), *Die politische Funktion des Reichskammergerichts* (Cologne, 1993); B. Diestelkamp (ed.), *Das Reichskammergericht in der deutschen Geschichte* (Cologne, 1990); F. Hertz, 'Die Rechtsprechung im römisch-deutschen Reich und ihre politische Bedeutung', *Mitteilungen des Instituts für Österreichische Geschichtsforschung*, 69 (1961), 331–58.
51 Schmale, 'Das Heilige Römische Reich', pp. 245–8.
52 Dreitzel, *Absolutismus und ständische Verfassung*, pp. 92–100.
53 Pufendorf, *On the duty*, p. 148; Bireley, 'Antimachiavellianism', pp. 154–6.

3 Practice

1 N. Elias, *The court society* (New York, 1983; German original 1969), and his *Civilising process* (2 vols, New York, 1978–82; German original 1939; all references here are to the single-volume Oxford, 1994 edn); J.F. v. Krüdener, *Die Rolle des Hofes im Absolutismus* (Stuttgart, 1973).
2 Examples of the positive reception include R. Vierhaus, 'Höfe und höfische Gesellschaft in Deutschland im 17. und 18. Jahrhundert', in E. Hinrichs (ed.), *Absolutismus* (Frankfurt/M., 1986), pp. 116–137, and V. Bauer, *Die höfische Gesellschaft in Deutschland von der Mitte des 17. bis zum Ausgang des 18. Jahrhunderts* (Tübingen, 1993).
3 Elias, *Civilising process*, pp. 42–178.
4 Elias, *Court society*, p. 91.
5 Elias, *Civilising process*, pp. 475–513.
6 Ibid., pp. 390–421.
7 The chief revisionists are J. Adamson (ed.), *The princely courts of Europe 1500–1750* (London, 1999), and J. Duindam, *Myths of power. Norbert Elias and the early modern European court* (Amsterdam, 1995). For recent critique of Elias's wider civilising process see W. Ludwig-Mayerhofer, 'Disziplin oder Distinktion? Zur Interpretation der Theorie des Zivilisationsprozesses von Norbert Elias', *Kölner Zeitschrift für Soziologie und Sozialpsychologie*, 50 (1998), 217–37, and P. Burke, 'Civilisation, discipline, disorder. Three case studies in history and social theory', *Theoria* (June 1996), 21–35.
8 Vierhaus, 'Höfe und höfische Gesellschaft', pp. 123–4; C. Dipper, *Deutsche Geschichte 1648–1789* (Frankfurt/M., 1991), pp. 201–3. For a useful survey of a Protestant court see M. Völkel, 'The Hohenzollern court 1535–1740', in Adamson (ed.), *Princely courts*, pp. 210–29.

9 G. Klingenstein, 'Der Wiener Hof in der frühen Neuzeit', *Zeitschrift für Historische Forschung*, 22 (1995), 237–45. Volker Press provides insight into the Habsburg court in 'The Habsburg court as centre of the imperial government', *Journal of Modern History*, 58 (1986), supplement 23–45, and his 'The imperial court of the Habsburgs from Maximilian I to Ferdinand III, 1493–1657', in R.G. Asch and A.M. Birke (eds), *Princes, patronage and the nobility* (Oxford, 1991), pp. 289–312. See also J. Duindam, 'The court of the Austrian Habsburgs *c*.1500–1750', in Adamson (ed.), *Princely courts*, pp. 164–87.

10 J.P. Spielman, *The city and the crown. Vienna and the imperial court 1600–1740* (West Lafayette, 1993), pp. 102–11, 185–96.

11 C. Belschner, *Ludwigsburg im Wechsel der Zeiten* (3rd edn, Ludwigsburg, 1969). For the general political events see J.A. Vann, *The making of a state. Württemberg 1593–1793* (Ithaca, 1984); P.H. Wilson, *War, state and society in Württemberg, 1677–1793* (Cambridge, 1995).

12 R. Wagner-Rieger, 'Gedanken zum fürstlichen Schlossbau des Absolutismus', in F. Engel-Janosi *et al.* (eds), *Fürst, Bürger, Mensch* (Munich, 1975), pp. 42–70; H. Lorenz, 'The imperial Hofburg. The theory and practice of architectural representation in baroque Vienna', in Ingrao (ed.), *State and society*, pp. 93–109.

13 Dipper, *Deutsche Geschichte*, pp. 204–5; Bauer, *Höfische Gesellschaft*, pp. 90–1; P.-C. Hartmann, *Karl Albrecht, Karl VII: glücklicher Kurfürst, unglücklicher Kaiser* (Regensburg, 1985), p. 70; A. Pfister, 'Hof und Hoffeste', in *Herzog Karl Eugen und seiner Zeit* (issued by the Württembergischer Geschichts- und Altertumsverein, 2 vols, Esslingen, 1907–9), I, 103–18, plus papers in the Hauptstaatsarchiv Stuttgart, A8: Bü.66; A202: Bü.1870, 1872, 1873.

14 Figures extracted from Dipper, *Deutsche Geschichte*, p. 205; P.G.M. Dickson, *Finance and government under Maria Theresia 1740–1780* (2 vols, Oxford, 1987), II, 385; Frey and Frey, *Frederick I*, pp. 155–9; W. Ribbe (ed.), *Geschichte Berlins* (2 vols, Munich, 1988), I, 370; Duchhardt, *Absolutismus*, p. 50; Wilson, *War, state and society*, pp. 35–6, 127–8, 257–9.

15 H. Schnee, *Die Hoffinanz und der moderne Staat* (6 vols, Berlin, 1953–67), I, 62.

16 Hauptstaatsarchiv Stuttgart, A19a: Bd.52.

17 Krüdener, *Rolle des Hofes*, p. 20.

18 W. Sombart, *Krieg und Kapitalismus* (Munich, 1913). For the debate on the role of war in economic growth see J.M. Winter (ed.), *War and economic development* (Cambridge, 1975).

19 R. Sandgruber, '"Österreich über alles". Programmatik und Realität der Wirtschaft zur Zeit Prinz Eugens', in E. Zöllner and K. Gutkas (eds), *Österreich und die Osmanen – Prinz Eugen und seiner Zeit* (Vienna, 1988), pp. 153–71 at 153–5; Ribbe (ed.), *Geschichte Berlins*, I, 348–55.

20 H. Gaese, 'Zur Gründung der Stadt Ludwigsburg', *Ludwigsburger Geschichtsblätter*, 20 (1968), 7–30 at 28; W. Schmierer, 'Zur Entstehungsgeschichte von Ludwigsburg', *Ludwigsburger Geschichtsblätter*, 32 (1980), 79–94 at 90.

21 K. Gutkas *et al.* (eds), *Prinz Eugen und das barocke Österreich* (catalogue vol., Vienna, 1986); W. Fleischhauer, *Barock im Herzogtum Württemberg* (2nd edn, Stuttgart, 1981).

22 Wagner-Rieger, 'Fürstlicher Schlossbau', p. 45. The original town plan still structures the centre of modern Karlsruhe today.

23 F. Matsche, *Die Kunst im Dienst der Staatsidee Kaiser Karl VI* (2 vols, Berlin, 1981).

24 P. Burke, *The fabrication of Louis XIV* (New Haven, 1992), pp. 26, 44–5, 66, 130–1; C. Ingrao, *In quest and crisis. Emperor Joseph I and the Habsburg monarchy* (West Lafayette, 1979), p. 32.

25 G.L. Buelow (ed.), *The late baroque era from the 1680s to 1740* (Basingstoke, 1993); N. Zaslaw (ed.), *The classical era from the 1740s to the end of the 18th century* (London, 1989), esp. pp. 221–2; A. Yorke-Long, *Music at court. Four eighteenth century studies* (London, 1964).

26 Gestrich, *Absolutismus und Öffentlichkeit*, pp. 123–6; Buelow (ed.), *Late baroque era*, pp. 221–7.

27 Fauchier-Magnan, *Small German courts*, pp. 42–3, 53. French influence is also stressed by G. Livet, 'Louis XIV and the Germanies', in R. Hatton (ed.), *Louis XIV and Europe* (London, 1976), pp. 60–81. For a recent reappraisal of the wider reception of French court culture see Burke, *Fabrication of Louis XIV*, pp. 151–78.

28 Frey and Frey, *Frederick I*, p. 18.

29 Endres, 'Markgraf Christian', pp. 269–70.

30 S.J. Klingensmith, *The utility of splendor. Ceremony, social life, and architecture at the court of Bavaria 1600–1800* (Chicago, 1993), pp. 122–44 and the appendix of floor plans; Buelow (ed.), *Late baroque era*, pp. 139–41, 217–28, 297–318; E. Sagarra, *A social history of Germany 1648–1914* (London, 1977), pp. 24–5.

31 Buelow (ed.), *Late baroque era*, pp. 298–306, 324–5; Duindam, *Myths of power*, pp. 160–5. For a sustained critique of the functionalist approach, see John Adamson's 'Introduction' to his edited work *Princely courts*, pp. 7–41.

32 Vann, *Making of a state*, esp. p. 21; C. Ingrao, *The Hessian mercenary state. Ideas, institutions and reform under Frederick II 1760–1785* (Cambridge, 1987), esp. pp. 6–7.

33 Wilson, *German armies*, pp. 280–4; Wilson, *War, state and society*, pp. 5–6, 28.

34 R. Babel, 'The court of the Wittelsbachs c.1500–1750', in Adamson (ed.), *Princely courts*, pp. 188–209, esp. 197–8; G. Streidt and P. Feierabend (eds), *Prussia. Art and architecture* (Cologne, 1999), esp. pp. 76–153; K. Czok, *Am Hofe Augusts des Starken* (Stuttgart, 1990); A. Boroviczény, *Graf von Brühl* (Zürich, 1930), pp. 358–97.

35 Endres, 'Markgraf Christian', pp. 279–80.

36 Further discussion in W. Roosen, 'Early modern diplomatic ceremonial', *Journal of Modern History*, 52 (1980), 452–76; Gestrich, *Absolutismus und Öffentlichkeit*, pp. 157–68. For the influence of science and geometry see the two articles by H. Eichberg, 'Geometrie als barocke Verhaltensnorm. Fortifikation und Exerzitien', *Zeitschrift für Historische Forschung*, 4 (1977), 17–50, and his 'Ordnen, messen, disziplinieren. Moderner Herrschaftsstaat und Fortifikation', in J. Kunisch (ed.), *Staatsverfassung*

und Heeresverfassung in der europäische Geschichte der frühen Neuzeit (Berlin, 1986), pp. 347–75.

37 Duindam, *Myths of power*, pp. 134–5.
38 For Becher, see P.H. Smith, *The business of alchemy. Science and culture in the Holy Roman Empire* (Princeton, 1994), pp. 106–9, 126–40. For France see O. Ranum, 'Courtesy, absolutism and the rise of the French state 1630–60', *Journal of Modern History*, 52 (1980), 426–51.
39 W.H. McNeill, *Keeping together in time. Dance and drill in human history* (Cambridge, Mass., 1995), pp. 132–4; R. Wohlfeil, 'Ritter – Söldnerführer – Offizier. Versuch eines Vergleiches', in J. Bärmann (ed.), *Geschichtliche Landeskunde*, vol. 3 (Wiesbaden, 1966), pp. 45–70; K. Demeter, *The German officer corps in society and state 1650–1945* (London, 1965), pp. 116–55.
40 Gawthrop, *Pietism*, pp. 230–46; Willems, *Way of life and death*, p. 17.
41 Sagarra, *Social history of Germany*, p. 36.
42 Duindam, *Myths of power*, pp. 126–33; J.P. Spielman, *Leopold I of Austria* (London, 1977), pp. 31–6. For the difference between French and central European ceremonial, see Klingensmith, *Utility of splendor*, pp. 7–18; Duindam, 'Courts of the Austrian Habsburgs', pp. 174–8.
43 Gestrich, *Absolutismus und Öffentlichkeit*, pp. 162–6.
44 A good contemporary example of such gossip is C.L. v. Pöllnitz, *Das galante Sachsen* (Munich, 1992; first published 1734).
45 Prohibitions against duelling had to be repeated throughout the eighteenth century; see Hauptstaatsarchiv Stuttgart, A30c: Bü.3; A202: Bü.2418. For the problem generally see V.G. Kiernan, *The duel in European history. Honour and the reign of aristocracy* (Oxford, 1989).
46 Gestrich, *Absolutismus und Öffentlichkeit*, pp. 57–74, 115–17. For an example of Pietism criticism, see T. Kevorkian, 'Piety confronts politics: Philipp Jacob Spener in Dresden, 1686–1691', *German History*, 16 (1998), 145–66.
47 Ribbe (ed.), *Geschichte Berlins*, I, 376–7, 388–9; Ingrao, *Hessian mercenary state*, pp. 164–87; G. Kleemann, *Schloß Solitude bei Stuttgart* (Stuttgart, 1966).
48 Wagner-Rieger, 'Fürstlicher Schlossbau', pp. 69–70; W.H. Bruford, *Culture and society in classical Weimar 1775–1806* (Cambridge, 1962); M. Umbach, 'Visual culture, scientific images and German small-state politics in the late Enlightenment', *Past and Present*, 158 (1998), 110–45.
49 This has not been as fully explored for central Europe as for France: P. Mansel, *The court of France 1789–1830* (Cambridge, 1988).
50 R. Koselleck, *Critique and crisis. Enlightenment and the pathogenesis of modern society* (Oxford, 1988); J. Habermas, *The structural transformation of the public sphere* (Cambridge, Mass., 1989).
51 For example, Poggi, *Development of the modern state*, pp. 77–85 and D. Outram, *The Enlightenment* (Cambridge, 1995), pp. 10–12, 26 both follow Habermas explicitly.
52 A. Farge, *Subversive voices. Public opinion in eighteenth-century France* (Cambridge, 1994).
53 These criticisms are voiced in Gestrich's excellent *Absolutismus und Öffentlichkeit*, on which much of the following is based.

54 On the latter see U. Danker, 'Bandits and the state: robbers and the authorities in the Holy Roman Empire', in R.J. Evans (ed.), *The German underworld* (London, 1988), pp. 75–107.

55 P.L.H. Röder, *Geographie und Statistik Wirtembergs* (Laibach in Krain, 1787), pp. 186, 196–8; M. Erbe, *Deutsche Geschichte 1713–1790* (Stuttgart, 1985), pp. 58–9. The problems of censorship are exemplified in P.S. Spalding, *Seize the book, jail the author. Johann Lorenz Schmidt and censorship in eighteenth-century Germany* (West Lafayette, 1998).

56 P.H. Wilson, 'Violence and the rejection of authority in eighteenth-century Germany: the case of the Swabian mutinies in 1757', *German History*, 12 (1994), 1–26. For subculture see C. Küther, *Räuber und Gauner in Deutschland. Das organisierte Bandenwesen im 18. und 19. Jahrhundert* (2nd edn, Göttingen, 1987). For the itinerants see the literature cited in n. 116 below.

57 For examples see the songs commenting on Prussian military service in J. Kloosterhuis (ed.), *Bauern, Bürger und Soldaten. Quellen zur Sozilaisation des Militärsystems im preußischen Westfalen 1713–1803* (2 vols, Münster, 1992), I, 593–9.

58 Frederick II, *Anti-Machiavel*, p. 112.

59 See the two articles by F.L. Carsten, 'The Great Elector and the foundation of Hohenzollern despotism', *English Historical Review*, 65 (1950), 175–202 and 'The resistance of Cleves and Mark to the despotic policy of the Great Elector', *English Historical Review*, 66 (1951), 219–41. For a general introduction to early modern estates see A.R. Myers, *Parliaments and estates in Europe to 1789* (London, 1975). For central Europe see V. Press, 'The system of estates in the Austrian Hereditary Lands and in the Holy Roman Empire', in R.J.W. Evans and T.V. Thomas (eds), *Crown, Church and estates* (New York, 1991), pp. 1–22.

60 Ertman, *Birth of the Leviathan*, pp. 20–5, 267–78, 285–92, 300–3; O. Subeltny, *Domination of eastern Europe. Native nobilities and foreign absolutism 1500–1715* (Gloucester, 1986).

61 F.L. Carsten, 'The causes of the decline of the German estates', reprinted in his *Essays in German history* (London, 1985), pp. 119–26. See also his *Princes and parliaments*.

62 Good coverage in D. Gerhard (ed.), *Ständische Vertretungen im 17. und 18. Jahrhundert* (Göttingen, 1969). See also P. Baumgart (ed.), *Ständetum und Staatsbildung in Brandenburg-Preußen* (Berlin, 1983) and W. Grube, *Der Stuttgarter Landtag 1457–1957. Von den Landständen zum demokratischen Parlament* (Stuttgart, 1957).

63 M. Hughes, *Law and politics in 18th-century Germany. The Imperial Aulic Council in the reign of Charles VI* (Woodbridge, 1988); G. Haug-Moritz, *Württembergischer Ständekonflikt und deutscher Dualismus* (Stuttgart, 1992); Asch, 'Estates and princes after 1648'.

64 P. Blickle, *Obedient Germans? A rebuttal. A new view of German history* (Charlottesville, 1997; German original 1981). For a critical overview of Blickle's work, see R.W. Scribner, 'Communalism: universal category or ideological construct?', *Historical Journal*, 37 (1994), 199–207.

65 Blickle, *Obedient Germans?*, pp. 40–58.

66 P. Blickle, *The revolution of 1525. The German Peasants War from a new perspective* (Baltimore, 1981).

67 Blickle, *Obedient Germans?*, pp. 25–32, 59–60, 78–9, 94–100.
68 Statistics from P.-C. Hartmann, *Geld als Instrument europäischer Macht-politikim Zeitalter des Merkantilismus 1715–1740* (Munich, 1978), p. 63. Blickle attempted to clarify the link in his 'Kommunalism, Parliamentarismus, Republikanismus', *Historische Zeitschrift*, 242 (1986), 529–56 where he disputes the assumption made by other historians after the 1960s that the territorial estates (*Stände*) were forerunners of later parliaments because this placed the origins of modern democracy in institutions dominated by nobles and high clerics. Instead, Blickle argues that only those estates he terms *Landstände* or *Landschaften*, where the 'common man' was represented, had the potential to develop towards parliamentary democracy or even republicanism, because popular participation transformed them along communal lines. However, his evidence comes almost exclusively from Switzerland rather than territories remaining part of the Reich.
69 H. Gabel and W. Schulze, 'Peasant resistance and politicization in Germany in the eighteenth century', in E. Hellmuth (ed.), *The transformation of political culture* (Oxford, 1990), pp. 119–46 at 141–5.
70 B. Kappelhoff, *Absolutisches Regiment oder Ständeherrschaft? Landesherr und Landstände in Ostfriesland im ersten Drittel des 18. Jahrhunderts* (Hildesheim, 1982); Wick, *Versuche zur Errichtung des Absolutismus*, Hughes, *Law and politics*.
71 R. Scribner, 'Communities and the nature of power', in Scribner (ed.), *Germany. A new social and economic history*, pp. 291–326; M. Walker, *German home towns. Community, state and general estate 1648–1871* (Ithaca, 1971).
72 D. Sabean, 'The communal basis of pre-1800 peasant uprisings in western Europe', *Comparative Politics*, 8 (1975/76), 355–64; Y.-M. Bercé, *Revolt and revolution in early modern Europe* (Manchester, 1987); C.R. Friedrichs, 'Urban politics and urban social structures in seventeenth-century Germany', *European History Quarterly*, 22 (1992), 187–216 and his 'Urban conflicts and the imperial constitution in seventeenth-century Germany', *Journal of Modern History*, 58 (1986), supplement 98–123.
73 Blickle, *Obedient Germans?*, pp. 27–32, 92–3.
74 L. Enders, 'Die Landgemeinde in Brandenburg. Grundzüge ihre Funktion und Wirkungsweise vom 13. bis zum 18. Jahrhundert', *Blätter deutscher Landesgeschichte*, 129 NF (1993), 195–256; Hagen, 'Village life in East-Elbian Germany', pp. 160–82.
75 Scribner, 'Communities and the nature of power', pp. 293–4; T. Barnett-Robisheaux, 'Peasant revolts in Germany and central Europe after the Peasants War', *Central European History*, 17 (1984), 384–403 at 393.
76 For example, Ertman, *Birth of the Leviathan*, pp. 224–42.
77 See the contributions by K. Benda and S. Vilfan in Evans and Thomas (eds), *Crown, Church and estates*. For further arguments stressing bargaining with corporate groups as a significant factor in state formation, see most recently S. Ogilvie, 'The state in Germany. A non-Prussian view', in J. Brewer and E. Hellmuth (eds), *Rethinking Leviathan. The eighteenth-century state in Britain and Germany* (Oxford, 1999), pp. 167–202.
78 Dreitzel, *Absolutismus und ständische Verfassung*, pp. 100–23.

79 B. Wunder, *Geschichte der Bürokratie in Deutschland* (Frankfurt/M., 1986), p. 7.

80 H. Jacoby, *The bureaucratization of the world* (Berkeley, 1976), pp. 20–35; E. Kamencka, *Bureaucracy* (Oxford, 1989), pp. 76–118.

81 H. Duchhardt, *Deutsche Verfassungsgeschichte 1495–1806* (Stuttgart, 1991), pp. 180–90; W. Doyle, *The old European order 1660–1800* (2nd edn, Oxford, 1992), pp. 254–5.

82 R. Braun, 'Taxation, sociopolitical structure and state-building: Britain and Brandenburg-Prussia', in C. Tilly (ed.), *The formation of national states in western Europe* (Princeton, 1975), pp. 243–327 at 268; Ertman, *Birth of the Leviathan*, pp. 245–62; Downing, *Military revolution and political change*, pp. 9–12, 84–112.

83 For the latter view see H. Rosenberg, *Bureaucracy, aristocracy and autocracy. The Prussian experience 1660–1815* (Cambridge, Mass., 1966).

84 J.S. Wheeler, *The making of a world power. War and the military revolution in seventeenth-century England* (Stroud, 1999); J. Brewer, *The sinews of power. War, money and the English state 1688–1783* (New York, 1989); M.C. t'Hart, *The making of a bourgeois state. War, politics and finance during the Dutch revolt* (Manchester, 1993); P.T. Hoffman and K. Norberg (eds), *Fiscal crises, liberty and representative government* (Stanford, 1994).

85 H.C. Johnson, *Frederick the Great and his officials* (New Haven, 1975).

86 B. Simms, *The impact of Napoleon. Prussian high politics, foreign policy and the crisis of the executive 1797–1806* (Cambridge, 1997).

87 Mann, *Sources of social power*, II, 446; M. Weber, *Economy and society* (2 vols, Berkeley, 1978), I, 220–1. The relevance of Weber's theory to Prussia is discussed further by R. Vierhaus, 'The Prussian bureaucracy reconsidered', in Brewer and Hellmuth (eds), *Rethinking Leviathan*, pp. 149–65.

88 B. Wunder, *Privilegierung und Disziplinierung. Die Entstehung des Berufsbeamtentums in Bayern und Württemberg, 1780–1825* (Munich, 1978).

89 The term 'fiscal–military state' comes from Brewer, *Sinews of power*. For overviews of war and military developments in this period see J. Black, *European warfare 1660–1815* (London, 1994); J. Black (ed.), *European warfare 1453–1815* (London, 1999); F. Tallett, *War and society in early modern Europe 1495–1715* (London, 1992).

90 V.G. Kiernan, 'Foreign mercenaries and absolute monarchy', *Past and Present*, 11 (1957), 66–86; O. Rocholl, 'Das stehende Heer als Stütze der feudalen Reaktion', *Wissenschaftliche Zeitschrift der Karl-Marx-Universität Leipzig, Gesellschafts- und Staatswissenschaftliche Reihe*, 1 (1952/53), 499–510; Mooers, *Making of bourgeois Europe*, pp. 114–20. For royal guards see P. Mansel, *Pillars of monarchy. An overview of the political and social history of royal guards 1400–1984* (London, 1984).

91 O. Schuster and F.A. Francke, *Geschichte der sächsische Armee* (3 vols, Leipzig, 1885), I, 121–2; C. Jany, *Geschichte der Preußischen Armee vom 15. Jahrhundert bis 1914* (4 vols, Osnabrück, 1967), I, 296–8; A. v. Wrede, *Geschichte der kaiserlichen und königlichen Wehrmacht von 1618 bis zum Ende des XIX. Jahrhunderts* (5 vols, Vienna, 1898–1905). Though the Saxon units had French titles, many of their personnel were probably Germans.

92 H. Meier-Welcker, *Deutsches Heerwesen im Wandel der Zeit* (Frankfurt/ M., 1956); C.H. Hermann, *Deutsche Militärgeschichte* (2nd edn, Frankfurt/M., 1968); M. Kitchen, *A military history of Germany from the eighteenth century to the present day* (London, 1975).

93 O. Büsch, *Military system and social life in old regime Prussia 1713–1807. The beginnings of the social militarisation of Prusso-German society* (Atlantic Highlands, 1997; German original 1962). For an extended critique of this theory see P.H. Wilson, 'Social militarisation in eighteenth-century Germany', *German History*, 18, 1 (2000), 1–39.

94 For this latter point see M. Sikora, *Disziplin und Desertion. Strukturprobleme militärischer Organisation im 18. Jahrhundert* (Berlin, 1996). For recent revisionist work on early modern German armies see B.R. Kroener and R. Pröve (eds), *Krieg und Frieden. Militär und Gesellschaft in der frühen Neuzeit* (Paderborn, 1996); R. Pröve, *Stehendes Heer und städtische Gesellschaft im 18. Jahrhundert. Göttingen und seine Militärbevölkerung 1713–1756* (Munich, 1995); R. Pröve (ed.), *Klio in Uniform? Probleme und Perspektiven einer modernen Militärgeschichte der frühen Neuzeit* (Cologne, 1997).

95 Wilson, *War, state and society*, pp. 228–31; M. Hughes, 'Die Strafpreussen. Mecklenburg und der Bund der deutschen absolutistischen Fürsten, 1648–1719', *Parliaments, Estates and Representation*, 3 (1983), 101–13; W. Trossbach, 'Fürstenabsetzung im 18. Jahrhundert', *Zeitschrift für Historische Forschung*, 13 (1986), 425–54.

96 W. Kohl, *Christoph Bernhard von Galen. Politische Geschichte des Fürstbistums Münster 1650–1678* (Münster, 1964); W. Frhr. v. Tettau, 'Erfurts Unterwerfung unter die Mainzische Landeshoheit', *Neujahrsblätter herausgegeben von der Historischen Kommission der Provinz Sachsen*, 11 (1887), 3–56; H. Querfurth, *Die Unterwerfung der Stadt Braunschweig im Jahre 1671* (Braunschweig, 1953); R. van Dülmen, 'Bäuerlicher Protest und patriotische Bewegung. Der Volksaufstand in Bayern 1705/6', *Zeitschrift für Bayerische Landesgeschichte*, 45 (1982), 331–61.

97 F. Theuer, *Brennendes Land. Kuruzzenkriege* (Vienna, 1984); A. Várkonyi, 'Rákóczi's war of independence and the peasantry', in J.M. Bak and B.K. Kiraly (eds), *From Hunyadi to Rákóczi* (New York, 1982), pp. 369–91; Ingrao, *In quest and crisis*, pp. 126–60.

98 For the size of German armies see Wilson, *German armies*, pp. 26–32, 92–4, 108–11, 162, and P.H. Wilson, 'Warfare in the old regime', in Black (ed.), *European warfare*, pp. 69–95 at 80 (Table 3.1).

99 In addition to the literature cited in n. 84 above, see P.-C. Hartmann, *Das Steuersystem der europäischen Staaten am Ende des Ancien Régime* (Munich, 1979); H.V. Bowen, *War and British society 1688–1815* (Cambridge, 1998).

100 Anderson, *Lineages*, pp. 29–33, 57–9; Schnitter and Schmidt, *Absolutismus und Heer*, pp. 29–30; J.A. Schumpeter, *Imperialism and social classes* (New York, 1951).

101 J. Kunisch, *Staatsverfassung und Mächtekonflikt. Zur Genese von Staatenkonflikten im Zeitalter des Absolutismus* (Berlin, 1979).

102 Quotation from M. Howard, *The causes of war and other essays* (Oxford, 1983), p. 13. Fuller discussion in P.H. Wilson, 'War in German thought from the Peace of Westphalia to Napoleon', *European History Quarterly*,

28 (1998), 5–50. The Silesian Wars and Seven Years War are reappraised in Wilson, *German armies*, pp. 247–80, and D.E. Showalter, *The wars of Frederick the Great* (Harlow, 1996).

103 U. Müller-Weil, *Absolutismus und Aussenpolitik in Preußen* (Stuttgart, 1992); H.M. Scott, 'Prussia's royal foreign minister: Frederick the Great and the administration of Prussian diplomacy', in R. Oresko *et al.* (eds), *Royal and republican sovereignty in early modern Europe* (Cambridge, 1997), pp. 500–26.

104 For example, G. Ortenburg (ed.), *Heerwesen der Neuzeit* (10 vols, Koblenz, 1984–93), III, *Das Zeitalter des Kabinettskriege*.

105 Wilson, *German armies*, pp. 331–40.

106 Oestreich, *Neostoicism*; W. Schulze, 'Gerhard Oestreichs Begriff "Sozial Disziplinierung in der frühen Neuzeit"', *Zeitschrift für Historische Forschung*, 14 (1987), 265–302; S. Breuer, 'Sozialdisziplinierung. Probleme und Problemverlagerungen eines Konzepts bei Max Weber, Gerhard Oestreich und Michel Foucault', in C. Sachße and F. Tennstedt (eds), *Soziale Sicherheit und soziale Disziplinierung* (Frankfurt/M., 1986), pp. 45–69.

107 The impact of drill is discussed by G.E. Rothenberg, 'Maurice of Nassau, Gustavus Adolphus, Montecuccoli and the "military revolution"', in P. Paret (ed.), *The makers of modern strategy* (Princeton, 1986), pp. 32–63.

108 R. Po-Chia Hsia, *Social discipline in the Reformation. Central Europe 1550–1750* (London, 1989).

109 M. Foucault, *Discipline and punish. The birth of the prison* (London, 1977).

110 Breuer, 'Sozialdisziplinierung', pp. 56–62; K. Vocelka, 'Public opinion and the phenomenon of *Sozialdisziplinierung* in the Habsburg monarchy', in Ingrao (ed.), *State and society*, pp. 119–38.

111 See the critique in Burke, 'Civilisation, discipline and disorder', pp. 23–8.

112 This is a charge levelled at Marc Raeff's *Well ordered police state* by J. Van Horn Melton, 'Absolutism and "modernity" in early modern central Europe', *German Studies Review*, 8 (1985), 383–98.

113 For example, R.A. Dorwart, *The Prussian welfare state before 1740* (Cambridge, Mass., 1971).

114 W. v. Hippel, *Armut, Unterschichten Randgruppen in der frühen Neuzeit* (Munich, 1995), p. 51; P. Nitschke, *Verbrechensbekämpfung und Verwaltung. Die Entstehung der Polizei in der Grafschaft Lippe 1700–1814* (Münster, 1990).

115 There is an informative discussion of this point in O. Ulbricht, 'The world of a beggar around 1775: Johann Gottfried Kästner', *Central European History*, 27 (1994), 153–84.

116 C. Küther, *Menschen auf der Straße. Vagierende Unterschichten in Bayern, Franken und Schwaben in der zweiten Hälfte des 18. Jahrhunderts* (Göttingen, 1983) and his *Räuber und Gauner in Deutschland*; E. Schubert, *Arme Leute, Bettler und Gauner im Franken des 18. Jahrhunderts* (Neustadt an der Aisch, 1983).

117 Introductions to the considerable literature on popular protest are provided by T. Scott, 'Peasant revolts in early modern Germany', *Historical Journal*, 28 (1985), 455–68, and Barnett-Robisheaux, 'Peasant revolts'. For specific examples see W.W. Hagen, 'The Junkers' faithless servants: peasant insubordination and the breakdown of serfdom in Brandenburg-

Prussia 1763–1811', in R.J. Evans and W.R. Lee (eds), *The German peasantry* (London, 1986), pp. 77–86.

118 For examples see W. Schulze, *Bäuerlicher Widerstand und feudale Herrschaft in der frühen Neuzeit* (Stuttgart, 1980); H. Gabel, *Widerstand und Kooperation. Studien zur politischen Kultur rheinischer und maasländischer Kleinterritorien (1648–1794)* (Tübingen, 1995), and his '"Äußerliche Verfolgung und innerliche Rebellion". Zur Ermordung des Abtes von Korneleimünster am 18. Juli 1699', *Zeitschrift des Aachener Geschichts Vereins*, 93 (1986), 87–126.

119 H. Rebel, 'Reimagining the *oikos*. Austrian cameralism in its social formation', in J. O'Brien and W. Roseberry (eds), *Golden ages, dark ages: reimagining the past* (Berkeley, 1991), pp. 48–80 at 55–61. See also his *Peasant classes. The bureaucratization of property and family relations under early Habsburg administration 1511–1636* (Princeton, 1983) and 'Peasantries under the Austrian empire, 1300–1800', in Scott (ed.), *Peasantries of Europe*, pp. 191–225.

120 Blickle, *Obedient Germans?*, pp. 21–5; Dipper, *Deutsche Geschichte*, pp. 21–41.

121 T. Robisheaux, *Rural society and the search for order in early modern Germany* (Cambridge, 1989); K. Wegert, *Popular culture, crime and social control in 18th century Württemberg* (Stuttgart, 1994).

122 Ingrao, *In quest and crisis*, pp. 10–15. See, generally, H.M. Scott, 'The rise of the first minister in eighteenth-century Europe', in T.C.W. Blanning and D. Cannadine (eds), *History and biography. Essays in honour of Derek Beales* (Cambridge, 1996), pp. 21–52; L.W.B. Brockliss and J.H. Elliott (eds), *The world of the favourite* (New Haven, 1999).

123 W. Jannen Jr, '"Das Liebe Teutschland" in the 17th century – Count George Frederick von Waldeck', *European Studies Review*, 6 (1979), 165–95.

124 Duindam, *Myths of power*, pp. 90–2, 126–34 especially stresses the role of personality.

4 Enlightened absolutism

1 Koser, 'Epochen der absoluten Monarchie'. For general overviews of the literature see Scott, *Enlightened absolutism*, pp. 7–12; Kunisch, *Absolutismus*, pp. 188–93.

2 Hartung, 'Aufgeklärter Absolutismus', p. 35.

3 Outram, *The Enlightenment*, pp. 1–15; J. Hardman, *French politics 1774–1789* (Harlow, 1995). This is not to argue that the later Bourbon monarchy was devoid of reforming impulses, or that these did not prefigure many of those associated with the revolution. Further discussion is provided by P.M. Jones, *Reform and revolution in France. The politics of transition, 1774–1791* (Cambridge, 1995).

4 C. Scharf, *Katharina II., Deutschland und die Deutschen* (Mainz, 1995).

5 Cited by Dreitzel, *Absolutismus und ständische Verfassung*, p. 111.

6 Views expressed by Epstein, *Genesis of German conservatism*, pp. 254–5, and Durchhardt, *Verfassungsgeschichte*, p. 214.

7 Sophisticated examples of this view are provided by I. Mittenzwei, *Friedrich II. Von Preußen* (3rd edn, Cologne, 1983), esp. p. 35, and I. Mittenzwei and

E. Herzfeld, *Brandenburg-Preußen 1648–1789* (Cologne, 1987), pp. 350–406. Dorpalen, *German history in Marxist perspective*, pp. 159–65, gives a good overview of this interpretation.

8 Epstein, *Genesis of German conservatism*, pp. 265–76.

9 H.U. Wehler, *Deutsche Gesellschaftsgeschichte* (3 vols, Munich, 1987–95). Wehler's ideas are endorsed in Dipper, *Deutsche Geschichte*, pp. 237–42, 310–14. They have much in common with the influential work of Barrington Moore, *The social origins of dictatorship and democracy* (Boston, 1966), esp. pp. 432–55.

10 Cited in Hartung, 'Aufgeklärter Absolutismus', p. 41.

11 D. Beales, 'The false Joseph II', *Historical Journal*, 18 (1975), 467–95; M.S. Anderson, *Europe in the eighteenth century 1713–1783* (1st edn, London, 1961), pp. 121–9; C.B.A. Behrens, 'Enlightened absolutism', *Historical Journal*, 18 (1975), 401–8 at 402.

12 Important monographs included T.C.W. Blanning, *Reform and revolution in Mainz 1743–1803* (Cambridge, 1974) and K.O. Frhr. v. Aretin (ed.), *Der aufgeklärte Absolutismus* (Cologne, 1974). Those who changed their views included C.B.A. Behrens, *Society, government and the enlightenment. The experiences of eighteenth-century France and Prussia* (London, 1985), p. 178, and M.S. Anderson, *Europe in the eighteenth century 1713–1783* (3rd edn, London, 1987), pp. 206–7.

13 Scott (ed.), *Enlightened absolutism*, p. 12; Outram, *The Enlightenment*, p. 101.

14 S.C. Brown, *Benjamin Thompson, Count Rumford* (Cambridge, Mass., 1979).

15 See D. Beales, 'Social forces and enlightened policies', in Scott (ed.), *Enlightened absolutism*, pp. 37–54 at 52, and T.C.W. Blanning, 'Frederick the Great and enlightened absolutism', in ibid., pp. 265–88 at 285–6.

16 Quoted in W. Kohl (ed.), *Westfälische Geschichte*, vol. 1 (Düsseldorf, 1983), pp. 620–1.

17 P. Mansel, 'Monarchy, uniform and the rise of the *frac*', *Past and Present*, 96 (1982), 103–32 at 111.

18 B. Holl, *Hofkammerpräsident Gundaker Thomas Graf Starhemberg und die österreichische Finanzpolitik der Barockzeit (1703–1715)* (Vienna, 1976); J.W. Stoye, 'Emperor Charles VI: the early years of the reign', *Transactions of the Royal Historical Society*, 5th series, 12 (1962), 63–84. For works stressing the military and international imperative behind the reforms see M. Hochedlinger, ' "Bella gerant alii . . ." '? On the state of early modern military history in Austria', *Austrian History Yearbook*, 30 (1999), 237–77.

19 On the latter point see J. Burkhardt, 'Geschichte als Argument in der habsburgisch–französischen Diplomatie', in R. Babel (ed.), *Frankreich im europäischen Staatensystem der frühen Neuzeit* (Sigmaringen, 1995), pp. 191–217.

20 K.O. Frhr. v. Aretin, *Das alte Reich 1648–1806* (3 vols, Stuttgart, 1993–7), I and II.

21 Here I follow F.A.J. Szabo, *Kaunitz and enlightened absolutism 1753–1780* (Cambridge, 1994), esp. pp. 210–57, 347–8.

22 J. Bérenger, *A history of the Habsburg empire 1700–1918* (Harlow, 1997), p. 64.

23 See Szabo, *Kaunitz*, pp. 74–7.

24 E. Bruckmüller, 'Die Habsburgische Monarchie im Zeitalter des Prinzen Eugen zwischen 1683 und 1740', in Zöllner and Gutkas (eds), *Österreich und die Osmanen*, pp. 88–119 at 113.

25 For differing perspectives see D. Beales, *Joseph II in the shadow of Maria Theresa* (Cambridge, 1987); T.C.W. Blanning, *Joseph II* (London, 1994); S.K. Padover, *The revolutionary emperor. Joseph the second 1741–1790* (London, 1938).

26 Overviews in W. Hubatsch, *Frederick the Great. Absolutism and administration* (London, 1975), pp. 148–89; T. Schieder, *Friedrich der Grosse* (Berlin, 1987), pp. 331–40, now available in a fine English translation edited by H.M. Scott, *Frederick the Great* (Harlow, 1999).

27 Aretin summarises his view in his *Das Reich. Friedensordnung und europäische Gleichgewicht 1648–1806* (Stuttgart, 1992), pp. 12–16, 36–8.

28 Hartung, 'Aufgeklärter Absolutismus', pp. 31–5.

29 C. Ingrao, 'The smaller German states', in Scott (ed.), *Enlightened absolutism*, pp. 221–43 and his *Hessian mercenary state*. See also M. Hughes, *Early modern Germany 1477–1806* (London, 1992), p. 149.

30 Ingrao, 'Smaller German states', p. 223.

31 For examples see P.K. Taylor, *Indentured to liberty. Peasant life and the Hessian military state 1688–1815* (Ithaca, 1994), and V. Müller, 'Das alte wiedische Militärwesen', *Heimatkalender des Landkreises Neuwied* (1970), 41–4.

32 For the Catholic Enlightenment see Blanning, *Reform and revolution in Mainz*; K.O. Frhr. v. Aretin, *Heiliges Römisches Reich 1776–1806* (2 vols, Wiesbaden, 1967), I, 38–43, 375–452. For Wörlitz, see Umbach, 'Visual culture'.

33 F.W. Schaer, 'Der Absolutismus in Lippe und Schaumburg-Lippe', *Lippische Mitteilungen*, 37 (1968), 154–99.

34 W. Trossbach, 'Widerstand als Normalfall: Bauernunruhen in der Grafschaft Sayn-Wittgenstein-Wittgenstein 1696–1806', *Westfälische Zeitschrift*, 135 (1985), 25–111.

35 S. Mörz, *Aufgeklärter Absolutismus in der Kurpfalz während der Mannheimer Regierungszeit des Kurfürsten Karl Theodor (1742–1777)* (Stuttgart, 1991); Bruford, *Culture and society in classical Weimar*; R. Uhland, *Geschichte der Hohen Karlsschule in Stuttgart* (Stuttgart, 1953); A. Kuhn et al., *Revolutionsbegeisterung an der Hohen Carlsschule* (Stuttgart, 1989).

36 T.C.W. Blanning, 'The French Revolution and the modernization of Germany', *Central European History*, 22 (1989), 109–29; J. Gagliardo, *Reich and nation. The Holy Roman Empire as idea and reality 1763–1806* (Bloomington, 1980), pp. 49–140; Whitman, *Legacy of Roman law*, pp. 66–91.

37 Koselleck, *Critique and crisis*.

38 J. Lukowski, *The partitions of Poland. 1772, 1793, 1795* (Harlow, 1999).

39 J.-P. Lavandier, *Le livre au temps de Joseph II et de Leopold II* (Bern, 1995); P.P. Bernard, *From the Enlightenment to the police state. The public life of Johann Anton Pergen* (Urbana, 1991); K.A. Roider Jr, *Baron Thugut and Austria's response to the French Revolution* (Princeton, 1987).

40 Dipper, *Deutsche Geschichte*, pp. 310–12; Durchhardt, *Deutsche Verfassungsgeschichte*, p. 242.

41 L. Gall, *Von der ständischen zur bürgerlichen Gesellschaft* (Munich, 1993);
    O. Büsch and M. Neugebauer-Wölk (eds), *Preussen und die revolutionäre
    Herausforderung seit 1789* (Berlin, 1989).
42 For good overviews of this transition see T. Nipperdey, *Deutsche Geschichte
    1800–1866. Bürgerwelt und starker Staat* (Munich, 1983), and J.J. Sheehan,
    German history 1770–1866 (Oxford, 1989).

5 Conclusions

1 Henshall, 'Early modern absolutism', p. 52.
2 G. Durand, 'What is absolutism?', in Hatton (ed), *Louis XIV and absolutism*,
    pp. 18–34 at 18–19, 21. See also Parker, *Making of French absolutism*, p. xvi,
    and Vincent, *Theories of the state*, p. 47.

Select bibliography

Adamson, J. (ed.), *The princely courts of Europe. Ritual, politics and culture under the Ancien Régime 1500–1750* (London, 1999).

Albrecht, D., *Maximilian I. Von Bayern 1573–1651* (Munich, 1998).

Althusius, J., *Politica* (transl. and ed. F.S. Carney, Indianapolis, 1995).

Anderson, J. and S. Hall, 'Absolutism and other ancestors', in J. Anderson (ed.), *The rise of the modern state* (Brighton, 1986), pp. 21–40.

Anderson, M.S., *Europe in the eighteenth century* (1st edn, London, 1961, and 3rd edn, 1987).

Anderson, P. *Lineages of the absolutist state* (London, 1974).

—— *Passages from antiquity to feudalism* (London, 1974).

Aretin, K.O. Frhr. v., *Das alte Reich 1648–1806* (3 vols, Stuttgart, 1993–7).

—— *Das Reich. Friedensordnung und europäische Gleichgewicht 1648–1806* (Stuttgart, 1992).

—— *Heiliges Römisches Reich 1776–1806* (2 vols, Wiesbaden, 1967).

—— (ed.), *Der aufgeklärte Absolutismus* (Cologne, 1974).

Arnold, B., *Medieval Germany, 500–1300* (Basingstoke, 1997).

—— *Princes and territories in medieval Germany* (Cambridge, 1991).

Asch, R.G., 'Estates and princes after 1648: the consequences of the Thirty Years War', *German History*, 6 (1988), 113–32.

—— *The Thirty Years War: the Holy Roman Empire and Europe, 1618–1648* (London, 1997).

—— and A.M. Birke (eds), *Princes, patronage and the nobility* (Oxford, 1991).

—— and H. Duchhardt (eds), *Der Absolutismus – ein Mythos? Strukturwandel monarchischer Herrschaft* (Cologne, 1996).

Aston, T.H. and C.H.E. Philpin (eds), *The Brenner debate* (Cambridge, 1985).

Barnett-Robisheaux, T., 'Peasant revolts in Germany and central Europe after the Peasants War', *Central European History*, 17 (1984), 384–403.

Bauer, V., *Die höfische Gesellschaft in Deutschland von der Mitte des 17. bis zum Ausgang des 18. Jahrhunderts* (Tübingen, 1993).

Baumgart, P. (ed.), *Ständetum und Staatsbildung in Brandenburg-Preußen* (Berlin, 1983).

Beales, D., *Joseph II in the shadow of Maria Theresa* (Cambridge, 1987).

Beales, D., 'The false Joseph II', *Historical Journal*, 18 (1975), 467–95.

Behrens, C.B.A., 'Enlightened absolutism', *Historical Journal*, 18 (1975), 401–8.

—— *Society, government and the Enlightenment. The experiences of eighteenth-century France and Prussia* (London, 1985).

Beller, S., *Francis Joseph* (London, 1996).

Belschner, C., *Ludwigsburg im Wechsel der Zeiten* (3rd edn, Ludwigsburg, 1969).

Berbig, H.J., 'Der Krönungsritus im alten Reich (1648–1806)', *Zeitschrift für Bayerische Landesgeschichte*, 38 (1975), 639–700.

Bercé, Y.-M., *Revolt and revolution in early modern Europe* (Manchester, 1987).

Bérenger, J., *A history of the Habsburg monarchy 1273–1918* (2 vols, London, 1994–7).

Bernard, P.P., *From the Enlightenment to the police state. The public life of Johann Anton Pergen* (Urbana, 1991).

Bireley, R., 'Antimachiavellianism, the baroque and Maximilian of Bavaria', *Archivum Historicum Societatis Jesu*, 103 (1984), 137–59.

Black, J., *European warfare 1660–1815* (London, 1994).

—— (ed), *European warfare 1453–1815* (London, 1999).

Blanning, T.C.W., *Joseph II* (London, 1994).

—— *Reform and revolution in Mainz 1743–1803* (Cambridge, 1974).

—— 'The French Revolution and the modernization of Germany', *Central European History*, 22 (1989), 109–29.

Blickle, P., 'Kommunalismus, Parliamentarismus, Republikanismus', *Historische Zeitschrift*, 242 (1986), 529–56.

—— *Obedient Germans? A rebuttal. A new view of German history* (Charlottesville, 1997).

Bodin, J., *On sovereignty* (ed. J.H. Franklin, Cambridge, 1992; first published 1576).

Boldt, H., *Deutsche Verfassungsgeschichte*, vol. I (3rd edn, Munich, 1994).

Borovczény, A., *Graf von Brühl* (Zürich, 1930).

Bosbach, F., *Monarchia universalis. Ein politischer Leitbegriff der frühen Neuzeit* (Göttingen, 1988).

Bossuet, J.-B., *Politics drawn from the very words of Holy Scripture* (Cambridge, 1990; first published 1709).

Breuer, S., 'Sozialdisziplinierung. Probleme und Problemverlagerung eines Konzepts bei Max Weber, Gerhard Oestreich und Michel Foucault', in C. Sachße and F. Tennstedt (eds), *Soziale Sicherheit und soziale Disziplinierung* (Frankfurt/M., 1986), pp. 45–69.

Brewer, J., *The sinews of power. War, money and the English state 1688–1783* (New York, 1989).

—— and E. Hellmuth (eds), *Rethinking Leviathan. The eighteenth-century state in Britain and Germany* (Oxford, 1999).

Brockliss, L.W.B. and J.H. Elliott (eds), *The world of the favourite* (New Haven, 1999).

Brown, S.C., *Benjamin Thompson, Count Rumford* (Cambridge, Mass., 1979).
Bruford, W.H., *Culture and society in classical Weimar 1775–1806* (Cambridge, 1962).
—— *Germany in the eighteenth century* (Cambridge, 1935).
Buelow, G.L. (ed.), *The late baroque era from the 1680s to 1740* (Basingstoke, 1993).
Burke, P. 'Civilisation, discipline, disorder. Three case studies in history and social theory', *Theoria* (June 1996), 21–35.
—— *The fabrication of Louis XIV* (New Haven, 1992).
Büsch, O., *Military system and social life in old regime Prussia 1713–1807. The beginnings of the social militarisation of Prusso-German society* (Atlantic Highlands, 1997; German original 1962).
—— and M. Neugebauer-Wölk (eds), *Preussen und die revolutionäre Herausforderung seit 1789* (Berlin, 1989).
Callinicos, A., *Theories and narratives. Reflections on the philosophy of history* (Cambridge, 1995).
Carsten, F.L., *Essays in German history* (London, 1985).
—— *Princes and parliaments in Germany from the fifteenth to the eighteenth century* (Oxford, 1959).
—— 'The Great Elector and the foundation of Hohenzollern despotism', *English Historical Review*, 65 (1950), 175–202.
—— *The origins of Prussia* (Oxford, 1954).
—— 'The resistance of Cleves and Mark to the despotic policy of the Great Elector', *English Historical Review*, 66 (1951), 219–41.
Church, W.F. (ed.), *The greatness of Louis XIV. Myth or reality?* (Lexington, 1959).
Collins, J.B., *Fiscal limits of absolutism: direct taxation in seventeenth-century France* (Berkeley, 1988).
—— *The state in early modern France* (Cambridge, 1995).
Corvisier, A., *Armies and societies in Europe 1494–1789* (Bloomington, 1979).
Czok, K., *Am Hofe Augusts des Starken* (Stuttgart, 1990).
Danker, U., 'Bandits and the state: robbers and the authorities in the Holy Roman Empire', in R.J. Evans (ed.), *The German underworld* (London, 1988), pp. 75–107.
Demeter, K., *The German officer corps in society and state 1650–1945* (London, 1965; German original 1962).
Dickson, P.G.M., *Finance and government under Maria Theresia 1740–1780* (2 vols, Oxford, 1987).
Diestelkamp, B. (ed.), *Das Reichskammergericht in der deutschen Geschichte* (Cologne, 1990).
—— (ed.), *Die politische Funktion des Reichskammergerichts* (Cologne, 1993).
Dipper, C., *Deutsche Geschichte 1648–1789* (Frankfurt/M., 1991).
Dorpalen, A., *German history in Marxist perspective. The East German approach* (London, 1985).

Dorwart, R.A., *The administrative reforms of Frederick William I of Prussia* (Westport, 1953).

—— *The Prussian welfare state before 1740* (Cambridge, Mass., 1971).

Downing, B.M., *The military revolution and political change in early modern Europe* (Princeton, 1991).

Doyle, W., *Origins of the French Revolution* (2nd edn, Oxford, 1988).

Dreitzel, H., *Absolutismus und ständische Verfassung in Deutschland* (Mainz, 1992).

—— 'Ständestaat und absolute Monarchie in der politischen Theorie des Reiches in der frühen Neuzeit', in G. Schmidt (ed.), *Stände und Gesellschaft im alten Reich* (Stuttgart, 1989), pp. 19–50.

Duchhardt, H., 'Absolutismus – Abschied von einem Epochenbegriff?', *Historische Zeitschrift*, 258 (1994), 113–22.

—— *Das Zeitalter des Absolutismus* (Munich, 1989).

—— *Deutsche Verfassungsgeschichte 1495–1806* (Stuttgart, 1991).

—— *Protestantisches Kaisertum und altes Reich* (Wiesbaden, 1977).

Duindam, J., *Myths of power. Norbert Elias and the early modern European court* (Amsterdam, 1995).

Dülmen, R. van, 'Bäuerlicher Protest und patriotische Bewegung. Der Volksaufstand in Bayern 1705/6', *Zeitschrift für Bayerische Landesgeschichte*, 45 (1982), 331–61.

Eichberg, H. 'Geometrie als barocke Verhaltensnorm. Fortifikation und Exerziten', *Zeitschrift für Historische Forschung*, 4 (1977), 17–50.

Elias, N., *The civilising process* (Oxford, 1994; German original 1939).

—— *The court society* (New York, 1983; German original 1969).

Enders, L., 'Die Landgemeinde in Brandenburg. Grundzüge ihre Funktion und Wirkungsweise vom 13. bis zum 18. Jahrhundert', *Blätter deutscher Landesgeschichte*, 129 NF (1993), 195–256.

Endres, R., 'Markgraf Christian Ernst von Bayreuth', *Fränkische Lebensbilder*, 2 (1968), 260–90.

Epstein, K., *The genesis of German conservatism* (Princeton, 1966).

Erbe, M., *Deutsche Geschichte 1713–1790* (Stuttgart, 1985).

Ertman, T., *Birth of the Leviathan. Building states and regimes in medieval and early modern Europe* (Cambridge, 1997).

Evans, R.J.W., *The making of the Habsburg monarchy, 1550–1700* (Oxford, 1979).

—— and T.V. Thomas (eds), *Crown, Church and estates. Central European politics in the sixteenth and seventeenth centuries* (New York, 1991).

Fauchier-Magnan, A., *The small German courts in the eighteenth century* (London, 1958; first published Paris, 1947).

Fleischhauer, W., *Barock im Herzogtum Württemberg* (2nd edn, Stuttgart, 1981).

Foucault, M., *Discipline and punish. The birth of the prison* (London, 1977).

Frederick II, *Anti-Machiavel* (transl. and ed. P. Sonnino, Athens, 1981).

Frey, L. and M. Frey, *Frederick I. The man and his times* (New York, 1984).

Friedrichs, C.R., 'Urban conflicts and the imperial constitution in seventeenth-century Germany', *Journal of Modern History*, 58 (1986), supplement, 98–123.

—— 'Urban politics and urban social structures in seventeenth-century Germany', *European History Quarterly*, 22 (1992), 187–216.

Fulbrook, M., *Piety and politics. Religion and the rise of absolutism in England, Württemberg and Prussia* (Cambridge, 1983).

Gabel, H., *Widerstand und Kooperation. Studien zur politischen Kultur rheinischer und maasländischer Kleinterritorien (1648–1794)* (Tübingen, 1995).

—— and W. Schulze, 'Peasant resistance and politicization in Germany in the eighteenth century', in E. Hellmuth (ed.), *The transformation of political culture* (Oxford, 1990), pp. 119–46.

Gagliardo, J., *Reich and nation. The Holy Roman Empire as idea and reality 1763–1806* (Bloomington, 1980).

Gall, L., *Von der ständischen zur bürgerlichen Gesellschaft* (Munich, 1993).

Gawthrop, R.L., *Pietism and the making of eighteenth-century Prussia* (Cambridge, 1993).

Gerhard, D. (ed.), *Ständische Vertretungen im 17. und 18. Jahrhundert* (Göttingen, 1969).

Gestrich, A., *Absolutismus und Öffentlichkeit. Politische Kommunikation in Deutschland zu Beginn des 18. Jahrhunderts* (Göttingen, 1994).

Giddens, A., *The nation-state and violence* (Berkeley, 1985).

Grube, W., *Der Stuttgarter Landtag 1457–1957. Von den Landständen zum demokratischen Parlament* (Stuttgart, 1957).

Gutkas, K. (ed.), *Prinz Eugen und das barocke Österreich* (2 vols, Salzburg, 1985).

Habermas, J., *The structural transformation of the public sphere* (Cambridge, Mass., 1989).

Hagen, W.W., 'Seventeenth-century crisis in Brandenburg. The Thirty Years War, the destabilization of serfdom and the rise of absolutism', *American Historical Review*, 94 (1989), 302–35.

—— 'The Junkers' faithless servants: peasant insubordination and the breakdown of serfdom in Brandenburg-Prussia 1763–1811', in R.J. Evans and W.R. Lee (eds), *The German peasantry. Conflict and community in rural society from the eighteenth to the twentieth centuries* (London, 1986), pp. 77–86.

—— 'Working for the Junker. The standard of living of manorial labourers in Brandenburg 1584–1810', *Journal of Modern History*, 58 (1986), 143–58.

Harrington, J.F. and H.W. Smith, 'Confessionalization, community, and state building in Germany 1555–1870', *Journal of Modern History*, 69 (1997), 77–101.

Hartmann, P.-C., *Das Steuersystem der europäischen Staaten am Ende des Ancien Régime* (Munich, 1979).

—— *Karl Albrecht, Karl VII: glücklicher Kurfürst, unglücklicher Kaiser* (Regensburg, 1985).

Hartung, F., 'Der aufgeklärte Absolutismus', *Historische Zeitschrift*, 180 (1955), 15–42.

—— 'Die Epochen der absoluten Monarchie in der neueren Geschichte', *Historische Zeitschrift*, 145 (1932), 46–52.

Hatton, R. (ed.), *Louis XIV and Europe* (London, 1976).

Haug-Moritz, G., *Württembergischer Ständekonflikt und deutscher Dualismus* (Stuttgart, 1992).

Henshall, N., *The myth of absolutism. Change and continuity in early modern European monarchy* (London, 1992).

Hertz, F., 'Die Rechtssprechung im römisch-deutschen Reich und ihre politische Bedeutung', *Mitteilungen des Instituts für Österreichische Geschichtsforschung*, 69 (1961), 331–58.

Herzog Karl Eugen und seiner Zeit (issued by the Württembergischer Geschichts- und Altertumsverein, 2 vols, Esslingen, 1907–9).

Hinrichs, E., *Preussentum und Pietismus. Der Pietismus in Brandenburg-Preussen als religiös-soziale Reformbewegung* (Göttingen, 1971).

—— (ed.), *Absolutismus* (Frankfurt/M., 1986).

Hintze, O., *Die Hohenzollern und ihr Werke. Fünfhundert Jahre vaterländische Geschichte* (Berlin, 1915).

—— *The historical essays of Otto Hintze* (ed. F. Gilbert, Oxford, 1975).

Hippel, W.v., *Armut, Unterschichten, Randgruppen in der frühen Neuzeit* (Munich, 1995).

Hoffman, P.T. and K. Norberg (eds), *Fiscal crises, liberty and representative government* (Stanford, 1994).

Holl, B., *Hofkammerpräsident Gundaker Thomas Graf Starhemberg und die österreichische Finanzpolitik der Barockzeit (1703–1715)* (Vienna, 1976).

Holton, R.J., *The transition from feudalism to capitalism* (London, 1984).

Hubatsch, W., *Frederick the Great. Absolutism and administration* (London, 1975).

Hughes, M., 'Die Strafpreussen. Mecklenburg und der Bund der deutschen absolutistischen Fürsten, 1648–1719', *Parliaments, Estates and Representation*, 3 (183), 101–13.

—— *Early modern Germany 1477–1806* (London, 1992).

—— *Law and politics in 18th-century Germany. The Imperial Aulic Council in the reign of Charles VI* (Woodbridge, 1988).

Hüttl, L., *Friedrich Wilhelm von Brandenburg, der Große Kurfürst, 1620–1688* (Munich, 1981).

Ingrao, C., *In quest and crisis. Emperor Joseph I and the Habsburg monarchy* (West Lafayette, 1979).

—— *The Hessian mercenary state. Ideas, institutions and reform under Frederick II 1760–1785* (Cambridge, 1987).

—— (ed.), *The state and society in early modern Austria* (West Lafayette, 1994).

Jacoby, H., *The bureaucratization of the world* (Berkeley, 1976).

Jannen Jr, W., '"Das Liebe Teutschland" in the 17th century – Count George Frederick von Waldeck', *European Studies Review*, 6 (1979), 165–95.

Jeserich, K.G.A., *et al.* (eds), *Deutsche Verwaltungsgeschichte*, vol. I (Stuttgart, 1983).

Johnson, H.C., *Frederick the Great and his officials* (New Haven, 1975).

Jones, P.M., *Reform and revolution in France. The politics of transition 1774–1791* (Cambridge, 1995).

Kamen, H., *European society 1500–1700* (London, 1984).

Kamencka, E., *Bureaucracy* (Oxford, 1989).

Kampmann, C., *Reichsrebellion und kaiserliche Acht. Politische Strafjustiz im Dreißigjährigen Krieg und das Verfahren gegen Wallenstein 1634* (Münster, 1992).

Kappelhoff, B., *Absolutistisches Regiment oder Ständeherrschaft? Landesherr und Landstände in Ostfriesland im ersten Drittel des 18. Jahrhunderts* (Hildesheim, 1982).

Kennedy, P.M., *The rise and fall of the great powers: economic change and military conflict from 1500 to 2000* (New York, 1987).

Kiernan, V.G., 'Foreign mercenaries and absolute monarchy', *Past and Present*, 11 (1957), 66–86.

—— *The duel in European history. Honour and the reign of aristocracy* (Oxford, 1989).

Kimmel, M.S., *Absolutism and its discontents. State and society in seventeenth-century France and England* (New Brunswick, 1988).

Klingensmith, S.J., *The utility of splendor. Ceremony, social life, and architecture at the court of Bavaria 1600–1800* (Chicago, 1993).

Klingensten, G., 'Der Wiener Hof in der frühen Neuzeit', *Zeitschrift für Historische Forschung*, 22 (1995), 237–45.

Kohl, W., *Christoph Bernhard von Galen. Politische Geschichte des Fürstbistums Münster 1650–1678* (Münster, 1964).

—— (ed.), *Westfälische Geschichte*, vol. 1 (Düsseldorf, 1983).

Koselleck, R., *Critique and crisis. Enlightenment and the pathogenesis of modern society* (Oxford, 1988).

Koser, R., 'Die Epochen der absoluten Monarchie in der neueren Geschichte', *Historische Zeitschrift*, 61 (1889), 246–88.

Krieger, L., *Ranke. The meaning of history* (Chicago, 1977).

—— *The German idea of freedom* (Chicago, 1957).

Kroener, B.R. and R. Pröve (eds), *Krieg und Frieden. Militär und Gesellschaft in der frühen Neuzeit* (Paderborn, 1996).

Krüdener, J.v., *Die Rolle des Hofes im Absolutismus* (Stuttgart, 1973).

Kunisch, J., *Absolutismus. Europäische Geschichte vom Westfälischen Frieden bis zur Krise des Ancien Regime* (Göttingen, 1986).

—— *Staatsverfassung und Mächtekonflikt. Zur Genese von Staatenkonflikten im Zeitalter des Absolutismus* (Berlin, 1979).

—— (ed.), *Staatsverfassung und Heeresverfassung in der europäische Geschichte der frühen Neuzeit* (Berlin, 1986).

Küther, C., *Menschen auf der Straße. Vagierende Unterschichten in Bayern, Franken und Schwaben in der zweiten Hälfte des 18. Jahrhunderts* (Göttingen, 1983).

—— *Räuber und Gauner in Deutschland. Das organisierte Bandenwesen im 18. und 19. Jahrhundert* (2nd edn, Göttingen, 1987).

Leibniz, G.W. Frhr. v., *Political writings* (transl. and ed. P. Riley, Cambridge, 1988).

Locke. J., *Two treatises on government* (ed. P. Laslett, Cambridge, 1988).

Lossky, A., 'Maxims of state in Louis XIV's foreign in the 1680s', in R. Hatton and J.S. Bromley (eds), *William III and Louis XIV. Essays 1680–1720* (Liverpool, 1968), pp. 7–23.

Ludwig-Mayerhofer, W., 'Disziplin oder Distinktion? Zur Interpretation der Theorie des Zivilisationsprozesses von Norbert Elias', *Kölner Zeitschrift für Soziologie und Sozialpsychologie*, 50 (1998), 217–37.

Lukowski, J., *Liberty's folly. The Polish–Lithuanian Commonwealth in the eighteenth century, 1697–1795* (London, 1991).

Macartney, C.A. (ed.), *The Habsburg and Hohenzollern dynasties in the seventeenth and eighteenth centuries* (London, 1970).

McNeill, W.H., *Keeping together in time. Dance and drill in human history* (Cambridge, Mass., 1995).

Mann, M., *The sources of social power* (2 vols, Cambridge, 1986–93).

Mansel, P., 'Monarchy, uniform and the rise of the *frac*', *Past and Present*, 96 (1982), 103–32.

—— *Pillars of monarchy. An overview of the political and social history of royal guards 1400–1984* (London, 1984).

Matsche, F., *Die Kunst im Dienst der Staatsidee Kaiser Karl VI* (2 vols, Berlin, 1981).

Melton, E., 'Population structure, the market economy, and the transformation of *Gutsherrschaft* in east central Europe, 1650–1800: the cases of Brandenburg and Bohemia', *German History*, 16 (1999), 297–327.

Mettam, R., *Power and faction in Louis XIV's France* (New York, 1988).

Miller, J. (ed.), *Absolutism in seventeenth-century Europe* (Basingstoke, 1990).

Mittenzwei, I. and E. Herzfeld, *Brandenburg-Preußen 1648–1789* (Cologne, 1987).

Mommsen, W., 'Zur Beurteilung des Absolutismus', *Historische Zeitschrift*, 158 (1938), 52–76.

Monod, P.K., *The power of kings. Monarchy and religion in Europe, 1589–1715* (New Haven, 1999).

Mooers, C., *The making of bourgeois Europe. Absolutism, revolution and the rise of capitalism in England, France and Germany* (London, 1991).

Moore, B., *The social origins of dictatorship and democracy* (Boston, 1966).

Mörz, S., *Aufgeklärter Absolutismus in der Kurpfalz während der Mannheimer Regierungszeit des Kurfürsten Karl Theodor (1742–1777)* (Stuttgart, 1991).

Müller-Weil, U., *Absolutismus und Aussenpolitik in Preußen* (Stuttgart, 1992).

Münch, P., 'Die "Obrigkeit im Vaterstand". Zu Definition und Kritik des "Landesvaters" während der Frühen Neuzeit', *Daphnis*, 11 (1982), 15–40.

Münkler, H., *Im Namen des Staates. Die Begründung der Staatsraison in der frühen Neuzeit* (Frankfurt/M., 1987).

Myers, A.R., *Parliaments and estates in Europe to 1789* (London, 1975).

Neuhaus, H., *Das Reich in der frühen Neuzeit* (Munich, 1997).

—— 'Zwänge und Entwicklungsmöglichkeiten reichsständischer Beratungsformed in der zweiten Hälfte des 16. Jahrhunderts', *Zeitschrift für Historische Forschung*, 10 (1983), 279–98.

Nipperdey, T., *Deutsche Geschichte 1800–1866. Bürgerwelt und starker Staat* (Munich, 1983).

Nitschke, P., *Verbrechensbekämpfung und Verwaltung. Die Entstehung der Polizei in der Grafschaft Lippe 1700–1814* (Münster, 1990).

Oestreich, G., *Neostoicism and the early modern state* (Cambridge, 1982).

Oresko, R., *et al.* (eds), *Royal and republican sovereignty in early modern Europe* (Cambridge, 1997).

Outram, D., *The Enlightenment* (Cambridge, 1995).

Pamlényi, E., *A history of Hungary* (London, 1975).

Parker, D., *Class and state in ancien régime France. The road to modernity?* (London, 1996).

—— *The making of French absolutism* (London, 1983).

Parker, G., *Europe in crisis 1598–1648* (London, 1982).

—— *The military revolution. Military innovation and the rise of the West 1500–1800* (Cambridge, 1988).

Peters, J. (ed.), *Gutsherrschaft als soziales Modell. Vergleichende Betrachtungen zur Funktionsweise frühneuzeitlicher Agrargesellschaften* (Munich, 1995).

Po-Chia Hsia, R., *Social discipline in the Reformation. Central Europe 1550–1750* (London, 1989).

Poggi, G., *The development of the modern state. A sociological introduction* (London, 1978).

Pöllnitz, C.L.v., *Das gallante Sachsen* (Munich, 1992; first published 1734).

Porter, B.D., *War and the rise of the state. The military foundations of modern politics* (New York, 1994).

Porter, R. and M. Teich (eds), *The Renaissance in national context* (Cambridge, 1992).

—— (eds), *The scientific revolution in national context* (Cambridge, 1992).

Press, V., 'The Habsburg court as centre of the imperial government', *Journal of Modern History*, 58 (1986), supplement, 23–45.

Pröve, R. (ed.), *Klio in Uniform? Probleme und Perspektiven einer modernen Militärgeschichte der frühen Neuzeit* (Cologne, 1997).

Pufendorf, S., *On the duty of man and citizen* (transl. and ed. J. Tully, Cambridge, 1991; first published 1673).

Rabb, T.K., *The struggle for stability in early modern Europe* (New York, 1975).

Raeff, M., *The well-ordered police state. Social and institutional change through law in the Germanies and Russia 1600–1800* (New Haven, 1983).

Rebel, H., *Peasant classes. The bureaucratization of property and family relations under early Habsburg administration 1511–1636* (Princeton, 1983).
—— 'Reimagining the *oikos*. Austrian cameralism in its social formation', in J. O'Brien and W. Roseberry (eds), *Golden ages, dark ages: reimagining the past* (Berkeley, 1991), pp. 48–80.
Reinhard, W., 'Zwang zur Konfessionalisierung? Prologemena zu einer Theorie des konfessionellen Zeitalters', *Zeitschrift für Historische Forschung*, 10 (1983), 257–77.
Repgen, K. (ed.), *Das Herrscherbild im 17. Jahrhundert* (Münster, 1991).
Ribbe, W. (ed.), *Geschichte Berlins* (2 vols, Munich, 1988).
Robisheaux, T., *Rural society and the search for order in early modern Germany* (Cambridge, 1989).
Rocholl, O., 'Das stehende Heer als Stütze der feudalen Reaktion', *Wissenschaftliche Zeitschrift der Karl-Marx-Universität Leipzig, Gesellschaft- und Staatswissenschaftliche Reihe*, 1 (1952/53), 499–510.
Rogers, C.J. (ed.), *The military revolution debate* (Boulder, 1995).
Roider Jr, K.A., *Baron Thugut and Austria's response to the French Revolution* (Princeton, 1987).
Roosen, W., 'Early modern diplomatic ceremonial', *Journal of Modern History*, 52 (1980), 452–76.
Rosenberg, H., *Bureaucracy, aristocracy and autocracy. The Prussian experience 1660–1815* (Cambridge, Mass., 1966).
Rürup, R., *Johann Jakob Moser. Pietismus und Reform* (Wiesbaden, 1965).
Sabean, D., 'The communal basis of pre-1800 peasant uprisings in western Europe', *Comparative Politics*, 8 (1975/76), 355–64.
Schaer, F.W., 'Der Absolutismus in Lippe und Schaumburg-Lippe', *Lippische Mitteilungen*, 37 (1968), 154–99.
Scharf, C., *Katharina II., Deutschland und die Deutschen* (Mainz, 1995).
Schieder, T., *Friedrich der Grosse. Ein Königtum der Widersprüche* (Berlin, 1987).
Schilling, H., *Höfe und Allianzen. Deutschland 1648–1763* (Berlin, 1989).
Schindling, A. and W. Ziegler (eds), *Die Kaiser der Neuzeit 1519–1918* (Munich, 1990).
Schnee, H., *Die Hoffinanz und der moderne Staat* (6 vols, Berlin, 1953–67).
Schnitter, H. and T. Schmidt, *Absolutismus und Heer* (Berlin, 1987).
Schubert, E., *Arme Leute, Bettler und Gauner in Franken des 18. Jahrhunderts* (Neustadt an der Aisch, 1983).
Schulze, W., *Bäuerlicher Widerstand und feudale Herrschaft in der frühen Neuzeit* (Stuttgart, 1980).
—— 'Gerhard Oestreichs Begriff "Sozial Disziplinierung in der frühen Neuzeit"', *Zeitschrift für Historische Forschung*, 14 (1987), 265–302.
Schumpeter, J.A., *Imperialism and social classes* (New York, 1951).
Scribner, R., 'Communalism: universal category or ideological construct?', *Historical Journal*, 37 (1994), 199–207.

—— and S. Ogilvie (eds), *Germany. A new social and economic history* (2 vols, London, 1996).

Scott, H.M., 'The rise of the first minister in eighteenth-century Europe', in T.C.W. Blanning and D. Cannadine (eds), *History and biography. Essays in honour of Derek Beales* (Cambridge, 1996), pp. 21–52.

—— (ed.), *Enlightened absolutism. Reform and reformers in later eighteenth-century Europe* (London, 1990).

—— (ed.), *The European nobilities in the seventeenth and eighteenth centuries* (2 vols, London, 1995).

Scott, T., 'Peasant revolts in early modern Germany', *Historical Journal*, 28 (1985), 455–68.

—— (ed.), *The peasantries of Europe from the fourteenth to the eighteenth century* (Harlow, 1998).

Sheehan, J.J., *German history 1770–1866* (Oxford, 1989).

Simms, B., *The impact of Napoleon. Prussian high politics, foreign policy and the crisis of the executive 1797–1806* (Cambridge, 1997).

Smith, P.H., *The business of alchemy. Science and culture in the Holy Roman Empire* (Princeton, 1994).

Sombart, W., *Krieg und Kapitalismus* (Munich, 1913).

Southard, R., *Droysen and the Prussian school of history* (Lexington, 1995).

Spielman, J.P., *Leopold I of Austria* (London, 1977).

—— *The city and the crown. Vienna and the imperial court 1600–1740* (West Lafayette, 1993).

Stoye, J.W., 'Emperor Charles VI: the early years of the reign', *Transactions of the Royal Historical Society*, 5th series, 12 (1962), 63–84.

Streidt, G. and P. Feierabend (eds), *Prussia. Art and architecture* (Cologne, 1999).

Subetlny, O., *Domination of eastern Europe. Native nobilities and foreign absolutism 1500–1715* (Gloucester, 1986).

Sutter-Fichtner, P., *Protestantism and primogeniture in early modern Germany* (New Haven, 1989).

Szabo, F.A.J., *Kaunitz and enlightened absolutism 1753–1780* (Cambridge, 1994).

Tallett, F., *War and society in early modern Europe 1495–1715* (London, 1992).

Tanner, M., *The last descendant of Aeneas. The Hapsburgs and the mythic image of the emperor* (New Haven, 1993).

Taylor, P.K., *Indentured to liberty. Peasant life and the Hessian military state 1688–1815* (Ithaca, 1994).

te Brake, W., *Shaping history. Ordinary people in European politics, 1500–1700* (Berkeley, 1998).

t'Hart, M.C., *The making of a bourgeois state. War, politics and finance during the Dutch Revolt* (Manchester, 1993).

Theuer, F., *Brennendes Land. Kuruzzenkriege* (Vienna, 1984).

Thompson, J.E., *Mercenaries, pirates and sovereigns. State-building and extra-territorial violence in early modern Europe* (Princeton, 1994).

Tilly, C., *Coercion, capital and European states AD 990–1992* (Oxford, 1992).
—— 'War making and state making as organised crime', in P. Evans *et al.* (eds), *Bringing the state back in* (Cambridge, 1985), pp. 169–91.
—— (ed.), *The formation of national states in western Europe* (Princeton,1975).
Trossbach, W., 'Fürstenabsetzung im 18. Jahrhundert', *Zeitschrift für Historische Forschung*, 13 (1986), 425–54.
—— 'Widerstand als Normalfall: Bauernunruhen in der Grafschaft Sayn-Wittgenstein-Wittgenstein 1696–1806', *Westfälische Zeitschrift*, 135 (1985), 25–111.
Uhland, R., *Geschichte der Hohen Karlsschule in Stuttgart* (Stuttgart, 1953).
Ulbricht, O., 'The world of a beggar around 1775: Johann Gottfried Kästner', *Central European History*, 27 (1994), 153–84.
Umbach, M., 'Visual culture, scientific images and German small state politics in the late Enlightenment', *Past and Present*, 158 (1998), 110–45.
Van Horn Melton, J., 'Absolutism and "modernity" in early modern central Europe', *German Studies Reviews*, 8 (1985), 383–98.
Vann, J.A., *The making of a state. Württemberg 1593–1793* (Ithaca, 1984).
Vincent, A., *Theories of the state* (Oxford, 1987).
Wagner-Rieger, R., 'Gedanken zum fürstlichen Schlossbau des Absolutismus', in F. Engel-Janosi *et al.* (eds), *Fürst, Bürger, Mensch* (Munich, 1975), pp. 45–70.
Walker, M., *German home towns. Community, state and general estate 1648–1871* (Ithaca, 1971).
—— *Johann Jakob Moser and the Holy Roman Empire of the German Nation* (Chapel Hill, 1981).
—— 'Rights and functions: the social categories of eighteenth-century German jurists and cameralists', *Journal of Modern History*, 50 (1978), 234–51.
Weber, M., *Economy and society* (2 vols, Berkeley, 1978).
Wegert, K., *Popular culture, crime and social control in 18th century Württemberg* (Stuttgart, 1994).
Wehler, H.-U., *Deutsche Gesellschaftsgeschichte* (3 vols, Munich, 1987–95).
Whitman, J.Q., *The legacy of Roman law in the German Romantic era* (Princeton, 1990).
Wick, P., *Versuche zur Einrichtung des Absolutismus in Mecklenburg in der ersten Hälfte des 18. Jahrhunderts* (Berlin, 1964).
Willems, E., *A way of life and death: three centuries of Prussian-German militarism – an anthropological approach* (Nashville, 1986).
Wilson, P.H., 'European warfare 1450–1815', in J. Black (ed.), *War in the early modern world 1450–1815* (London, 1999).
—— *German armies. War and German politics 1648–1806* (London, 1998).
—— 'The German "soldier trade" of the seventeenth and eighteenth century: a reassessment', *International History Review*, 18 (1996), 757–92.
—— *The Holy Roman Empire 1495–1806* (London, 1999).
—— 'War in German thought from the Peace of Westphalia to Napoleon', *European History Quarterly*, 28 (1998), 5–50.

—— *War, state and society in Württemberg, 1677–1793* (Cambridge, 1995).

Wohlfeil, R., 'Ritter – Söldnerführer – Offizier. Versuch eines Vergleiches', in J. Bärmann (ed.), *Geschichtliche Landeskunde*, vol. 3 (Wiesbaden, 1966), pp. 45–70.

Wunder, B., *Geschichte der Bürokratie in Deutschland* (Frankfurt/M., 1986).

—— *Privilegierung und Disziplinierung. Die Entstehung des Berufsbeamtententums in Bayern und Württemberg, 1780–1825* (Munich, 1978).

Yorke-Long, A., *Music at court. Four eighteenth-century case studies* (London, 1964).

Zaslaw, N. (ed.), *The classical era from the 1740s to the end of the 18th century* (London, 1989).

Zeumer, K. (ed.), *Quellensammlung zur Geschichte der deutschen Reichsverfassung in Mittelalter und Neuzeit* (2 vols, Tübingen, 1913).

Zöllner, E. and K. Gutkas (eds), *Österreich und die Osmanen – Prinz Eugen und seiner Zeit* (Vienna, 1988).

Index